Responsive Web Design with HTML5 and CSS

Third Edition

Develop future-proof responsive websites
using the latest HTML5 and CSS techniques

Ben Frain

BIRMINGHAM - MUMBAI

Responsive Web Design with HTML5 and CSS
Third Edition

Producer: Jonathan Malysiak

Acquisition Editor – Peer Reviews: Suresh Jain

Content Development Editors: Alex Patterson, Bhavesh Amin

Technical Editor: Saby D'silva

Project Editor: Radhika Atitkar

Proofreader: Safis Editing

Indexer: Pratik Shirodkar

Presentation Designer: Pranit Padwal

First published: April 2012
Second Edition: August 2015
Third Edition: April 2020

Production reference: 3120520

Published by Packt Publishing Ltd.
Livery Place
35 Livery Street
Birmingham B3 2PB, UK.

ISBN 978-1-83921-156-0

www.packt.com

packt.com

Subscribe to our online digital library for full access to over 7,000 books and videos, as well as industry leading tools to help you plan your personal development and advance your career. For more information, please visit our website.

Why subscribe?

- Spend less time learning and more time coding with practical eBooks and Videos from over 4,000 industry professionals
- Learn better with Skill Plans built especially for you
- Get a free eBook or video every month
- Fully searchable for easy access to vital information
- Copy and paste, print, and bookmark content

Did you know that Packt offers eBook versions of every book published, with PDF and ePub files available? You can upgrade to the eBook version at www.Packt.com and as a print book customer, you are entitled to a discount on the eBook copy. Get in touch with us at customercare@packtpub.com for more details.

At www.Packt.com, you can also read a collection of free technical articles, sign up for a range of free newsletters, and receive exclusive discounts and offers on Packt books and eBooks.

Contributors

About the author

Ben Frain has been a web designer/developer since 1996. He is currently employed as a UI-UX Technical Lead at bet365. Before the web, he worked as an underrated (and modest) TV actor and technology journalist, having graduated from Salford University with a degree in Media and Performance. He has written four equally underrated (his opinion) screenplays and still harbors the (fading) belief he might sell one. Outside of work, he enjoys simple pleasures: playing indoor football while his body and wife still allow it, and wrestling with his two sons.

About the reviewers

J. Pedro Ribeiro is a Brazilian front-end engineer living in the heart of London. He has been working on the web for several years focusing on performant, accessible websites that deliver great user experience.

Alongside web development, Pedro has worked as a technical reviewer for other Packt Publishing titles, *Mastering Responsive Web Design* and *Responsive Web Design Patterns*.

He is also the author of Baseliner, a Chrome extension with over 6,000 weekly users.

- **Blog** – https://jpedroribeiro.com/
- **Twitter** – https://twitter.com/jpedroribeiro
- **GitHub** – https://github.com/jpedroribeiro

Clarissa Peterson is a user experience designer and strategist who has spent more than 15 years creating effective and intuitive experiences. She originally started out as a front-end web developer, and then spent many years as a "web team of one" at nonprofit and advocacy organizations in Washington, DC. More recently, she has focused on design education by writing, speaking, and teaching.

Clarissa is the author of *Learning Responsive Web Design: A Beginner's Guide* (O'Reilly Media). She has created online courses for LinkedIn Learning and taught at the Southern Alberta Institute of Technology (SAIT). She has also spoken at design and tech conferences around the world

Clarissa is especially interested in inclusion and accessibility, and she is currently working on a new project that looks at the intersection of civil rights and technology.

Table of Contents

Preface

When I wrote the first edition of this book in 2011 and 2012, it was by no means certain that responsive web design would become the de facto approach for web design for the foreseeable future. Here we are, 9 years and two editions later and its popularity and utility show no signs of abating.

There's a saying apt for authors of technical books, "When one person teaches, two people learn". That's certainly been the case for me while writing this third edition. I've learned so much more covering these topics than I imagined I would. In my day-to-day work, I already find myself coming back to certain chapters and sections when trying to refresh my memory on how to do one thing or another that I have subsequently forgotten! I hope these pages prove as resourceful for you!

Thinking back on the contents of the first edition, it also struck me just how capable the technologies we have at our disposal have become. If you are an old hand at the web development game, feel free to jump right into some of the newest topics, such as CSS Grid layout or variable fonts and I'd be shocked if you didn't come away in the least bit excited by the possibilities they offer. These are things that would have blown my mind a decade ago.

I won't waste any more of your precious time here. Thank you for taking the time to read this book. I hope you enjoy this latest edition and take plenty from it. Please reach out to me with your thoughts, both good and bad, and any questions that arise. They will naturally inform the content of any future editions.

Finally, while the publishers mention it again in a moment, if you do enjoy it, please consider adding a review on Amazon or your book store of choice. From a commercial point of view, it really does help with sales. From a personal perspective, it's really lovely to read them and know people around the world are making use of something you spent so long working on.

It should go without saying here that if you don't enjoy it, please keep your opinions to yourself!

Who this book is for

Are you a full-stack developer who needs to gen up on their front-end skills? Perhaps you work on the front-end and need a definitive overview of everything that modern HTML and CSS has to offer? Maybe you have done a little website building but you need a deep understanding of responsive web designs and how to achieve them? This is the book for you!

All you need to take advantage of this book is a working understanding of HTML and CSS. No JavaScript knowledge is needed.

What this book covers

Chapter 1, The Essentials of Responsive Web Design, is a whistle-stop tour of the key ingredients in coding a responsive web design.

Chapter 2, Writing HTML Markup, covers all the semantic elements of HTML5, text-level semantics, and considerations of accessibility. We also cover how to insert media such as video into our pages.

Chapter 3, Media Queries – Supporting Differing Viewports, covers everything you need to know about CSS media queries: their capabilities, the syntax, and the various ways in which you can wield them.

Chapter 4, Fluid Layout, Flexbox, and Responsive Images, shows you how to code proportional layouts and responsive images and provides a thorough exploration of Flexbox layouts.

Chapter 5, Layout with CSS Grid, is a deep dive into the two-dimensional layout system of CSS Grid.

Chapter 6, CSS Selectors, Typography, Color Modes, and More, covers the endless possibilities of CSS selectors, HSLA and RGBA color, web typography including variable fonts, viewport-relative units, and a whole lot more.

Chapter 7, Stunning Aesthetics with CSS, covers CSS filters, box shadows, linear and radial gradients, multiple backgrounds, and how to target background images to high-resolution devices.

Chapter 8, Using SVGs for Resolution Independence, covers everything we need to use SVG graphics inside documents and as background images, as well as how to interact with them using JavaScript.

Chapter 9, Transitions, Transformations, and Animations, gets our CSS moving as we explore how to make interactions and animations using CSS.

Chapter 10, Conquer Forms with HTML5 and CSS, explains how web forms have always been tough but the latest HTML5 and CSS features make them easier to deal with than ever before.

Chapter 11, Bonus Techniques and Parting Advice, explores the essential considerations before embarking on responsive web design and also provides a few last-minute nuggets of wisdom to aid you in your responsive quest.

Get the most out of this book

To get the most from this book, you'll need:

- A text editor such as Sublime Text, Vim, or Visual Studio Code.
- A modern browser such as Firefox, Edge, Safari, or Chrome.
- An appreciation for mediocre jokes and obscure popular film references.

Download the example code files

You can download the example code files for this book from your account at www.packt.com/. If you purchased this book elsewhere, you can visit www.packtpub.com/support and register to have the files emailed directly to you.

You can download the code files by following these steps:

1. Log in or register at http://www.packt.com.
2. Select the **Support** tab.
3. Click on **Code Downloads**.
4. Enter the name of the book in the **Search** box and follow the on-screen instructions.

Once the file is downloaded, please make sure that you unzip or extract the folder using the latest version of:

- WinRAR/7-Zip for Windows

- Zipeg/iZip/UnRarX for Mac
- 7-Zip/PeaZip for Linux

The code bundle for the book is also hosted on GitHub at `https://github.com/PacktPublishing/Responsive-Web-Design-with-HTML5-and-CSS-Third-Edition`. In case there's an update to the code, it will be updated on the existing GitHub repository.

We also have other code bundles from our rich catalog of books and videos available at `https://github.com/PacktPublishing/`. Check them out!

Download the color images

We also provide a PDF file that has color images of the screenshots/diagrams used in this book. You can download it here: `https://static.packt-cdn.com/downloads/9781839211560_ColorImages.pdf`.

Conventions used

There are a number of text conventions used throughout this book.

`CodeInText`: Indicates code words in text, folder names, filenames, file extensions, pathnames, dummy URLs, user input, and Twitter handles. For example: "We can fix that prior problem easily by adding this snippet in the `<head>`."

A block of code is set as follows:

```
img {
  max-width: 100%;
}
```

When we wish to draw your attention to a particular part of a code block, the relevant lines or items are set in bold:

```
img {
  max-width: 100%;
  display: inline-flex;
}
```

Bold: Indicates a new term, an important word, or words that you see on screen, for example, in menus or dialog boxes, also appear in the text like this. For example: "At its simplest, you pick a URL and click on **START TEST**."

Warnings or important notes appear like this.

 Tips and tricks appear like this.

Get in touch

Feedback from our readers is always welcome.

General feedback: If you have questions about any aspect of this book, mention the book title in the subject of your message and email us at `customercare@packtpub.com`.

Errata: Although we have taken every care to ensure the accuracy of our content, mistakes do happen. If you have found a mistake in this book, we would be grateful if you could report this to us. Please visit `www.packtpub.com/support/errata`, select your book, click on the **Errata Submission Form** link, and enter the details.

Piracy: If you come across any illegal copies of our works in any form on the Internet, we would be grateful if you could provide us with the location address or website name. Please contact us at `copyright@packt.com` with a link to the material.

If you are interested in becoming an author: If there is a topic that you have expertise in and you are interested in either writing or contributing to a book, please visit `authors.packtpub.com`.

Reviews

Please leave a review. Once you have read and used this book, why not leave a review on the site that you purchased it from? Potential readers can then see and use your unbiased opinion to make a purchase decision, we at Packt can understand what you think about our product, and our author can see your feedback on their book. Thank you!

For more information about Packt, please visit `packt.com`.

1
The Essentials of Responsive Web Design

By the end of this first chapter, we will have covered everything needed to author a fully responsive web page.

You might be wondering, why the other 10 chapters? By the end of this chapter, that should be apparent too.

When the first edition of this book came out in 2012, responsive web design was a new and exciting possibility to address the needs of the ever-growing list of devices that could access the internet. In 2020 it's simply the de facto standard. Unless you have a good reason, if you're building a website or web application and it isn't responsive, you're probably doing it wrong!

Perhaps you're reading this because you need to understand what makes a responsive web design, and get a better handle on the capabilities of HTML and CSS? Or perhaps you're already building websites responsively and need a steer on features and techniques you may have missed along the way—not to mention all the new techniques that will be at our disposal in 2020 and beyond?

Either way, we have you covered. If you're in that latter camp, this first chapter should serve as a quick and basic refresher. If you're in the former, think of it as a "boot camp" of sorts, so we're all on the same page.

Here's what we will cover in this first chapter:

- The browser and device landscape

- Defining responsive web design
- Setting browser support levels
- A brief discussion on development tools and text editors
- Our first responsive example: a simple HTML5 page
- The viewport `meta` tag
- Fluid images
- Writing CSS3 media queries to make pages adapt
- The shortfalls in our basic example
- Why our journey has only just begun

Are you sitting comfortably? Then we will begin!

The browser and device landscape

Less than 10 years ago, it was reasonable to build a website at a fixed width. The expectation was that all end users would get a fairly consistent experience. This fixed width (typically 960px wide or thereabouts) wasn't too wide for laptop screens, and users with large resolution monitors merely had an abundance of space on either side.

But in 2007, Apple's iPhone ushered in the first truly usable phone browsing experience, and the way people access and interact with the web changed forever.

In the first edition of this book, published in early 2012, the following was noted about the percentage of total browser usage by device type:

> *"In the 12 months from July 2010 to July 2011, global mobile browser use had risen from 2.86 to 7.02 percent."*

In the second edition of this book, I noted:

> *"As these words are written, in mid 2014, the same statistics system gs.statcounter.com reports that figure has risen to 29.48% (by way of comparison, North America's mobile figure is at 24%). It's a rising trend that shows no sign of abating."*

As I write these latest words in September 2019, again using StatCounter, mobile accounts for a whopping 51.11% of total browser usage, desktop 45.18%, and tablet 3.71%.

The indisputable fact is that the number of people using smaller-screen devices to view the internet is growing at an ever-increasing rate, whilst at the other end of the scale, 27- and 30-inch displays are now also commonplace (along with various tablet and console devices). There is now more of a difference between the smallest screens browsing the web and the largest than ever before.

Thankfully, there is a solution to this ever-expanding browser and device landscape. A responsive web design, built with HTML and CSS allows a website to "just work" across multiple devices and screens. It enables the layout and capabilities of a website to respond to their environment (screen size, input type, and device/browser capabilities).

Originally, before responsive web design was a thing, it was not uncommon for businesses to have a separate mobile site with its own unique URL. That was something that required detecting the user-agent on the host server before sending the browser to the relevant desktop or mobile URL. Another bonus with a responsive website is that it can be implemented without the need for server-based/backend solutions.

Defining responsive web design

The term "responsive web design" was coined by Ethan Marcotte in 2010. In his seminal *A List Apart* article `http://www.alistapart.com/articles/responsive-web-design`, he consolidated three existing techniques (flexible grid layout, flexible images/media, and media queries) into one unified approach and named it responsive web design.

Responsive web design in a nutshell

To attempt to put the philosophy of responsive web design into a "nutshell," I would say it's the presentation of web content in the most relevant format for the viewport and device accessing it.

In its infancy, it was typical for responsive design to be implemented by starting with a fixed-width desktop design before trying to scale the design down as needed for smaller screens. However, processes evolved and it became apparent there was a better way. Namely, that everything from design to content management and development worked better when starting with the smallest screens first, and then "progressively enhancing" the design and content for larger screens and/or more capable devices. If the term "progressive enhancement" makes no sense right now, fear not. We'll be talking about that again in a moment.

Before we get into things fully, there are a few subjects I'd like to address and get squared away before we continue: browser support, text editors, and tooling.

Browser support

The sheer volume of disparate devices that access the web means most people understand the need for technical solutions that cater for most devices.

The popularity and ubiquity of responsive web design usually makes the approach an easy sell to clients and stakeholders. Nowadays, most people have some idea what responsive web design is about, even if that understanding amounts to little more than "a website that looks good on phones as well as computers."

However, one question that almost always comes up when starting a responsive design project is browser support. With so many browser and device variants it's not always pragmatic to support every single browser permutation fully. Perhaps time is a limiting factor; perhaps money—perhaps both.

Typically, the older the browser, the greater the amount of work and code required to get feature or aesthetic parity with modern browsers.

We are going to practice progressive enhancement. In essence, starting with a functional and accessible website for the most basic browsers, which will be progressively enhanced with features for more capable browsers. It should be a very rare occasion indeed that you are forced to create a website that isn't at least functional on an old browser/device.

 If working on a greenfield project, where there is no existing browser usage data, you can at least think about the demographics of your target audience and make some broad assumptions about likely devices/browsers being used based on those demographics.

Before considering any web project it makes sense to decide, in advance, what platforms you need to fully support and which you are happy to concede visual/functional anomalies for.

For example, if you're unlucky enough to have 25% of your website visitors using Internet Explorer 11, you'll need to consider what features that browser supports and tailor your solution accordingly. The same caution is required if a large number of your users are visiting with older mobile phone platforms such as Android 4.

To this end, if you aren't already, become familiar with websites such as `http://caniuse.com`. *Can I use* provides a simple interface for establishing the browser support for each web platform feature.

Generally speaking, when starting a project, as a simple and broad way to determine what browsers to support, I apply the following crude piece of logic: if the cost of developing and supporting browser X is more than the revenue/benefit created by the users of browser X, don't develop specific solutions for browser X.

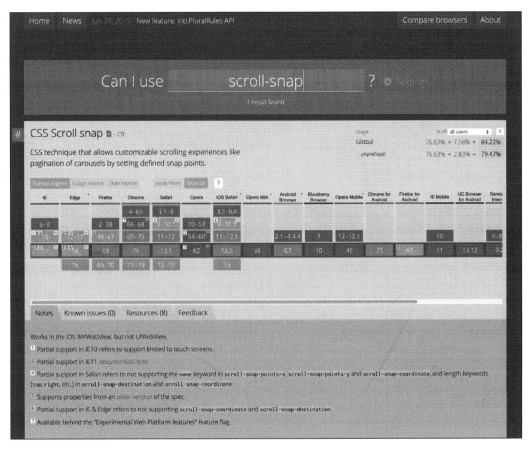

Figure 1.1: Can I Use provides browser support data for every web platform feature

Text editors

It makes no difference what tool you use to write your code. If the simplest of text editors allows you to write your HTML, CSS, and JavaScript efficiently, that's absolutely fine. Whether your preference is Sublime Text, Vim, Emacs, Nova, Visual Studio Code, or Notepad, it matters little. Just use what works best for you.

Tools for software development

Similarly, there are no requisite tools that are essential to get a responsive web design out of the door. That said, you should be aware that there are many, often free, tools available to eliminate many of the manual and time-intensive tasks of building websites. For example, CSS preprocessors such as Sass can help with code organization, variables, color manipulations, and arithmetic. CSS postprocessors such as PostCSS can automate horrible and thankless jobs like CSS vendor prefixing. Linting and validation tools can check your HTML, JavaScript, and CSS code against standards as you work, eliminating many time-wasting errors that are the result of nothing more than a typo. More recently, code formatters have changed the way we work day to day. Tools like Prettier, for example, automatically format your code with indentation and spacing when you save. None of these tools are essential but they may afford you some benefits.

New tools come out constantly and they are continually evolving. Therefore, whilst some relevant and beneficial tools will be mentioned by name as we go, be aware that something better may be just around the corner. Hence we won't be relying on anything other than standards-based HTML and CSS in our examples. You should, however, use whatever tools you can bring to bear to produce your frontend code as quickly and reliably as possible.

Our first responsive example

In the first paragraph, I promised that by the end of this chapter you would know all you needed to build a fully responsive web page. So far, I've just been talking around the issue at hand. It's time to walk the walk.

Code samples

You can download all the code samples from this book by visiting `https://rwd.education/`. It's worth knowing that where individual examples are built up throughout a chapter, only the final version of the example is provided in the code download. For example, if you download the code samples for *Chapter 2*, the examples will be in the state they are at by the end of that chapter. No intermediate states are provided other than in the text.

Our basic HTML file

We will start with a simple HTML5 structure. Don't worry at this point what each of the lines do, especially the content of `<head>`, as we will cover that in detail in *Chapter 2*, *Writing HTML Markup*.

For now, concentrate on the elements inside the `<body>` tag. There we have a few `div` elements, a graphic for a logo, a paragraph or two of text, and a list of items. Although you can see more content in the screengrabs, a shorter version of the code follows. For brevity, I have removed the paragraphs of text as we only need to concern ourselves with the core structure.

However, what you should know is that the text is a recipe and description of how to make scones—a quintessentially British dessert.

Remember, if you want to get your hands on the full HTML file, you can download the example code from the `https://rwd.education/` website.

```html
<!DOCTYPE html>
<html class="no-js" lang="en">
  <head>
    <meta charset="utf-8" />
    <title>Our first responsive web page with HTML5 and CSS3</title>
    <meta name="description" content="A basic responsive web page -
an example from Chapter 1" />
    <link rel="stylesheet" href="css/styles.css" />
  </head>
  <body>
    <div class="Header">
      <a href="/" class="LogoWrapper"><img src="img/SOC-Logo.png"
alt="Scone O'Clock logo"/></a>
      <p class="Strap">Scones: the most resplendent of snacks</p>
    </div>
    <div class="IntroWrapper">
      <p class="IntroText">Occasionally maligned and misunderstood;
the scone is a quintessentially British classic.</p>
      <div class="MoneyShot">
        <p class="ImageCaption">Incredible scones, picture from
Wikipedia</p>
      </div>
    </div>
    <p>Recipe and serving suggestions follow.</p>
    <div class="Ingredients">
      <h3 class="SubHeader">Ingredients</h3>
      <ul></ul>
    </div>
    <div class="HowToMake">
      <h3 class="SubHeader">Method</h3>
      <ol class="MethodWrapper"></ol>
    </div>
  </body>
</html>
```

By default, web pages are inherently flexible. If I open the example page, even as it is at this point, with no special work done to make it responsive, and resize the browser window, the text reflows as needed.

What about on different devices? Again, with no CSS whatsoever added to the page, this is how that renders on an iPhone XR:

Figure 1.2: Not pretty but by default all web pages are inherently flexible

As you can see, it's rendering, but like a desktop page shrunken down to fit the space available. The reason for that is that iOS renders web pages at 980px wide by default and shrinks them down into the "viewport."

Before responsive design was a thing, it was commonplace to see websites render like that on an iPhone. Nowadays, thanks to the ubiquity of responsive web design, they are as rare as rocking horse droppings!

 The area of a browser window that allows a web page to be viewed is known technically as the viewport. To be clear, the viewport area excludes the browser toolbars, URL bar, and so on. From now on, we will generally use this more accurate term.

We can make the page more mobile-friendly by adding this snippet in the `<head>`:

```
<meta name="viewport" content="width=device-width,initial-scale=1.0" />
```

This viewport `meta` tag is the non-standard, but de facto, way of telling the browser how to render the page. Although introduced to the web by Apple, rather than a standards process, it remains essential for responsive web design. We will cover the `meta` tag and its various settings and permutations in *Chapter 3, Media Queries – Supporting Differing Viewports*.

For now, you just need to know that in this case, our viewport `meta` tag is effectively saying "make the content render at the width of the device."

In fact, it's probably easier to just show you the effect this line has on applicable devices:

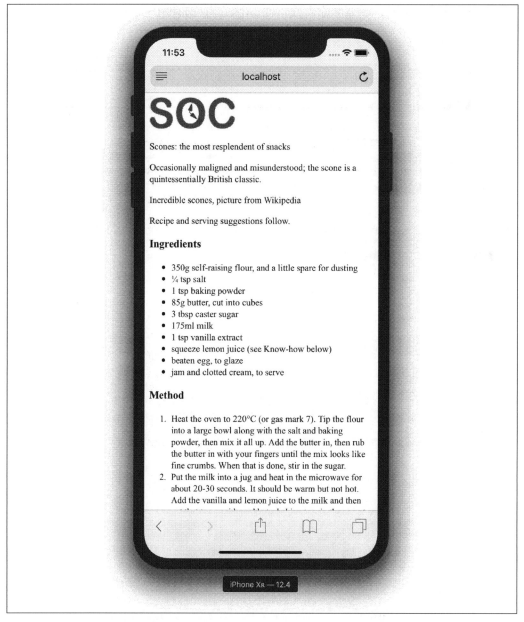

Figure 1.3: With just one line added, already things are improving dramatically

Great! Another snag fixed; the text is now rendering and flowing at a more "native size." Let's move on.

Taming images

They say a picture speaks a thousand words. All this writing about scones on our sample page and there's no image of the beauties! I'm going to add in an image of a scone near the top of the page; a sort of "hero" image to entice users to read the page.

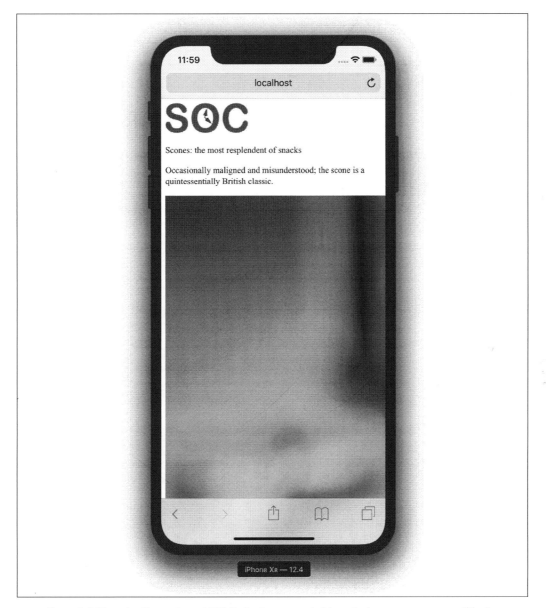

Figure 1.4: There is a line or two of CSS that's always needed to make images appear a sensible size

Oh! That nice big image (2000px wide) is forcing our page to render more than a little wonky. We clearly need to fix that.

Ideas? Well, we could add a fixed width to the image via CSS but the problem there is that we want the image to scale to different screen sizes. For example, in CSS, our iPhone XR is 414px wide by 896px high. If we set a width of 414px to that image, what happens if a user rotates the screen? On this device, the 414px wide viewport is now 896px wide. Thankfully, it's pretty easy to achieve fluid images with a single line of CSS.

I'm going to create the `css/styles.css` CSS file now that's already linked in the `head` of the HTML page.

In our blank `styles.css` file, here is the first thing I'm adding. Although this could be written as a single line, I'm actually going to write it as three for the sake of legibility. Ordinarily, I'd be setting a few other defaults, and we'll discuss those defaults in later chapters, but for our purposes, I'm happy to open with just this:

```
img {
    max-width: 100%;
}
```

With that file saved and the page refreshed, we see something more akin to what we might expect.

Figure 1.5: With a little CSS, our images will never exceed their bounds

All this `max-width` based rule does is stipulate that all images should grow to be a maximum of 100% of their size. Where a containing element (such as the `body` or a `div` it sits within) is less than the full intrinsic width of the image, the image will simply scale up to display as large as it can within that constraint.

A brief tangent on width/max-width for images

To make images fluid, you could also use the more widely used `width` property. For example, `width: 100%`, but this has a different effect. When a property of `width` is used, then the image will be displayed at that width, relative to its container if using percentages, regardless of its own inherent size. The result in our example would be that the logo (also an image) would stretch beyond its intrinsic size to fill 100% of its container. With a container far wider than the image, as is the case with our logo, this leads to a massively oversized image.

Excellent. Everything is now laid out as expected. No matter the viewport size, nothing is overflowing the page horizontally.

The code samples provided throughout this book do not include "vendor prefix" styles. Vendor prefixes have been employed historically to prefix experimental CSS properties in different browsers; for example, `-webkit-backface-visibility`. Including vendor prefixes in CSS is often essential to achieve support for certain properties in older browsers. There are now tools to automate this prefixing and, as you might imagine, the tools perform the task faster and more accurately than we can.

Therefore, I'm refraining from including any vendor-prefixed code in the samples, in the hope you will adopt a similar painless approach. The topic of vendor prefixing, and the tools to automate it, is detailed more fully in *Chapter 7, Stunning Aesthetics with CSS*.

However, if we look at the page in larger viewports, the basic styles start to get both literally and figuratively stretched. Take a look at the example page at a size of around 1400px:

Figure 1.6: We clearly need to fix the size of this image at larger viewports!

Oh, dear! In fact, even at around 800px wide it's starting to suffer. Around this point, it would be handy if we could rearrange a few things. Maybe resize the image and position it off to one side. Perhaps alter some font sizes and background colors of elements.

Thankfully, we can achieve all this functionality quite easily by employing CSS media queries to bend things to our will.

Enter media queries

As we have established, somewhere beyond the 800px wide point, our current layout starts to look stretched. We'll use CSS media queries at this point to adjust the layout depending upon the screen width. We will cover media queries in great depth in *Chapter 3*, which is inventively titled *Media Queries*. For now, all you need to appreciate is that media queries are directives in CSS that allow us to isolate CSS rules to certain environmental conditions; the size of the screen in this instance.

Breakpoints

Before we proceed, it's worth familiarizing yourself with the term "breakpoint."

The term "breakpoint" is web developer vernacular for defining a particular viewport width or height at which a responsive design should change significantly.

When people first started making use of media queries, it was common to see designs built with specific breakpoints to cater to the popular devices of the day. At the time, it was typically iPhone (320px × 480px) and iPad (768px × 1024px) devices.

That practice was a bad decision then, and it would be an even worse one now. The problem is that doing that caters a design to specific screen sizes. We want a responsive design—something that is agnostic of the screen size viewing it, responding to any size viewport it finds itself in, not something that only looks at its best at specific sizes.

Imagine me as your well-intentioned Dad at this point. I'm furrowing my brow and insisting that "There are no specific breakpoints—use a breakpoint if your design needs it, not for a specific device!". OK, I'm taking my "Dad" hat off again now; I promise to not crack any jokes while your friends are around.

To conclude this little aside, it's important to remember that you will enjoy better results if you are guided by your design when deciding where to introduce "breakpoints."

For the purpose of whipping our basic example into shape, however, we will concentrate on just one type of media query: a minimum width media query. CSS rules within this type of media query only get applied if the viewport is or exceeds a certain width. The exact minimum width can be specified using a raft of different length units, including percent, em, rem, and px. In CSS, a minimum width media query is written like this:

```css
@media screen and (min-width: 800px) {
  /* styles */
}
```

The `@media` directive tells the browser we are starting a media query, the `screen` part (declaring `screen` is technically not needed in this situation but we will deal with that in detail in *Chapter 3, Media Queries – Supporting Differing Viewports*) tells the browser these rules should be applied to all screen types. We then have the `and` keyword, which chains together another set of conditionals, which in this case is `(min-width: 800px)`. That tells the browser that the rules should also be limited to all viewports at least 800px wide.

I believe it was Bryan Rieger, `http://www.slideshare.net/bryanrieger/ rethinking-the-mobile-web-by-yiibu`, who first wrote that "The absence of support for media queries is in fact the first media query." What he meant by that is that the first rules we write outside of a media query should be our starter or "base" rules for the most basic devices, which we then enhance for more capable devices and larger screens.

That is what we are doing in this example. The basic styles are written first. It is only when we need to do something different that we introduce a media query.

This approach also facilitates a "smallest screen first" mentality and allows us to progressively layer on detail as and when the design needs to change for bigger screens.

Amending the example for a larger screen

We've already established that our design is starting to suffer at around 800px wide.

Therefore, let's mix things up a little by way of a simple example of how we can lay things out differently at different viewport sizes.

First off, we will stop that main "hero" image from getting too big and keep it over on the right. Then the intro text can sit to the left.

We will then have the main portion of the text (the "method" that describes how to make the scones) on the left below, with a small boxed-out section detailing the ingredients over on the right.

All these changes can be achieved relatively simply by encapsulating these specific styles within a media query. Here's what things look like with the relevant styles added:

Figure 1.7: With a few rules added within a media query we get a different layout for larger screens

It still looks essentially the same as it did before on smaller screens but adjusts to the new layout if the viewport is 800px or wider.

There are some further visual embellishments that don't add to the understanding of what's happening responsively, hence I have omitted them here, but if you'd like to view the relevant code, download the chapter code at http://rwd.education.

Here are the layout styles that were added:

```
@media screen and (min-width: 800px) {
  .IntroWrapper {
    display: table;
    table-layout: fixed;
    width: 100%;
  }
}
```

```css
.MoneyShot,
.IntroText {
  display: table-cell;
  width: 50%;
  vertical-align: middle;
  text-align: center;
}

.IntroText {
  padding: 0.5rem;
  font-size: 2.5rem;
  text-align: left;
}

.Ingredients {
  font-size: 0.9rem;
  float: right;
  padding: 1rem;
  margin: 0 0 0.5rem 1rem;
  border-radius: 3px;
  background-color: #fffdf;
  border: 2px solid #e8cfa9;
}

.Ingredients h3 {
  margin: 0;
  }
}
```

That wasn't too bad, was it? With only minimal code we have built a page that responds to the viewport size and offers a preferable layout as needed. By adding just a few more styles things look even easier on the eye.

With those in place, our basic responsive page now looks like this on an iPhone:

Figure 1.8: A few more styles added and our basic page is palatable

And like this when the viewport is 800px or wider:

SOC

Scones: the most resplendent of snacks

Occasionally maligned and misunderstood; the scone is a quintessentially British classic.

Incredible scones, picture from Wikipedia

Recipe and serving suggestions follow.

Method

1. Heat the oven to 220°C (or gas mark 7). Tip the flour into a large bowl along with the salt and baking powder, then mix it all up. Add the butter in, then rub the butter in with your fingers until the mix looks like fine crumbs. When that is done, stir in the sugar.

2. Put the milk into a jug and heat in the microwave for about 20-30 seconds. It should be warm but not hot. Add the vanilla and lemon juice to the milk and then put that to one side and but a baking tray in the oven to warm.

Ingredients

- 350g self-raising flour, and a little spare for dusting
- ¼ tsp salt
- 1 tsp baking powder
- 85g butter, cut into cubes
- 3 tbsp caster sugar
- 175ml milk
- 1 tsp vanilla extract
- squeeze lemon juice (see Know-how below)
- beaten egg, to glaze
- jam and clotted cream, to serve

Figure 1.9: Same HTML and CSS but different layout for larger viewports

This has been a very basic example but it has encapsulated the essential methodology of building out a responsive web design.

Let's just go over the important parts of what we have covered in this chapter and in this basic example again:

- Use whatever text editor you like
- Tools exist to make writing code easier but don't get hung up on what to use
- Responsive designs are made possible with a flexible layout, fluid images, and media queries
- A `meta` tag is needed in the head of your HTML so a browser knows how to render the page
- You'll want all images to be set with a `max-width` of 100% in the CSS by default

- A breakpoint is just a point, typically a screen-width, at which we use a media query to alter the design

- When you write CSS for a responsive design, start with base styles that can work on any device—typically the smallest screen and then use media queries to adapt it for larger screens

- Scones with clotted cream and jam are really tasty

 You can find the full specifications for CSS Media Queries (Level 3) here: `http://www.w3.org/TR/css3-mediaqueries/`.

There is also a working draft for CSS Media Queries (Level 4) here: `http://dev.w3.org/csswg/mediaqueries-4/`.

The shortcomings of our example

In this chapter, we've covered all the essential component parts of building a basic responsive web page with HTML and CSS. Granted, it's not what I'd call a real looker. I'd forgive you for using words like "infantile," "lazy," and "ugly" but just do it quietly amongst yourselves; I have feelings, you know!

The point here is you and I both know that this basic responsive example is far from what we will likely be tasked with building day to day. Nor should it reflect the limit of what we are capable of building.

We need to cover typography, color, shadows, and hover styles; semantic markup; accessibility concerns; animation; scalable graphics; forms; and so much more!

You get the picture; the truth is we have barely scratched the surface. But don't worry. That's what the rest of the book is for.

Summary

Well done—you now know and understand the essential elements needed to create a fully responsive web page. However, as we have just discovered, there are plenty of places where things could be improved.

But that's fine. We don't just want the ability to make competent responsive web designs, we want to be able to create "best of breed" experiences. And as you're here, investing your time in the betterment of websites everywhere, I know you're up to the challenge. So let's press on.

In the next chapter, *Chapter 2*, *Writing HTML Markup*, we are going to take a deep dive into HTML5 markup. HTML is the very skeleton of any web page or application, the bedrock on which to build anything meaningful, the oxygen a website breathes, the... OK, I'm out of analogies—suffice it to say, HTML is pretty important, so let's press on and get stuck in.

2
Writing HTML Markup

HTML stands for Hypertext Markup Language. It is a language that allows content to be marked up in a manner that makes it more understandable to technology, and then in turn to humans.

You can have content on the web without CSS or without JavaScript. But you can't have content without HTML.

It's a common misconception that HTML is the easy part of authoring web pages and applications. Writing HTML is often dismissed out of hand as something anyone can do easily. My experience tells me HTML is easy to get wrong and not a lot else.

Also consider that for users of the web without sight or who have impaired vision, the way you author HTML can turn content from a confusing unusable mess, into a meaningful, useful, and delightful experience. Sighted users who rely on assistive technology for other reasons can also enjoy web pages far more easily if they have been marked up correctly.

Writing good quality HTML is not a specific need of responsive web design. It's far more important than that. It's a prerequisite of anything that you want to be accessible to all users of the web.

This chapter is therefore going to be about writing HTML markup. We will be considering the vocabulary of HTML, its semantics, or, more succinctly, the way we can use the elements of HTML to describe the content we place in markup.

HTML is what's known as a living standard. A few years back, the latest version was typically referred to as HTML5, a buzzword that helped identify modern web techniques and approaches. It's the reason this book is named "Responsive Web Design with HTML5 and CSS" instead of simply "Responsive Web Design with HTML and CSS." Back in 2012, you could more easily highlight that your techniques were modern by using the terms HTML5 and CSS3. As I write this in 2020, this distinction is less important. To read the living standard, head over here: `http://www.w3.org/TR/html5/`.

The topics we will cover in this chapter are:

- Starting HTML pages correctly
- The forgiving nature of HTML5 markup
- Sectioning, grouping, and text-level elements
- Putting HTML elements to use
- WCAG accessibility conformance and WAI-ARIA for more accessible web applications
- Embedding media
- Responsive video and iframes

HTML also provides specific tools for handling forms and user input. This set of features takes much of the burden away from more resource heavy technologies like JavaScript for things like form validation. However, we're going to look at HTML forms separately in *Chapter 10, Conquer Forms with HTML5 and CSS*.

The basic structure of an HTML page is like this:

```
<!DOCTYPE html>
<html lang="en">
<head>
    <meta charset="utf-8" />
    <title>Web Page Structure</title>
</head>
<body></body>
</html>
```

When writing HTML, you will typically be "marking up" or writing content inside a series of tags or elements. The majority of elements in HTML have an opening and closing tag. A few, like the preceding meta example, are void and hence "self-closing."

 There's only a limited number of self-closing or void elements, defined here: `https://html.spec.whatwg.org/multipage/syntax.html#void-elements`.

They are referred to as void elements because they have no contents. Presently the void tags are `area`, `base`, `br`, `col`, `embed`, `hr`, `img`, `input`, `link`, `meta`, `param`, `source`, `track`, and `wbr`.

To exemplify the opening and closing nature of HTML tags, a paragraph of text would be most suitably marked up with an opening `<p>` at the beginning and a closing `</p>` at the end. Note the forward slash on the closing tag, as that's the differentiator between the opening and closing tags.

Although we are about to cover the `head` section, which is the content between the opening `<head>` and closing `</head>` tags, be aware that the lion's share of HTML authoring is done in the `body` section.

Getting the start of HTML pages right

We will begin at the start, which seems the logical place to start. Let's consider the opening elements of an HTML page and ensure we fully understand all the essential component parts.

Like so many things with the web, remembering the exact syntax of each thing inside the `head` section is not particularly important. Understanding what each thing is for is important, however. I generally copy and paste the opening code each time, or have it saved in a text snippet, and I would recommend you do too.

The first few lines of an HTML page should look something like this:

```
<!DOCTYPE html>
<html lang="en">
<head>
    <meta charset="utf-8" />
```

The doctype

So, what do we actually have there? First of all, we opened our document with the HTML5 Doctype declaration:

```
<!DOCTYPE html>
```

If you're a fan of lowercase, then `<!doctype html>` is just as good. It makes no difference.

The html tag and lang attribute

After the Doctype declaration, we open the `html` tag; the first and therefore root tag for our document. We also use the `lang` attribute to specify the language for the document, and then we open the `<head>` section:

```
<html lang="en">
<head>
```

Specifying alternate languages

According to the W3C specifications (`http://www.w3.org/TR/html5/dom.html#the-lang-and-xml:lang-attributes`), the `lang` attribute specifies the primary language for the element's contents and for any of the element's attributes that contain text. You can imagine how useful this will be to assistive technology such as screen readers. If you're not writing pages in English, you'd best specify the correct language code. For example, for Japanese, the HTML tag would be `<html lang="ja">`.

For a full list of languages, take a look at `http://www.iana.org/assignments/language-subtag-registry`.

Character encoding

Finally, we specify the character encoding, which in simple terms tells the browser how to parse the information contained within. As the `meta` tag is a void element, it doesn't require a closing tag:

```
<meta charset="utf-8" />
```

Unless you have a good reason to specify otherwise, the value for the charset is always `utf-8`.

The forgiving nature of HTML5 markup

If you're conscientious about how you write HTML markup, you'll typically use lowercase for the most part, wrap attribute values in straight quotation marks (not curly ones!), and declare a type for the scripts and style sheets you link to. For example, perhaps you link to a style sheet like this:

```
<link href="CSS/main.css" rel="stylesheet" type="text/css" />
```

The fact is that HTML5 doesn't require such precision. It's just as happy to see this:

```
<link href=CSS/main.css rel=stylesheet >
```

Did you notice that? There's no end forward slash at the end of the tag, there are no quotation marks around the attribute values, and there is no type declaration. However, easy-going HTML5 doesn't care. The second example is just as valid as the first.

This more lax syntax applies across the whole document, not just linked assets. For example, specify a `div` like this if you like:

```
<div id=wrapper>
```

That's perfectly valid HTML5. The same goes for inserting an image:

```
<img SRC=frontCarousel.png aLt=frontCarousel>
```

That's also valid HTML5. No end tag/slash, no quotes (although you would still need quotes if the value had white space in), and a mix of capitalization and lowercase characters. You can even omit things such as the opening `<head>` tag and the page still validates!

 Want a shortcut to great HTML5 code? Consider the HTML5 Boilerplate (`http://html5boilerplate.com/`). It's a premade best practice HTML5 file. You can also custom build the template to match your specific needs.

A sensible approach to HTML markup

Personally, I like writing my markup quite strictly. That means closing tags, quoting attribute values, and adhering to a consistent letter case. One could argue that ditching some of these practices would save a few bytes of data but that's what tools are for (any needless characters/data could be stripped if needed). I want my markup to be as legible as possible and I would encourage others to do the same. I'm of the opinion that clarity in authoring code should trump brevity.

When writing HTML documents, therefore, I think you can write clean and legible code while still embracing the economies afforded by HTML5. To exemplify, for a CSS link, I'd go with the following:

```
<link href="CSS/main.css" rel="stylesheet" />
```

I've kept the closing forward slash at the end of the element and the quotation marks but omitted the `type` attribute. The point to make here is that you can find a level you're happy with yourself. HTML5 won't be shouting at you, flagging up your markup in front of the class, and standing you in a corner for not validating. However you want to write your markup is just fine. No, who am I kidding, I can't let it go—I want you to know that if you're writing your code without quoting attribute values and closing your tags, I am silently judging you!

 Despite HTML5's looser syntax, it's always worth checking whether your markup is valid. Checking that markup validates catches basic human errors like missing or mismatched tags, missing `alt` attributes on images, incorrectly nested elements, and so on. The W3C validator was created for just this reason: `http://validator.w3.org/`.

Enough of me berating writers of slacker markup. Let's look at some more benefits of HTML5.

All hail the mighty <a> tag

The `<a>` tag is arguably the most important and defining tag of HTML. The anchor tag is the tag used to link from the document a user is on to another document elsewhere on the internet, or another point in the same document.

 You can read the specification for the `<a>` element here: `https://www.w3.org/TR/html52/textlevel-semantics.html#the-a-element.`

A welcome benefit of HTML5 is that we can wrap multiple elements in an `<a>` tag. Previously, if you wanted your markup to validate, it was necessary to wrap each element in its own `<a>` tag. For example, look at the following code:

```
<h2><a href="index.html">The home page</a></h2>
<p><a href="index.html">This paragraph also links to the home page</a></p>
<a href="index.html"><img src="home-image.png" alt="A rendering of the home page" /></a>
```

Nowadays, we can ditch all the individual `<a>` tags and instead wrap the group, as demonstrated in the following code:

```
<a href="index.html">
  <h2>The home page</h2>
  <p>This paragraph also links to the home page</p>
  <img src="home-image.png" alt="A rendering of the home page" />
</a>
```

The only limitations to keep in mind with `<a>` tags are that, understandably, you can't wrap one `<a>` tag within another `<a>` tag or other interactive element (such as a `button`) and you can't wrap a form in an `<a>` tag either.

That's not to say you can't physically do it. I doubt your text editor is going to start a fight with you about it, but don't be surprised if things don't work as expected in the browser if you do!

New semantic elements in HTML5

My dictionary defines semantics as "the branch of linguistics and logic concerned with meaning." For our purposes, semantics is the process of giving our markup meaning. Why is this important?

Most websites follow fairly standard structural conventions; typical areas include a header, a footer, a sidebar, a navigation bar, and so on. As web authors, we will often name the `div` elements we use to more clearly designate these areas (for example, `<div class="Header">`). However, as far as the code itself goes, any user agent, and that includes a web browser, screen reader, or search engine crawler, parsing that content couldn't say for sure what the purpose of each of these `div` elements is. HTML5 solves that problem with new semantic elements.

 For the full list of HTML5 elements, get yourself (very) comfy and point your browser here: `http://www.w3.org/TR/html5/semantics.html#semantics`.

We won't cover every one of the new elements here, merely those I feel are the most beneficial or interesting in day-to-day responsive web design use. After we have gone through the elements and gained an understanding of their intended use, we will look at some content examples, and consider how they might be best marked up. Then, to end the chapter I'm going to set you a bigger challenge!

In terms of the HTML specification, the elements we will be looking at fall into one of three groups:

- **Sectioning elements**, for the broadest strokes in a HTML page. These are the kind of elements to use for header, footer, and sidebar areas.

- **Grouping elements**, which are used to wrap associated elements. Think of paragraphs, blockquotes, and content of that nature.

- **Text-level semantics**, which are the elements we use to designate particulars, like a section of bold or italic text or code.

We will now look at the most useful from each of these sections in turn.

The <main> element

For a long time, HTML5 had no element to demarcate the main content of a page. It was argued that the content that wasn't inside one of the other new semantic HTML5 elements would, by negation, be the main content. Thankfully, we now have a more declarative way to group the main content: the aptly named `<main>` tag. Whether you're wrapping the main content of a page or the main section of a web-based application, the `main` element is what you should be grouping it all with. Here's a particularly useful line from the specification:

> *"The main content area of a document includes content that is unique to that document and excludes content that is repeated across a set of documents such as site navigation links, copyright information, site logos and banners and search forms (unless the document or application's main function is that of a search form)."*

It's also worth noting that there shouldn't be more than one `main` on each page (after all, you can't have two main pieces of content) and it shouldn't be used as a descendent child element of some of the other semantic HTML5 elements, such as `article`, `aside`, `header`, `footer`, `nav`, or `header`.

 Read the official line on the `main` element at `http://www.w3.org/TR/html5/grouping-content.html#the-main-element`.

The <section> element

The `<section>` element is used to define a generic section of a document or application. For example, you may choose to create sections around your content: one section for contact information, another section for news feeds, and so on. It's important to understand that it isn't intended for styling purposes.

If you need to wrap an element merely to style it, you should continue to use a `div` as you would have before.

When working on web-based applications, I tend to use `section` as the wrapping element for visual components. It provides a simple way to see the beginning and end of components in the markup.

You can also qualify for yourself whether you should be using a `section` based upon whether the content you are sectioning has a natural heading within it (for example, an `h1-h6`). If it doesn't, it's likely you'd be better off opting for a `div`.

 To find out what the W3C specification says about `<section>`, go to the following URL: `http://www.w3.org/TR/html5/sections.html#the-section-element`.

The <nav> element

The `<nav>` element is used to wrap major navigational links to other pages or parts within the same page. As it is for use in major navigational blocks it isn't strictly intended for use in footers (although it can be) and the like, where groups of links to other pages are common. If you usually mark up your navigational elements with an unordered list (`<ul>`) and a bunch of list tags (`<li>`), you may be better served with a `nav` and a number of nested `<a>` tags instead.

 To find out what the W3C specification says about `<nav>`, go to the following URL: `http://www.w3.org/TR/html5/sections.html#the-nav-element`.

The <article> element

The `<article>` element, alongside `<section>`, can easily lead to confusion. I certainly had to read and re-read the specifications of each before it sank in. Here's my reiteration of the specification. The `<article>` element is used to wrap a self-contained piece of content. When structuring a page, ask whether the content you're intending to use within an `<article>` tag could be taken as a whole lump and pasted onto a different site and still make complete sense. Another way to think about it is, would the content that you are considering wrapping in an `<article>` actually constitute a separate article in an RSS feed? Obvious examples of content that should be wrapped with an `<article>` element would be blog posts or news stories. Be aware that if you are nesting `<article>` elements, it is presumed that the nested `<article>` elements are principally related to the outer article.

You can read the specification for the `<article>` element here: `http://www.w3.org/TR/html5/sections.html#the-article-element`.

The <aside> element

The `<aside>` element is used for content that is tangentially related to the content around it. In practical terms, I often use it for sidebars, or content as a little tip about a related subject in a blog post. It's also considered suitable for pull quotes, advertising, and groups of navigation elements; basically, anything not directly related to the main content would work well in an `aside`. If it was an e-commerce site, I'd consider areas like "Customers who bought this also bought" as prime candidates for an `<aside>`.

For more on what the W3C specification says about `<aside>`, visit `http://www.w3.org/TR/html5/sections.html#the-aside-element`.

The <header> element

Practically, the `<header>` can be used for the "masthead" area of a site's header but also as an introduction to other content, such as an introduction section within an `<article>` element. You can use it as many times on the same page as needed. You could have a `<header>` inside every `<section>` on your page for example.

Here's what the W3C specification says about `<header>`: `http://www.w3.org/TR/html5/sections.html#the-header-element`.

The <footer> element

Like the `<header>`, the `<footer>` element doesn't take part in the outline algorithm (more on that in the following section) so doesn't section content. Instead it should be used to contain information about the section it sits within. It might contain links to other documents or copyright information, for example. Like the `<header>`, it can be used multiple times within a page if needed. For example, it could be used for the footer of a blog but also a footer within a blog post `<article>`.

However, the specification notes that contact information for the author of a blog post should instead be wrapped by an `<address>` element.

 The W3C specification for the `<footer>` element can be found here: `http://www.w3.org/TR/html5/sections.html#the-footer-element`.

The HTML5 outline algorithm

Ordinarily, for an HTML document, headings would begin with an `h1` for the main page title and then progress to using lower hierarchy title tags as needed for subheadings and the like.

However, HTML5 introduced the ability for each sectioning container to have its own self-contained outline. That means it is not necessary to think about which level of heading tag you're at in terms of the entire document. You could just concentrate on the sectioning container you are currently working in.

To illustrate why this might be preferable, within a blog, post titles could be set to use `<h1>` tags, while the title of the blog itself could also have an `<h1>` tag. For example, consider the following structure:

```
<h1>Ben's site</h1>
<section>
  <h1>Ben's blog</h1>
  <p>All about what I do</p>
</section>
<article>
  <header>
    <h1>A post about something</h1>
    <p>Trust me this is a great read</p>
    <p>No, not really</p>
    <p>See. Told you.</p>
  </header>
</article>
```

Despite having multiple `<h1>` headings, the outline still appears as follows:

1. Ben's site
2. Ben's blog
3. A post about something

As such, theoretically you shouldn't need to keep track of the heading tag you need to use in terms of the whole document. It should be possible to use whatever the appropriate level of heading tag is needed within each piece of sectioned content and the HTML5 outline algorithm will order it accordingly.

You can test the outline of your documents using HTML5 outliners at one of the following URLs:

- `http://gsnedders.html5.org/outliner/`
- `http://hoyois.github.com/html5outliner/`

However, the reality is that search engines and the like make no use of the HTML5 outliner at present. Therefore, from a pragmatic standpoint, it probably makes more sense to continue thinking about headings in terms of the whole document. That will make your documents easier to read for search engines and also aid assistive technology to infer the correct meaning.

A note on h1-h6 elements

Something I wasn't aware of initially is that using `h1-h6` tags to mark up headings and subheadings is discouraged. I'm talking about this kind of thing:

```
<h1>Scones:</h1>
<h2>The most resplendent of snacks</h2>
```

Here's a quote from the HTML5 specification:

> *"h1–h6 elements must not be used to mark up subheadings, subtitles, alternative titles and taglines unless intended to be the heading for a new section or subsection."*

That's us told!

So, how should we author such content? The specification actually has a whole section, `http://www.w3.org/TR/html5/common-idioms.html#common-idioms`, dedicated to this. Personally, I preferred the old `<hgroup>` element, but sadly that has been deprecated (more info in the *Obsolete HTML features* section). So, to follow the advice of the specification, our prior example could be rewritten as:

```
<h1>Scones:</h1>
<p>The most resplendent of snacks</p>
```

Right, we've now covered the lion's share of the HTML sectioning elements. Let's now consider grouping elements.

The div element

The most ubiquitous grouping element is the `<div>`. The `<div>` is so widely used because it is opinion-less. It conveys nothing. The only implied meaning of a `div` is that it groups something. Despite that, you will often see a `div` wrapping nothing but a string of text.

You should only opt for a `div` as a last resort. It is the element to use when you can think of nothing better.

We have more elements in HTML than ever before, so as we continue, hopefully we will get acquainted with plenty of other elements that will be more suitable for the jobs you currently use a `div` for.

The p element

The `<p>` element is used to markup a paragraph. However, don't think that means it can only be used on text 3-4 lines long. On the contrary, use it to mark up any text that cannot be better marked up with one of the other elements. For non-specific text, the `p` element is definitely a better choice than a `div`.

The blockquote element

A `blockquote` is used to markup text that is quoted from somewhere else. You don't have to wrap the text with any other element, but you can. For example, knowing what we now do about the `p` tag, we can use that inside a `blockquote` too if we wish. Here is a simple example using `blockquote`. First, there's an introductory section of text in a `p` tag, and then a `blockquote`:

```
<p>I did like Ben's book, but he kept going on about scones. For
example:</p>
<blockquote>
All this writing about scones in our sample page and there's no
image of the beauties! I'm going to add in an image of a scone near
the top of the page; a sort of 'hero' image to entice users to read
the page.
</blockquote>
```

There's some good examples of how and when to use blockquotes over on the HTML specification too: `https://html.spec.whatwg.org/multipage/grouping-content.html#the-blockquote-element`.

The \<figure\> and \<figcaption\> elements

The HTML specification relates that the `<figure>` element:

> *"...can thus be used to annotate illustrations, diagrams, photos, code listings, etc."*

So we use it as an element to call out visuals of any sort, and the accompanying `<figcaption>` provides the means to add some text supporting the visuals. Now, it is worth pointing out here that while we should always provide text in the `alt` attribute of an `<img>` tag to support assistive technology or to mitigate problems if an image fails to load, it isn't a requirement to provide a `figcaption` with a figure. The `figcaption` is added if you want to add a visual description alongside the visuals. Here's how we could use it to revise a portion of markup from the first chapter:

```
<figure class="MoneyShot">
  <img
    class="MoneyShotImg"
    src="img/scones.jpg"
    alt="Incredible scones baked to perfection and ready to eat"
  />
  <figcaption class="ImageCaption">
    This image isn't of scones I have made, instead it's a stock
photo from Wikipedia
  </figcaption>
</figure>
```

You can see that the `<figure>` element is used to wrap this little self-contained block. Inside, the `<figcaption>` is used to provide a caption for the parent `<figure>` element.

It's perfect when images or code need a little caption alongside them (that wouldn't be suitable in the main text of the content).

 The specification for the `figure` element can be found here: `http://www.w3.org/TR/html5/grouping-content.html#the-figure-element`. The specification for the `figcaption` is here: `http://www.w3.org/TR/html5/grouping-content.html#the-figcaption-element`.

`<details>` and `<summary>` elements

How many times have you wanted to create a simple open and close widget on your page? A piece of summary text that when clicked, opens a panel with additional information? Modern HTML facilitates this pattern with the `details` and `summary` elements. Consider this markup (you can open `example3.html` from this chapter's code to play with it for yourself):

```
<details>
  <summary>I ate 15 scones in one day</summary>
  <p>
    Of course I didn't. It would probably kill me if I did. What
a way to go.
    Mmmmmm, scones!
  </p>
</details>
```

Opening this in Chrome, with no added styling, shows only the summary text by default:

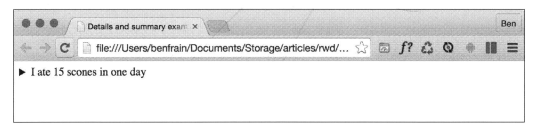

Figure 2.1: <details> and <summary> attempt to solve a common problem but their implementation is limited

Clicking anywhere on the `summary` text opens the panel. Clicking it again toggles it shut. If you want the panel open by default you can add the `open` attribute to the `details` element:

```
<details open>
  <summary>I ate 15 scones in one day</summary>
  <p>
    Of course I didn't. It would probably kill me if I did. What a
way to go.
    Mmmmmm, scones!
  </p>
</details>
```

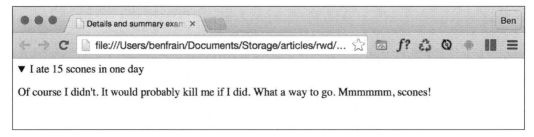

Figure 2.2: By adding the open attribute, the content is shown by default

Supporting browsers typically add some default styling to indicate the panel can be opened. Here in Chrome (and also Safari) that's a dark disclosure triangle. Different browsers have their own implementations of how we can deal with any marker for the details. As this is typically not a selector that has been defined in any W3C specification, to disable it in this instance, you need to use a proprietary pseudo class (note the `-webkit-` prefix):

```
summary::-webkit-details-marker {
   display: none;
}
```

You can of course use that same selector to style the marker differently.

Currently, there is no way of animating the open and close. Without JavaScript, there's also no way of toggling other details panels closed when another details/ summary combination is open. I'm not sure either of these desires will (or should) ever be addressed. However, I've therefore found the usefulness of these elements pretty limited by themselves. Rather than an all-in-one open/close drawer solution, you should think of them as a way to more semantically facilitate what you would have done previously with a `display: none;` toggle on a standard `div` with the help of JavaScript.

The <address> element

The `<address>` element is to be used explicitly for marking up contact information for its nearest `<article>` or `<body>` ancestor. To confuse matters, keep in mind that it isn't to be used for postal addresses and the like (unless they are indeed the contact addresses for the content in question). Instead, postal addresses and other arbitrary contact information should be wrapped in good ol' `<p>` tags. I'm not a fan of the `<address>` element. In my experience it would be far more useful to mark up a physical address with this element. However, hopefully it makes more sense to you.

For more on what the W3C specification says about `<address>`: `http://www.w3.org/TR/html5/sections.html#the-address-element`.

We have now covered the majority of the sectioning elements of HTML. We will now move on to the text-level elements. These are the elements used to mark up individual words, letters, and symbols to provide explicit meaning as to the intent.

HTML text-level semantics

Before HTML5, text-level semantic elements were referred to in the specifications as inline elements. Therefore, if you are familiar with that description, be aware that we are talking about the same thing here.

The section of the HTML specification that details text-level semantics can be found here: `http://www.w3.org/TR/html5/text-level-semantics.html#text-level-semantics`.

Let's take a look at the most common and useful text-level elements.

The <span> element

The `span` element is the text-level equivalent of a `div`. It is unopinionated and is the perfect element to reach for when you merely want to wrap text in an element for styling purposes.

The <b> element

Historically, visuals were defined in the markup and the `<b>` element meant "make this bold" (`http://www.w3.org/TR/html4/present/graphics.html#edef-B`). However, the specification now describes the `<b>` element like this:

> *"The b element represents a span of text to which attention is being drawn for utilitarian purposes without conveying any extra importance and with no implication of an alternate voice or mood, such as key words in a document abstract, product names in a review, actionable words in interactive text-driven software, or an article lede."*

Although no specific meaning is now attached to it, as it's text level, it's not intended to be used to surround large groups of markup. Use a `div` for that.

You should also be aware that because it was historically used to bold text, you'll typically have to reset the `font-weight` in CSS if you want content within a `<b>` tag to not appear bold.

For example:

```
b {
    font-weight: normal;
}
```

The \<strong\> element

If you do want to emphasize something for strength, urgency, or importance, `<strong>` is the element for you. Here is how the specification defines these use cases:

"**Importance**: *The strong element can be used in a heading, caption, or paragraph to distinguish the part that really matters from other parts that might be more detailed, more jovial, or merely boilerplate.*

Seriousness: *The strong element can be used to mark up a warning or caution notice.*

Urgency: *The strong element can be used to denote contents that the user needs to see sooner than other parts of the document.*"

You can read the full specification for `<strong>` here:

`https://www.w3.org/TR/html52/textlevel-semantics.html#the-strong-element`

The \<em\> element

I'll admit, in the past, I've often used `<em>` merely as a styling hook to provide italic text when I wanted it. I need to mend my ways as the HTML specification tells us:

"*The em element represents stress emphasis of its contents.*"

Therefore, unless you actually want the enclosed contents to be emphasized, consider using a `<b>` tag or, where relevant, an `<i>` or `span` tag instead.

The <i> element

The HTML5 specification describes the `<i>` as:

> *"A span of text in an alternate voice or mood, or otherwise offset from the normal prose in a manner indicating a different quality of text."*

Suffice it to say, it's not to be used to merely italicize something. For example, we could use it to mark up the odd name in this line of text:

```
<p>However, discussion on the hgroup element is now frustraneous
as it's now gone the way of the <i>Raphus cucullatus</i>.</p>
```

Or, perhaps if you were marking up a button in a food ordering web application, you might do this:

```
<button type="button">
    French Fries <i>No Salt Added</i>
</button>
```

There are plenty of other text-level semantic tags in HTML; for the full rundown, take a look at the relevant section of the specification at the following URL: `http://www.w3.org/TR/html5/text-level-semantics.html#text-level-semantics`.

Obsolete HTML features

If you have been writing HTML for a few years, you might be surprised to learn there are parts of HTML that are now considered obsolete. It's important to be aware that there are two camps of obsolete features in HTML: conforming and non-conforming. Conforming features will still work but will generate warnings in validators. Realistically, avoid them if you can but they aren't going to make the sky fall down if you do use them. Non-conforming features may still render in certain browsers but they may not. It's certainly not guaranteed.

In terms of obsolete and non-conforming features, there is quite a raft. I'll confess that there are many I have never used, and some I've never even seen! It's possible you may experience a similar reaction. However, if you're curious, you can find the full list of obsolete and non-conforming features at `http://www.w3.org/TR/html5/obsolete.html`. Notable obsolete and non-conforming features that you may occasionally encounter are `strike`, `center`, `font`, `acronym`, `frame`, and `frameset`.

There are also features that were present in earlier drafts of HTML5 that have now been dropped. `hgroup` is one such example. The `hgroup` element was originally proposed to wrap groups of headings: an `h1` for a title and an `h2` for a subtitle might have been wrapped in an `hgroup` element. However, discussion on the `hgroup` element is now frustraneous as it's now gone the way of the *Raphus cucullatus*.

Putting HTML elements to use

It's time to practice using some of the elements we have just looked at. Let's revisit the example from *Chapter 1*. If we compare the following markup to the original markup in *Chapter 1* (remember, you can download all the examples from `http://rwd.education`) you can see where the new elements we've looked at have been employed:

```html
<article>
  <header class="Header">
    <a href="/" class="LogoWrapper"
      ><img src="img/SOC-Logo.png" alt="Scone O'Clock logo"
    /></a>
    <h1 class="Strap">Scones: the most resplendent of snacks</h1>
  </header>
  <section class="IntroWrapper">
    <p class="IntroText">
      Occasionally maligned and misunderstood; the scone is
a quintessentially British classic.
    </p>
    <figure class="MoneyShot">
      <img class="MoneyShotImg" src="img/scones.jpg" alt="Incredible
scones" />
      <figcaption class="ImageCaption">
        Incredible scones, picture from Wikipedia
      </figcaption>
    </figure>
  </section>
  <p>Recipe and serving suggestions follow.</p>
  <section class="Ingredients">
    <h3 class="SubHeader">Ingredients</h3>
  </section>
  <section class="HowToMake">
    <h3 class="SubHeader">Method</h3>
  </section>
  <footer>
    Made for the book,
    <a href="http://rwd.education"
      >'Responsive web design with HTML5 and CSS'</a
    >
    by
```

```
    <address><a href="http://benfrain">Ben Frain</a></address>
  </footer>
</article>
```

I've removed a good portion of the inner content so we can concentrate on the structure. Hopefully you will agree that it's easy to discern different sections of markup from one another. However, at this point I'd also like to offer some pragmatic advice; it isn't the end of the world if you don't always pick the correct element for every single given situation.

For example, whether or not I used a `<section>` or `<div>` in the earlier example is of little real consequence. If we use an `<em>` when we should actually be using an `<i>`, I certainly don't feel it's a crime against humanity; the folks at the W3C won't hunt you down and tar and feather you for making the wrong choice. Just apply a little common sense. That said, if you can use elements like the `<header>` and `<footer>` when relevant, there are inherent accessibility benefits in doing so. I certainly think you're better than using nothing but `div` elements in your markup!

WCAG accessibility conformance and WAI-ARIA for more accessible web applications

Even since writing the first edition of this book in 2011/2012, the W3C has made great strides in making it easier for authors to make the necessary adjustments to code to make web pages more accessible.

Web Content Accessibility Guidelines (WCAG)

The **Web Content Accessibility Guidelines (WCAG)** exists to provide:

> *"a single shared standard for web content accessibility that meets the needs of individuals, organizations, and governments internationally"*

When it comes to more pedestrian web pages (as opposed to single-page web applications and the like) it makes sense to concentrate on the WCAG documentation. They offer a number of (mostly common sense) guidelines for how to ensure your web content is accessible. Each recommendation is rated by a conformance level: A, AA, or AAA. For more on these conformance levels, visit `http://www.w3.org/TR/UNDERSTANDING-WCAG20/conformance.html#uc-levels-head`.

You'll probably find that you are already adhering to many of the guidelines, like providing alternative text for images, for example. However, you can get a brief rundown of the guidelines at `http://www.w3.org/WAI/WCAG20/glance/Overview.html` and then build your own custom quick reference list of checks here: `http://www.w3.org/WAI/WCAG20/quickref/`.

I'd encourage everyone to spend an hour or two to look down the list. Many of the guidelines are simple to implement and offer real benefits to users.

WAI-ARIA

The aim of **Web Accessibility Initiative – Accessible Rich Internet Applications (WAI-ARIA)** is principally to solve the problem of making dynamic content on a web page accessible. It provides a means of describing roles, states, and properties for custom widgets (dynamic sections in web applications) so that they are recognizable and usable by assistive technology users. For example, if an on-screen widget displays a constantly updating stock price, how would a blind user accessing the page know that? WAI-ARIA attempts to solve this problem.

How to implement ARIA fully in something like a web application is outside the scope of this book. However, if that's the kind of project you are building, head over to `http://www.w3.org/WAI/intro/aria` for more information. Instead, let's just go over some of the most important headline points to consider about ARIA.

The first important point to note is that it used to be advisable to add landmark roles to headers and footers like this: `<header role="banner">` A header with ARIA landmark banner role `</header>`. However, `role="banner"` is now considered surplus to requirements. Look at the specifications for any of the elements we have looked at and you will see a dedicated *Allowed ARIA role attributes* section. Here is the relevant quote from the `<section>` element as an example:

> *"Allowed ARIA role attribute values: region role (default - do not set), alert, alertdialog, application, contentinfo, dialog, document, log, main, marquee, presentation, search or status."*

The key part there is "role (default - do not set)." This means explicitly adding an ARIA role to the element is pointless as it is implied by the element itself. A note in the specification now makes this clear:

> *"In the majority of cases setting an ARIA role and/or aria-* attribute that matches the default implicit ARIA semantics is unnecessary and not recommended as these properties are already set by the browser."*

Therefore, the easiest thing you can do to aid assistive technologies is use the correct elements where possible. A `header` element is going to be far more useful than `div class="Header"`. Similarly, if you have a button on your page, use the `<button>` element (rather than a `span` or another element styled to look like a button).

Taking ARIA further

If you want to explore a solid set of accessible design patterns, the W3C has a published set you can peruse here: `https://www.w3.org/TR/wai-aria-practices-1.1/examples/#examples_by_props_label`.

Test your designs for free with NonVisual Desktop Access (NVDA)

If you develop on the Windows platform and you'd like to test your ARIA enhanced designs on a screen reader, you can do so for free with NVDA. You can get it at the following URL: `http://www.nvda-project.org/`.

Google now also ships the free Accessibility Developer Tools for the Chrome browser (available cross-platform), which is well worth checking out.

There's also a growing number of tools that help quickly test your own designs against things like color blindness. For example, `https://michelf.ca/projects/sim-daltonism/` is a macOS app that lets you switch color blindness types and see a preview in a floating palette.

Hopefully, this brief introduction to WAI-ARIA and WCAG has given you a little background information on supporting assistive technologies. Perhaps adding assistive technology support to your next HTML project will be easier than you think. As a final resource for all things accessibility, there are handy links and advice galore on *The A11Y Project* homepage at `http://a11yproject.com/`.

Embedding media in HTML5

For many, HTML5 first entered their vocabulary when Apple refused to add support for Flash technology in their iOS devices. Flash had gained market dominance (some would argue a market stranglehold) as the plugin of choice to serve video through a web browser. However, rather than using Adobe's proprietary technology, Apple decided to rely on HTML5 instead to handle rich media rendering. While HTML5 was making good headway in this area anyway, Apple's public support of HTML5 gave it a major leg up and helped its media tools gain greater traction in the wider community.

We've discussed already that people tend to just use the term HTML rather than HTML5 these days, but that label was important historically in relation to media. Before HTML5, adding video and audio into markup was a bit of a pain. These days it's easy.

Adding video and audio in HTML

Video and audio in HTML is easy. Here's a "simple as can be" example of how to link to a video file in your page:

```
<video src="myVideo.mp4"></video>
```

HTML allows a single `<video></video>` tag (or `<audio></audio>` for audio) to do all the heavy lifting. It's also possible to insert text between the opening and closing tag to inform users when there is a problem. There are also additional attributes you'd ordinarily want to add, such as the height and width. Let's add these:

```
<video src="myVideo.mp4" width="640" height="480">If you're reading
this either the video didn't load or your browser is waaaayyyyyy
old!</video>
```

Now, if we add the preceding code snippet into our page and look at it in some browsers, it will appear but there will be no controls for playback. To ensure we show the default playback controls we need to add the `controls` attribute. For the sake of illustration, we could also add the `autoplay` attribute. However, I'd recommend against that in real-world scenarios—everyone hates videos that auto-play! Here's an example with the `controls` and `autoplay` attributes added:

```
<video src="myVideo.mp4" width="640" height="480" controls
autoplay>If you're reading this either the video didn't load or your
browser is waaaayyyyyy old!</video>
```

The result of the preceding code snippet is shown in the following screenshot:

Figure 2.3: With minimal code we have inserted a video into our page

Further attributes include `preload` to control preloading of media, `loop` to repeat the video, and `poster` to define a poster frame for the video, the image that shows while a video loads. To use an attribute, simply add it to the tag. Here's an example including all these attributes:

```
<video src="myVideo.mp4" width="640" height="480" controls autoplay
preload="auto" loop poster="myVideoPoster.png"> If you're reading
this either the video didn't load or your browser is waaaayyyyyy
old!</video>
```

Providing alternate media sources

The `<source>` tag enables us to provide alternate sources for media. For example, alongside providing an MP4 version of a video, if we wanted to provide support for a new format, we could easily do so. Furthermore, if the user didn't have any suitable playback technology in the browser, we could provide download links to the files themselves. Here's an example:

```
<video width="640" height="480" controls preload="auto" loop
poster="myVideoPoster.png">
    <source src="myVideo.sp8" type="video/super8" />
    <source src="myVideo.mp4" type="video/mp4" />
    <p><b>Download Video:</b> MP4 Format: <a href="myVideo.
mp4">"MP4"</a></p>
</video>
```

In that case, we first specified the source of a made-up video format called `super8`. The browser goes top to bottom deciding what to play, so if it doesn't support `super8`, it moves on to the next source, `mp4` in this case. And on and on it goes, moving down to the download link if it can't reconcile any of the sources listed. The `type` attribute tells the browser the MIME type of the resource. If you fail to specify this, the browser will fetch the content and try to play it anyway. But if you know the MIME type, you should add it in the `type` attribute. The prior code example and the sample video file (which, incidentally, is me appearing in the UK soap *Coronation Street* back when I had hair and hopes of starring alongside DeNiro) in MP4 format are in the `example2` section of the chapter's code.

Audio and video tags work almost identically

The `<audio>` tag works on the same principles as the `video` tag, with the same attributes (excluding `width`, `height`, and `poster`). The main difference between the two is the fact that `<audio>` has no playback area for visible content.

Responsive HTML5 video and iframes

The only problem with our lovely HTML video implementation is it's not responsive. That's right, an example in a book about responsive web design with HTML5 and CSS that doesn't respond. Thankfully, for HTML embedded video, the fix is easy. Simply remove any `height` and `width` attributes in the markup (for example, remove `width="640" height="480"`) and add the following in the CSS:

```
video {
  max-width: 100%;
  height: auto;
}
```

However, while that works fine for files that we might be hosting locally, it doesn't solve the problem of videos embedded within an iframe (take a bow YouTube, Vimeo, et al.) The following code will add a film trailer for *Midnight Run* from YouTube:

```
<iframe width="960" height="720" src="https://www.youtube.com/
embed/B1_N28DA3gY" frameborder="0" allowfullscreen></iframe>
```

However, if you add that to a page as is, even if adding that earlier CSS rule, if the viewport is less than 960px wide, things will start to get clipped.

The easiest way to solve this problem is with a little CSS trick pioneered by Gallic CSS maestro Thierry Koblentz here: `http://alistapart.com/article/creating-intrinsic-ratios-for-video`. Essentially, he is creating a box of the correct aspect ratio for the video it contains. I won't spoil the magician's own explanation, go take a read.

If you're feeling lazy, you don't even need to work out the aspect ratio and plug it in yourself; there's an online service that can do it for you. Just head to `http://embedresponsively.com/` and paste your iframe URL in. It will spit you out a simple chunk of code you can paste into your page.

For example, our *Midnight Run* trailer results in this (note the `padding-bottom` value to define the aspect ratio):

```
<style>
  .embed-container {
    position: relative;
    padding-bottom: 56.25%;
    height: 0;
    overflow: hidden;
    max-width: 100%;
    height: auto;
  }
  .embed-container iframe,
  .embed-container object,
  .embed-container embed {
    position: absolute;
    top: 0;
    left: 0;
    width: 100%;
    height: 100%;
  }
</style>
<div class="embed-container">
  <iframe
    src="http://www.youtube.com/embed/B1_N28DA3gY"
    frameborder="0"
    allowfullscreen
  ></iframe>
</div>
```

That's all there is to it! Simply add it to your page and you're done: we now have a fully responsive YouTube video (note: kids, don't pay any attention to Mr. DeNiro; smoking is bad)!

Summary

We've covered a lot in this chapter: everything from the basics of creating a page that validates as HTML5, through to embedding rich media (video) into our markup and ensuring it behaves responsively. Although not specific to responsive designs, we've also covered how we can write semantically rich and meaningful code and considered how we might ensure pages are meaningful and usable for users that are relying on assistive technology.

An exercise

In this chapter we covered a raft of HTML elements. We didn't cover them all, but we certainly covered all the elements you are likely to need day to day. I think you're ready to try a little exercise to see how much you have understood. Here is a screenshot of the site design used to create the website for this book:

Figure 2.4: A design of the website made for this book

If you have a Mac and you'd rather look at the original Sketch file, it's included in the download code as `RWD3e_design.sketch`.

Take a look at the design to try and create an HTML page for it. Consider the head section and what you need in there. Think about the language the content is in and any meta tags you might need. Then think about the visuals themselves. What might be the best elements to use to create the navigation section? Or each of those little sections below the book image? And what about that **DOWNLOAD CODE** box; any ideas how you might mark that up?

You can see the choices I made by visiting the live site at `https://rwd.education`, but do yourself a favor and don't peek until you've tried it for yourself!

3

Media Queries – Supporting Differing Viewports

This chapter will look in detail at CSS media queries, hopefully providing all that's needed to fully understand their capability, syntax, and future development. Where appropriate, we will use media queries to adjust the basic layout of our test site, adding relevant styles for wider screen sizes.

We ended the last chapter with a design for the `https://rwd.education/` website. For the sake of this chapter, I have written some preliminary markup and added some corresponding basic "mobile" styles.

If you open the `index.html` file inside this chapter's `start` folder in a web browser, you will see that the design looks acceptable on devices with slim viewports, such as mobile phones:

Figure 3.1: The design looks fine at smaller viewports

However, it quickly starts to look a little stretched when you widen the browser window:

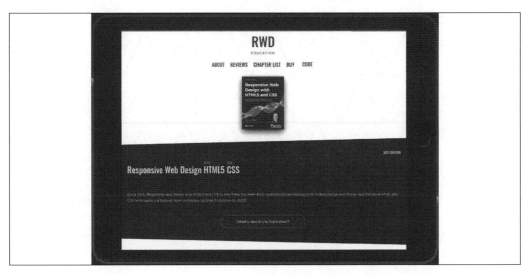

Figure 3.2: We definitely need to change the styles for wider viewports

The initial styles are written using a fluid/proportional approach. This means widths are generally written as percentages rather than fixed pixel sizes—the upshot being that the content at least grows and shrinks to fill the browser window regardless of how large or small it gets.

However, this still leaves you with the problem that when you go wide enough, you need to do something a little more drastic than just making things wider still!

We can fix this problem with media queries.

Media queries allow us to target specific CSS styles depending upon the capabilities of a device. For example, with just a few lines of CSS we can change the way content is displayed based upon things such as viewport width, screen aspect ratio, orientation (landscape or portrait), and so on.

In this chapter, we will:

- Understand the use of the viewport `meta` tag to make media queries work on mobile devices
- Learn why media queries are essential for a responsive web design
- Understand the media query syntax
- Learn how to use media queries in links, in `@import` statements, and within CSS files
- Understand what device features we can test for
- Consider whether to author similar media queries in one block or wherever it suits
- Consider the latest capabilities added in Media Queries Level 4 that we can use today—media features like `pointer`, `hover`, and `prefers-color-scheme`

Back in *Chapter 1, The Essentials of Responsive Web Design*, we inserted a `meta` tag into the head of our web page to make it work on mobile devices. At that point, I made the promise that *Chapter 3* would explain exactly what that tag was, what it does, and why we still have it. It's time to make good on that promise.

The viewport meta tag

When Apple released the iPhone in 2007, they introduced a proprietary `meta` tag called the viewport `meta` tag. Its purpose was to provide a way for web pages to communicate to mobile browsers how they would like the web browser to render the page.

Without this `meta` tag, iPhones would render web pages as a 980px wide window that the user would then have to zoom in or out of.

With this `meta` tag, it's possible to render a web page at its actual size and then adapt the layout to provide the kind of web page we now all expect to see when we browse the internet on our phones.

For the foreseeable future, any web page you want to be responsive, and render well across small screen devices, will still need to make use of this `meta` tag as Android and a growing number of other platforms also support it.

As you are now aware, the viewport `<meta>` tag is added within the `<head>` tags of the HTML. It can be set to a specific width (which we could specify in pixels, for example) or as a scale, for example, 2.0 (twice the actual size). Here's an example of the viewport `meta` tag set to show the browser at twice (200 percent) the actual size:

```
<meta name="viewport" content="initial-scale=2.0,width=device-width"
/>
```

Let's break the preceding `<meta>` tag down and understand what's going on. The `name="viewport"` attribute tells the browser this tag is dealing with the viewport. The `content="initial-scale=2.0` section is then saying, "scale the content to twice the size" (where 0.5 would be half the size, 3.0 would be three times the size, and so on), while the `width=device-width` part tells the browser that the width of the page should be equal to `device-width`. The `<meta>` tag can also be used to control the amount a user can zoom in and out of the page. This example allows users to go as large as three times the device's width and as small as half the device's width:

```
<meta name="viewport" content="width=device-width, maximum-scale=3,
minimum-scale=0.5" />
```

You could also disable users from zooming at all:

```
<meta name="viewport" content="initial-scale=1.0, user-scalable=no"
/>
```

`user-scalable=no` is the relevant part here.

However, with zooming being an important accessibility requirement, it would rarely be appropriate to prevent zooming. In addition, many browsers disable the ability to prevent zooming for that very reason.

Right, we'll change the scale to 1.0, which means that the mobile browser will render the page at 100 percent of its viewport. Setting it to the device's width means that our page should render at 100 percent of the width of all supported mobile browsers. For the majority of responsive web design cases, this `<meta>` tag would be appropriate:

```
<meta name="viewport" content="width=device-width,initial-scale=1.0"
/>
```

That should be all you need to know about viewport `meta` tags from a responsive design perspective. In short, ensure you have one added or things are unlikely to look and behave as you might expect! To be certain everything is in order, ensure you test at some point on an actual device.

Noticing the ubiquity of the viewport `meta` element, the W3C has attempted to bring the same capability into CSS. Head over to `http://dev.w3.org/csswg/css-device-adapt/` and read all about the `@viewport` declaration. The idea is that rather than writing a `<meta>` tag in the `<head>` section of your markup, you would declare the viewport settings in the CSS instead. To exemplify, something like `@viewport { width: 320px; }` in the CSS would set the browser width to 320 pixels. However, browser support is scant. As I write this, there seems little value in adding this to your CSS when all browsers understand the viewport `meta` tag.

Why media queries are needed for a responsive web design

If you head over to the W3C specification of the CSS3 media queries module (`http://www.w3.org/TR/css3-mediaqueries/`), you'll see that this is their official introduction to what media queries are all about:

> *"A media query consists of a media type and zero or more expressions that check for the conditions of particular media features. Among the media features that can be used in media queries are 'width', 'height', and 'color'. By using media queries, presentations can be tailored to a specific range of output devices without changing the content itself."*

While a fluid layout, created with percentages rather than fixed widths, can carry a design a substantial distance (we cover fluid layouts in full in the next chapter), given the gamut of screen sizes we have to cover, there are times when we need to revise the layout more substantially. Media queries make this possible—think of them as basic conditional logic for CSS.

Basic conditional logic in CSS

True programming languages all have some facility in which one of two or more possible situations is catered for. This usually takes the form of conditional logic, also known as "control flow," typified by an if/else statement.

If programming vernacular makes your eyes itch, fear not; it's a very simple concept. You probably dictate conditional logic every time you ask a friend to order for you when visiting a cafe, "If they've got triple chocolate muffins I'll have one of those; if not, I'll have a slice of carrot cake." It's a simple conditional statement with two possible results.

At the time of writing, CSS does not facilitate true conditional logic or programmatic features. Loops, functions, iteration, and complex math are still the sole domain of CSS preprocessors (did I mention a fine book on the subject of the Sass preprocessor, called *Sass and Compass for Designers*?). However, media queries are one mechanism that allows us to author basic conditional logic—styles applied depending upon whether certain media-based conditions are met.

Media query syntax

So what does a CSS media query look like and more importantly, how does it work?

Following is a complete but simple web page with no content but some basic styles and media queries:

```html
<!DOCTYPE html>
<html class="no-js" lang="en">
  <head>
    <meta charset="utf-8" />
    <title>Media Query Test</title>
    <meta name="viewport" content="width=device-width, initial-scale=1.0"/>
    <style>
      body {
        background-color: grey;
      }
      @media screen and (min-width: 320px) {
        body {
          background-color: green;
        }
      }
      @media screen and (min-width: 550px) {
```

```
      body {
        background-color: yellow;
      }
    }
    @media screen and (min-width: 768px) {
      body {
        background-color: orange;
      }
    }
    @media screen and (min-width: 960px) {
      body {
        background-color: red;
      }
    }
  </style>
 </head>
 <body></body>
</html>
```

Copy and save that into a new file, or, if you have the downloaded code for the book, you can find it in example_03-01.

Now, open the file in a browser and resize the window. The background color of the page will vary depending upon the current viewport size.

A default color is defined first, outside of a media query; when any of the media queries are true, the styles inside the media query overwrite the default.

The basic syntax of a media query is simple when you get used to it. You use the @media at-rule to communicate a media query and then write the media test in parentheses. The test must pass in order for the styles within the curly braces to be applied.

You can write media queries in links in HTML — to load particular style sheets if the media query passes. You can write media queries on CSS @import at-rules to determine which style sheets should be imported. You can also write media queries directly into a CSS file to determine which rules should be applied on the basis of which media queries resolve to true.

Let's look at each in turn.

Media queries in link tags

Here's what a media query looks like on a link you'd find in the `<head>` section of markup:

```
<link rel="stylesheet" media="screen and (orientation: portrait)"
href="portrait-screen.css" />
```

This media query is asking "Are you a screen and is your orientation portrait?".

Media query on an @import at-rule

Here's the same rule on an `@import` statement:

```
@import url("portrait-screen.css") screen and (orientation:
portrait);
```

You can see all the same component parts there—the file to be loaded, and the test that has to be passed. Different syntax, same outcome.

 Using the `@import` at-rule in CSS makes the browser request the relevant file from the network and this can add to the number of HTTP requests. This can sometimes adversely affect site load speed.

Media queries in a CSS file

Finally, here's the same media query written inside a CSS file, or, within a `style` tag inside the HTML:

```
@media screen and (orientation: portrait) {
    /* styles here */
}
```

Inverting media query logic

It's possible to reverse the logic of any media query expression by adding `not` to the beginning of the media query. For example, the following code would negate the result in our prior example, loading the file for anything that wasn't a screen with a portrait orientation:

```
<link rel="stylesheet" media="not screen and (orientation:
portrait)" href="portrait-screen.css" />
```

Although using the `not` keyword is occasionally useful, I find it is far simpler to just think about applying styles when you do want them. This way, you can stick to writing the tersest and simplest forms of media queries.

Combining media queries

It's also possible to string multiple expressions together. For example, let's extend one of our prior examples and also limit the file to devices that have a viewport greater than 800 pixels:

```
<link rel="stylesheet" media="screen and (orientation: portrait) and
(min-width: 800px)" href="800wide-portrait-screen.css" />
```

A number of different media queries

Further still, we could have a list of media queries. If any of the listed queries are true, the file will be loaded. If none are true, it won't. Here is an example:

```
<link rel="stylesheet" media="screen and (orientation: portrait) and
(min-width: 800px), print" href="800wide-portrait-screen.css" />
```

There are two points to note here. Firstly, a comma separates each media query, effectively acting like an `or` command. Secondly, you'll notice that after `print`, there is no trailing `and` or feature/value combination in parentheses. That's because in the absence of these values, the media query is applied to all media types. In our example, the styles will apply to all print scenarios.

 You should be aware that you can use any CSS length unit to specify media queries. Pixels (`px`) are the most commonly used but ems (`em`) and rems (`rem`) are equally valid and applicable.

Everyday media queries

At this point it's probably prudent of me to repeat that in most situations, you don't actually need to specify `screen`. Here's the key point in the specification:

> *"A shorthand syntax is offered for media queries that apply to all media types; the keyword 'all' can be left out (along with the trailing 'and'). I.e. if the media type is not explicitly given it is 'all'."*

Therefore, unless you want to target styles to particular media types, just leave the `screen and` part out. That's the way we will be writing media queries in the example files from this point on. For example:

```
@media (min-width: 750px) {
    /* styles */
}
```

What can media queries test for?

When building responsive designs, the media queries that get used most usually relate to a device's viewport width (`width`). In my own experience, I have found little need, with the occasional exception of `resolution` and viewport height, to employ the other capabilities. However, just in case the need arises, here is a list of all capabilities that Media Queries Level 3 can test for. Hopefully, some will pique your interest:

- `width`: The viewport width.
- `height`: The viewport height.
- `device-width`: The rendering surface's width (for our purposes, this is typically the screen width of a device).
- `device-height`: The rendering surface's height (for our purposes, this is typically the screen height of a device).
- `orientation`: This capability checks whether a device is portrait or landscape in orientation.
- `aspect-ratio`: The ratio of width to height based upon the viewport width and height. A 16:9 widescreen display can be written as `aspect-ratio: 16/9`.
- `device-aspect-ratio`: This capability is similar to `aspect-ratio` but is based upon the width and height of the device rendering surface, rather than viewport.
- `color`: The number of bits per color component. For example, `min-color: 16` will check that the device has 16-bit color.
- `color-index`: The number of entries in the color lookup table (the table is how a device changes one set of colors to another) of the device. Values must be numbers and cannot be negative.
- `monochrome`: This capability tests how many bits per pixel are in a monochrome frame buffer. The value would be a number (integer), for example, `monochrome: 2`, and cannot be negative.

- `resolution`: This capability can be used to test screen or print resolution; for example, `min-resolution: 300dpi`. It can also accept measurements in dots per centimeter; for example, `min-resolution: 118dpcm`.

- `scan`: This can be either progressive or interlace features largely particular to TVs. For example, a 720p HDTV (the p part of 720p indicates "progressive") could be targeted with `scan: progressive`, while a 1080i HDTV (the i part of 1080i indicates "interlaced") could be targeted with `scan: interlace`.

- `grid`: This capability indicates whether or not the device is grid- or bitmap-based.

All the preceding features, with the exception of `scan` and `grid`, can be prefixed with `min` or `max` to create ranges. For example, consider the following code snippet:

```
@import url("tiny.css") screen and (min-width:200px) and (max-
width:360px);
```

Here, a minimum (`min`) and maximum (`max`) have been applied to `width` to set a range. The `tiny.css` file will only be imported for screen devices with a minimum viewport width of 200 pixels and a maximum viewport width of 360 pixels.

Features deprecated in CSS Media Queries Level 4

It's worth being aware that the draft specification for Media Queries Level 4 deprecates the use of a few features (`http://dev.w3.org/csswg/mediaqueries-4/#mf-deprecated`), most notably `device-height`, `device-width`, and `device-aspect-ratio`. Support for those queries will remain in browsers but it's recommended you refrain from writing any new style sheets that use them.

Using media queries to alter a design

If you've read and at least partially understood what we have been through so far in this chapter, you should be ready to start using media queries in earnest.

I'd suggest opening the `index.html` file and the associated `styles.css` file from the `start` folder of this chapter's code. Then add some media queries to alter some areas of the page at certain viewport widths. Let's make a couple of changes together and then you can practice some of your own.

Let's look at the header section of what we have currently (viewport around 1200px wide):

Figure 3.3: At wider screens what we have in the browser doesn't match the designs

And here is the same section of the design we are building from:

Figure 3.4: The design calls for a different layout at wider viewports

We need to keep the design as it is for smaller viewports but amend it for larger ones. Let's start by adding a media query that makes the navigation links and the logo sit either side at 1200px and above:

```
@media (min-width: 1200px) {
    .rwd-MastHead {
        flex-direction: row;
        justify-content: space-between;
        max-width: 1000px;
        margin: 0 auto;
    }
}
```

If any of those styles don't make sense now, don't worry. We will be covering Flexbox layout in *Chapter 4, Fluid Layout, Flexbox, and Responsive Images*. What is important to understand is the media query itself. What we are saying is, "apply this rule, but only at a minimum width of 1200px."

And here is the effect of that rule in the browser:

Figure 3.5: Our first media query gets our navigation links over to the right

Now, the keen-eyed among you may realize that despite this new rule, which spreads out our logo and navigation links, we have some styles applied that we no longer need at this size. The following grab shows the no-longer-needed margin above and padding within the main navigation links:

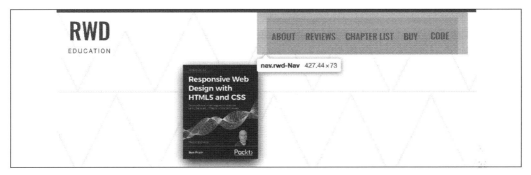

Figure 3.6: There are styles being applied we want to reset at this viewport

Let's write another media query to fix that. We'll make this change at a slightly smaller screen width:

```
@media (min-width: 1000px) {
    .rwd-Nav {
        margin: 0;
        padding: 0;
    }
}
```

In this instance, we are saying, "above 1000px, make the margin and padding zero for the `.rwd-Nav` element." Notice that each time, in our media query, we only amend the specific properties we need to change?

By writing our "base" styles as we have, outside of any media query, our actual media queries only need to encapsulate the differences needed.

It might seem a little reductive but the preceding process is essentially all there is to working with media queries. Write the basic styles without media queries and then work wider and wider, adding media queries and changes wherever needed to affect the design as required.

If you have the time, I implore you to try writing some media queries for yourself, whether it's by using the test page here or something of your own you want to work with. Pick something you want to change, pick a viewport width, and add a media query to make the change happen.

Testing responsive designs on emulators and simulators

Although there is no substitute for testing your development work on real devices, there are emulators for Android and a simulator for iOS (for the pedantic, a simulator merely simulates the relevant device whereas an emulator actually attempts to interpret the original device's code). The Android emulator for Windows, Linux, and Mac is available for free by installing Android Studio from https://developer.android.com/studio. The iOS simulator is only available to macOS users and comes as part of the Xcode package (free from the Mac App Store).

Browsers themselves are also including ever-improving tools for emulating mobile devices in their development tools. Both Firefox and Chrome currently have specific settings to emulate different mobile devices/viewports.

Advanced media query considerations

The following section deals with concerns for when you are highly proficient in writing media queries. Think of these topics as micro-optimizations. If you are just starting with media queries, you certainly shouldn't be worrying about any of these topics yet. Jump on to the Media Queries Level 4 section instead!

OK, media query uber-geekery, here we go...

Organizing media queries

Ordinarily, for a browser, CSS is considered to be a render-blocking asset. The browser needs to fetch and parse a linked CSS file before the rendering of the page can complete. This stands to reason as the browser needs to know what styles to apply for laying out and painting the page.

However, modern browsers are smart enough to discern which style sheets, (linked with media queries in the head) need to be analyzed immediately and which can be deferred until after the initial page rendering. The upshot of this is that for these browsers, CSS files that are linked with media queries that don't apply to the current environmental situation can be "deferred" until after the initial page load, providing some performance advantage. There's more on this topic over on Google's developer pages: `https://developers.google.com/web/fundamentals/performance/critical-rendering-path/render-blocking-css`.

However, I would like to draw your attention to this part in particular:

> *"...note that "render blocking" only refers to whether the browser will have to hold the initial rendering of the page on that resource. In either case, the CSS asset is still downloaded by the browser, albeit with a lower priority for non-blocking resources."*

To reiterate, all the linked files will still be downloaded; they just may not necessarily require the browser to hold the rendering of the page.

Therefore, a modern browser loading a responsive web page with four different style sheets linked with different media queries (to apply different styles for different viewport ranges) will download all four CSS files but probably only parse the applicable one initially before rendering the page. Take a look at `example_03-03` in the chapter's example code, which you may find more convenient to view at `https://benfrain.com/playground/mq-downloads/`. If you view that page with a slim viewport and you are proficient enough with your browser's developer tools, you can look in the network area and check that all files are downloaded, regardless of whether the media queries are actually being applied.

The practicalities of separating media queries

Apart from preference and/or compartmentalization of code, there is rarely a great tangible advantage in separating different media query styles into separate files. After all, using separate files increases the number of HTTP requests needed to render a page, which in turn can make pages slower in certain other situations. Nothing is ever easy on the Web! It's therefore really a question of evaluating the entire performance of your site and testing each scenario on different devices.

As a default approach, unless the project has considerable time available for performance optimizations, this is one of the last places I would look to make performance gains.

More practically, only once I am certain all images are compressed, all scripts are concatenated and minified, all assets are being served gzipped, all static content is being cached via CDNs, and all surplus CSS rules have been removed would I start looking to split up media queries into separate files for potential performance gains.

Nesting media queries "inline"

In all but exceptional circumstances, I recommend adding media queries within an existing style sheet alongside the "normal" rules. If you are happy to do the same, that leads to one further consideration: should media queries be declared underneath the associated selector? Or split off into a separate block of code at the end for all alike media queries? Glad you asked.

Combine media queries or write them where it suits?

I'm a fan of writing media queries underneath the original "normal" rule. For example, let's say I want to change the width of a couple of different elements, which are written at different places in the style sheet, depending upon the viewport width. I would typically do this:

```
.thing {
    width: 50%;
}

@media (min-width: 30rem) {
    .thing {
        width: 75%;
    }
}

/* A few more styles would go between them */

.thing2 {
    width: 65%;
}

@media (min-width: 30rem) {
    .thing2 {
        width: 75%;
    }
}
```

Can you see in this example, we have two separate media queries written testing for the same thing: `@media (min-width: 30rem)`? Surely duplicating media at-rules like this is overly verbose and wasteful? Shouldn't I be advocating grouping all the like media queries into a single block like this:

```css
.thing {
    width: 50%;
}

.thing2 {
    width: 65%;
}

@media (min-width: 30rem) {
    .thing {
        width: 75%;
    }
    .thing2 {
        width: 75%;
    }
}

/* A few more styles go after */
```

That is certainly one way to do it. However, from a maintenance point of view I find this more difficult. There is no "right" way to do this, but my preference is to define a rule for an individual selector once and have any variations of that rule (such as changes within media queries) defined immediately after. That way I don't have to search for separate blocks of code to find the declaration that is relevant to a particular selector.

 With CSS preprocessors, associating all alike rules can be even more convenient as the media query "variant" of a rule can be nested directly within the initial ruleset. But that's a technique for a different book. Curious? Take a look here: `https://ecss.io/chapter8.html#h-H2_1`.

It would seem fair to argue against the former technique on the grounds of verbosity. Surely file size alone should be enough reason not to write media queries in this manner? After all, no one wants a big bloated CSS file to serve their users. However, the simple fact is that gzip compression, which should be compressing all possible assets on your server, reduces the difference to a completely inconsequential amount.

I've done various tests on this in the past, so if it's something you would like to read more about, head over to `http://benfrain.com/inline-or-combined-media-queries-in-sass-fight/`. The bottom line is, I don't believe you should concern yourself with file size if you would rather write media queries directly after the "standard" styles.

As a final note on this, if you want to author your media queries directly after the original rule but have all alike media queries definitions merged into one, there are a number of build tools (at the time of writing Grunt and Gulp both have relevant plugins) that facilitate this.

That should give you everything you need to start wielding media queries like a pro. However, before we move on, there are a number of media query features in Media Queries Level 4 that we can actually start using today. Let's take a sneak peek!

Media Queries Level 4

Specifications at the W3C go through a ratification process, from **Working Draft (WD)**, to **Candidate Recommendation (CR)**, to **Proposed Recommendation (PR)**, before finally arriving, many years later, at W3C **Recommendation (REC)**. So modules at a greater maturity level than others are generally safer to use. For example, CSS Spatial Navigation Level 1 is in progress as I write this (`http://www.w3.org/TR/css-nav-1/`) at WD status with no support in browsers. Meanwhile the topic of this chapter, Media Queries Level 3, is implemented in every modern browser.

 If you have a spare day, you can knock yourself out reading all about the official explanation of the standards ratification process at `http://www.w3.org/2005/10/Process-20051014/tr`.

At the time of writing, while CSS Media Queries Level 4 enjoys a draft specification: `http://dev.w3.org/csswg/mediaqueries-4/`, not all the features it documents enjoy browser implementations. So in this section, we will concentrate on Media Queries Level 4 features that we can make use of—features already implemented in browsers.

Interaction media features

Interaction media queries are concerned with pointing devices and hover capability. Let's see what each of these can do for us.

The pointer media feature

Here is the W3C introduction to the `pointer` media feature:

> *"The pointer media feature is used to query about the presence and accuracy of a pointing device such as a mouse. If a device has multiple input mechanisms, the pointer media feature must reflect the characteristics of the "primary" input mechanism, as determined by the user agent."*

There are three possible states for the `pointer` features: `none`, `coarse`, and `fine`.

A `coarse` pointer device might be a finger on a touch screen device. However, it could equally be a cursor from a games console that doesn't have the fine-grained control of something like a mouse:

```
@media (pointer: coarse) {
    /* styles for when coarse pointer is present */
}
```

A `fine` pointer device might be a mouse but could also be a stylus pen or any future fine-grained pointer mechanism:

```
@media (pointer: fine) {
    /* styles for when fine pointer is present */
}
```

Browsers report whether the value of `pointer` is `fine`, `coarse`, or `none`, based on the "primary" pointing device. Therefore, consider that just because a device has the capability of a fine pointer, it doesn't mean that will be the primary pointing device. Think of tablets where the primary pointer is a finger (coarse), but that has an attached stylus—a fine pointing device.

 The safest bet is always to assume users are using touch-based input and to size user interface elements accordingly. That way, even if they are using a mouse they will have no difficulty using the interface with ease. If however you assume mouse input and don't provide affordance for coarse pointers, it might make for a difficult user experience.

Read the draft of this feature here: `https://www.w3.org/TR/mediaqueries-4/#pointer`.

The hover media feature

As you might imagine, the `hover` media feature tests a device's ability to hover over elements on the screen. If the user has multiple inputs at their disposal (touch and mouse, for example), characteristics of the primary input are used. Here are the possible values and example code.

For users that have no ability to hover, we can target styles at them with a value of `none`:

```
@media (hover: none) {
    /* styles for when the user cannot hover */
}
```

Or, as before, we might choose to make the non-hover scenario the default and then only add hover styles for devices that take advantage of them:

```
@media (hover) {
    /* styles for when user can hover */
}
```

Be aware that there are also `any-pointer` or `any-hover` media features. They are like the preceding `hover` and `pointer` but test the capabilities of any of the possible input devices.

That way, if you want to apply styles if any input device is capable of hover, regardless of whether that input device is the primary one:

```
@media (any-hover: hover) {
    /* styles if any input device is capable of hover*/
}
```

If you wanted to style an element a certain way based upon whether any attached pointer device was coarse, you could use `any-pointer` like this:

```
@media (any-pointer: coarse) {
    /* styles to be applied if any attached pointer is coarse */
}
```

The prefers-color-scheme media feature

In the last couple of years, popular operating systems for both desktop and mobile computers have given users the option of a "dark mode." To supplement this, operating systems expose this user preference to the browser by way of the `prefers-color-scheme` media feature. This media query is actually in Level 5 of the specification, not Level 4. However, it is in the odd situation of being implemented in most common browsers already.

At present there are three possible preferences: `light`, `dark`, and `no-preference`. To demonstrate this feature's use, we might amend the default colors for a page like this:

```
body {
    background-color: #e4e4e4;
    color: #545454;
}

@media (prefers-color-scheme: dark) {
    body {
        background-color: #333;
        color: #ddd;
    }
}
```

In the same vein as I'm recommending you to write your default "mobile" styles in the root of your style sheets, I would recommend writing the default colors in the root too and add one of these queries to cater for an alternative interface if needed or desired.

You can read the draft specification for the `prefers-color-scheme` media feature here: `https://drafts.csswg.org/mediaqueries-5/#prefers-color-scheme`.

Summary

In this chapter, we've learned what media queries are, why we need them, and how to include them in our CSS files. We've also learned how to use the viewport `meta` tag to make browsers render pages in the manner we'd like.

Don't worry about trying to memorize the syntax of media queries. Just get an understanding of the underlying principles and you can look up the syntax anytime; after all, that's what all developers do! As long as you understand what you can accomplish with media queries, our work here is largely done.

Back in *Chapter 1, The Essentials of Responsive Web Design* we noted that the three tenets of responsive web design are media queries, flexible layouts, and flexible media. We're three chapters in and we've only covered media queries! We're going to put that right in the next chapter.

In *Chapter 4, Fluid Layout, Flexbox, and Responsive Images*, we are going to take a deep dive into fluid layouts and images. We will cover how to convert a fixed-width design into a fluid proportional layout before laying out page elements with Flexbox, as well as covering flexible media in detail along with responsive images.

It's going to be another packed chapter, so get yourself comfy and I'll see you there!

4
Fluid Layout, Flexbox, and Responsive Images

At the end of the last chapter, we reminded ourselves that the three core tenets of responsive web design are fluid layout, media queries, and flexible media. We spent *Chapter 3, Media Queries – Supporting Differing Viewports*, learning all about media queries. Now we know how to wield them to change a layout at a particular "breakpoint."

In this chapter, we will focus on the other two pillars of responsive web design: fluid layout and flexible media. By the end of this chapter, we will be able to ensure any designs we code can flex easily between breakpoints, responding to the confines of their container.

Eons ago, in the mists of time (well, the late 1990s), websites were typically built with their widths defined as percentages. These percentage-based widths fluidly adjusted to the screen and were known as fluid layouts.

In the years after, in the mid-to-late 2000s, there was an intervening fixation on fixed-width designs (I blame those pesky print designers and their obsession with pixel-perfect precision). Nowadays, as we build responsive web designs, we need to look back to fluid layouts and remember all the benefits they offer.

Until fairly recently, web developers have used several CSS layout mechanisms to create great fluid layouts. If you've worked on the web for any length of time, you will be familiar with blocks, inline-blocks, tables, and other techniques to achieve any given layout. As I write this in 2020, there seems little benefit in giving those old techniques more than a cursory mention. We now have two powerful CSS layout mechanisms at our disposal: CSS Flexbox and CSS Grid.

This chapter will deal with CSS Flexbox. In *Chapter 5*, *Layout with CSS Grid*, I've got a feeling you can guess what we will be covering.

Flexbox is so useful because it can do more than merely provide a fluid layout mechanism. Do you want to center content easily, change the source order of markup, and generally create amazing layouts with ease? Flexbox has you covered.

In this chapter, we will:

- Learn how to convert fixed pixel layouts to proportional sizes
- Consider existing CSS layout mechanisms and their shortfalls
- Recognize Flexbox as a practical path beyond these limitations
- Understand the Flexible Box Layout Module and the benefits it offers
- Learn how to use responsive images and `srcset` for resolution switching and art direction

Let's crack on with our first task: converting fixed designs into fluid relationships. This is a task that you'll need to perform constantly when building responsive web designs.

Converting a fixed pixel design to a fluid proportional layout

Graphic composites, or "comps," as they are often called, exported from a program such as Photoshop, Illustrator, or Sketch all have fixed pixel dimensions. At some point, the designs need to be converted to proportional dimensions when recreating the design as a fluid layout for the browser.

There is a beautifully simple formula for making this conversion that the father of responsive web design, Ethan Marcotte, set down in his 2009 article, *Fluid Grids* (http://alistapart.com/article/FLUIDGRIDS):

$$target / context = result$$

Put another way, divide the units of the thing you want by the thing it lives in. Let's put that into practice. Understanding it will enable you to convert any fixed dimension layouts into responsive/fluid equivalents.

Consider a very basic page layout intended for desktop. In an ideal world, we would always be moving to a desktop layout from a smaller screen layout; however, for the sake of illustrating the proportions, we will look at the two situations back to front.

Here's an image of the layout:

Figure 4.1: A basic "desktop" layout

The layout is 960px wide. Both the header and footer are the full widths of the layout. The left-hand area is 200px wide, and the right-hand area is 100px wide. That leaves 660px for the main content area. Our job is to convert this fixed-width design into a fluid layout that retains its proportions as it is resized. For our first task, we need to convert the middle and side sections into proportional dimensions.

We will begin by converting the left-hand side. The left-hand side is 200 units wide. This value is our target value. We will divide that target size by 960 units, our context, and we have a result: .208333333. Now, whenever we get our result with this formula, we need to shift the decimal point two points to the right. That gives us a value that is the target value described as a percentage of its parent. In this case, the left-hand section is 20.8333333% of its parent.

Let's practice the formula again on the middle section. Our target value is 660. Divide that by our context of 960 and we get .6875. Move the decimal two points to the right and we have 68.75%.

Finally, let's look at the right-hand section. Our target is 100. We divide that by the context of 960 and we get .104166667. Move the decimal point and we have a value of 10.4166667%.

That's as difficult as it gets. Say it with me: target, divided by context, equals result.

 You can use values with long decimal values with no issues in the CSS. Or, if you would rather see more palatable numbers in your code, rounding them to two decimal points will work just as well for the browser.

To prove the point, let's quickly build that basic layout as blocks in the browser. To make it easier to follow along, I have added a class to the various elements that describes which piece of the "comp" they are referring to. It's not a good idea to name things based on their location ordinarily. The location can change, especially with a responsive design. In short, do as I say and not as I do here!

You can view the layout as example_04-01. Here is the HTML:

```html
<div class="Wrap">
  <header class="Header"></header>
  <div class="WrapMiddle">
    <aside class="Left"></aside>
    <main class="Middle"></main>
    <aside class="Right"></aside>
  </div>
  <footer class="Footer"></footer>
</div>
```

And here is the CSS:

```css
html,
body {
  margin: 0;
  padding: 0;
}

.Wrap {
  max-width: 1400px;
```

```css
    margin: 0 auto;
}

.Header {
  width: 100%;
  height: 130px;
  background-color: #038c5a;
}

.WrapMiddle {
  width: 100%;
  font-size: 0;
}

.Left {
  height: 625px;
  width: 20.83%;
  background-color: #03a66a;
  display: inline-block;
}

.Middle {
  height: 625px;
  width: 68.75%;
  background-color: #bbbf90;
  display: inline-block;
}

.Right {
  height: 625px;
  width: 10.41%;
  background-color: #03a66a;
  display: inline-block;
}

.Footer {
  height: 200px;
  width: 100%;
  background-color: #025059;
}
```

If you open the example code in a browser and resize the page, you will see that the dimensions of the .Left, .Middle, and .Right sections remain proportional to one another. You can also play around with the max-width of the .Wrap values to make the bounding dimensions for the layout bigger or smaller (in the example, it's set to 1400px).

Now, let's consider how we would have the same content on a smaller screen that flexes to a point and then changes to the layout we have already seen. You can view the final code of this layout in example_04-02.

The idea is that, for smaller screens, we will have a single "tube" of content. The left-hand area will only be viewable as an "off-canvas" area; typically, an area for a menu or similar, which sits off the viewable screen area and slides in when a menu button is pressed. The main content sits below the header, then the right-hand section below that, and finally the footer area. In our example, we can expose the left-hand menu area by clicking anywhere on the header. Typically, when making this kind of design pattern for real, a menu button would be used to activate the side menu.

As you would expect, when combining this with our newly mastered media query skills, we can adjust the viewport and the design just "responds" — effortlessly moving from one layout to another and stretching between the two. I'm not going to list all the CSS properties here; it's all in example_04-02. However, here's an example — the left-hand section:

```css
.Left {
  height: 625px;
  background-color: #03a66a;
  display: inline-block;
  position: absolute;
  left: -200px;
  width: 200px;
  font-size: 0.9rem;
  transition: transform 0.3s;
}

@media (min-width: 40rem) {
  .Left {
    width: 20.83%;
    left: 0;
    position: relative;
  }
}
```

You can see that, up first, without a media query, is the small screen layout. Then, at larger screen sizes, the width becomes proportional, the positioning relative, and the left value is set to zero. We don't need to rewrite properties such as `height`, `display`, or `background-color` as we aren't changing them.

This is progress. We have combined two of the core responsive web design techniques we have covered; converting fixed dimensions to proportions and using media queries to target CSS rules relevant to the viewport size.

 In a real project, we should be making some provision if JavaScript isn't available and we need to view the content of the menu. We deal with this scenario in detail in *Chapter 9, Transitions, Transformations, and Animations*.

We have now covered the essentials of fluid design. To summarize, where needed, make the dimensions of elements proportional rather than fixed. This way, designs adapt to the size of their container. And you now have the simple target / context = result formula to make the necessary calculations.

Before we go on to flexible media, we'll cover the CSS Flexbox layout mechanism.

Why do we need Flexbox?

We are now going to explore using CSS Flexible Box Layout, or Flexbox as it is more commonly known. However, before we do that, I think it will be prudent to first consider the shortfalls of existing layout techniques, such as inline-block, floats, and tables. Now, if you have never used floats, CSS tables, or inline-blocks to achieve layouts before, I'd likely advise you to not bother. As we will see, there are better ways to do it now. However, if you have used any of those techniques, it's worth reminding ourselves of the pain points.

Inline-block and white-space

The biggest issue with using inline-block as a layout mechanism is that it renders a space between HTML elements. This is not a bug (although most developers would welcome a sane way to remove the space), but it does require a few hacks to remove the space when it's unwanted, which, for me, is about 95% of the time. There are a bunch of ways to do this. However, rather than list each possible workaround for removing the white-space when using inline-block, refer to this article by the irrepressible Chris Coyier: `http://css-tricks.com/fighting-the-space-between-inline-block-elements/`.

It's also worth pointing out that there is no simple way to vertically center content within an inline-block. Using inline-block, there is also no way of having two sibling elements where one has a fixed width and another fluidly fills the remaining space.

Floats

I hate using floats for layout. There, I said it. In their favor, they work everywhere fairly consistently. However, there are two major irritations.

Firstly, when specifying the width of floated elements in percentages, their computed widths don't get rounded consistently across browsers (some browsers round up, some down). This means that, sometimes, sections will drop down below others when not intended, and at other times they can leave an irritating gap at one side.

Secondly, you usually have to "clear" the floats so that parent boxes/elements don't collapse. It's easy enough to do this, but it's a constant reminder that floats were never intended to be used as a robust layout mechanism.

Table and table-cell

Don't confuse `display: table` and `display: table-cell` with the equivalent HTML elements. These CSS properties merely mimic the layout of their HTML-based brethren. They in no way affect the structure of the HTML.

In years gone by, I've found enormous utility in using CSS tables for layout. For one, using `display: table` with a `display: table-cell` child enabled consistent and robust vertical centering of elements. Also, `table-cell` elements inside `table` elements space themselves perfectly; they don't suffer rounding issues like floated elements. You also get browser support all the way back to Internet Explorer 7!

However, there are limitations. Generally, it's necessary to wrap an extra element around items—to get perfect vertical centering, a table-cell must live inside an element set as a table. It's also not possible to wrap items set as `display: table-cell` on to multiple lines.

In conclusion, all of the existing layout methods have severe limitations. Thankfully, Flexbox overcomes them all.

Cue the trumpets and roll out the red carpet. Here comes Flexbox.

Introducing Flexbox

Flexbox addresses the shortfalls in each of the aforementioned display mechanisms. Here's a brief overview of its superpowers:

- It can easily center contents vertically.

- It can change the visual order of elements.

- It can automatically space and align elements within a box, automatically assigning available space between them.

- Items can be laid out in a row, a row going in the reverse direction, a column down the page, or a column going in reverse order up a page.

- It can make you look 10 years younger (probably not, but in low numbers of empirical tests (me), it has been proven to reduce stress).

The bumpy path to Flexbox

Flexbox has been through a few major iterations before arriving at the stable version we have today. For example, consider the changes from the 2009 version (`http://www.w3.org/TR/2009/WD-css3-flexbox-20090723/`), the 2011 version (`http://www.w3.org/TR/2011/WD-css3-flexbox-20111129/`), and the 2014 version we are basing our examples on (`http://www.w3.org/TR/css-flexbox-1/`). The syntax differences are marked.

These differing specifications mean there have been three major implementations across browsers. How many of these you need to concern yourself with depends on the level of browser support you need.

However, given the differing versions, we need to take a brief but essential tangent.

Leave prefixing to someone else

Writing Flexbox code to gain the widest possible browser support is a tough task by hand. Here's an example; I'm going to set three Flexbox-related properties and values. Consider this:

```css
.flex {
  display: flex;
  flex: 1;
  justify-content: space-between;
}
```

That's how the properties and values would look in the official syntax. However, if we want support for Android browsers (v4 and below) and IE 10, here is what would actually be needed:

```css
.flex {
  display: -webkit-box;
```

```
    display: -webkit-flex;
    display: -ms-flexbox;
    display: flex;
    -webkit-box-flex: 1;
    -webkit-flex: 1;
    -ms-flex: 1;
    flex: 1;
    -webkit-box-pack: justify;
    -webkit-justify-content: space-between;
    -ms-flex-pack: justify;
    justify-content: space-between;
}
```

I don't know about you, but I'd rather spend my time doing something more productive than writing out that little lot each time! In short, if you want or need the broadest level of browser support for Flexbox, take the time to set up an autoprefixing solution.

Choosing your autoprefixing solution

For the sake of your sanity, to accurately and easily add vendor prefixes to CSS, use some form of automatic prefixing solution. Right now, I favor Autoprefixer (https://github.com/postcss/autoprefixer). It's fast, easy to set up, and very accurate.

There are versions of Autoprefixer for most setups; you don't necessarily need a command line-based build tool (such as Gulp or Grunt). For example, if you use Sublime Text, there is a version that will work straight from the command palette: https://github.com/sindresorhus/sublime-autoprefixer. There are also versions of Autoprefixer for Atom, Brackets, Visual Studio Code, and more.

From this point on, unless essential to illustrate a point, there will be no more vendor prefixes in the code samples.

Getting Flexy

Flexbox has four key characteristics: direction, alignment, ordering, and flexibility. We'll cover all of these characteristics and how they relate to each other by way of a few examples.

The examples are deliberately simplistic; we are just moving some boxes and their content around so that we can understand the principles of how Flexbox works.

Perfect vertically centered text

Note that this first Flexbox example is `example_04-03`:

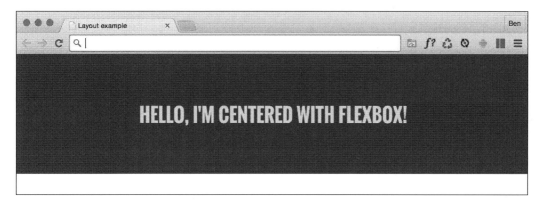

Figure 4.2: Centering is simple with Flexbox

Here's the markup:

```
<div class="CenterMe">
  Hello, I'm centered with Flexbox!
</div>
```

Here is the entire CSS rule that's styling that markup:

```
.CenterMe {
  background-color: indigo;
  color: #ebebeb;
  font-family: 'Oswald', sans-serif;
  font-size: 2rem;
  text-transform: uppercase;
  height: 200px;
  display: flex;
  align-items: center;
  justify-content: center;
}
```

The majority of the property/value pairs in that rule are merely setting the colors and font sizes. The three properties we are interested in are:

```css
.CenterMe {
  /* other properties */
  display: flex;
  align-items: center;
  justify-content: center;
}
```

If you have not used Flexbox or any of the properties in the related Box Alignment specification (http://www.w3.org/TR/css3-align/), these properties probably seem a little alien. Let's consider what each one does:

- `display: flex`: This is the bread and butter of Flexbox. This merely sets the item to be a Flexbox, as opposed to a block or inline-block.
- `align-items`: This aligns the items within a Flexbox in the cross axis, vertically centering the text in our example.
- `justify-content`: This sets the main axis, centering the content. With a Flexbox row, you can think of it as the button in a word processor that sets the text to the left, right, or center (although there are additional `justify-content` values we will look at shortly).

OK, before we get further into the properties of Flexbox, we will consider a few more examples.

> In some of these examples, I'm making use of the Google-hosted font "Oswald" (with a fallback to a sans serif font). In *Chapter 6, CSS Selectors, Typography, Color Modes, and More*, we will look at how we can use the @font-face rule to link to custom font files.

Offset items

How about a simple list of navigation items, but with one offset to one side?

Here's what it looks like:

Figure 4.3: Flexbox makes it simple to offset one link in a list

Here's the markup:

```
<div class="MenuWrap">
  <a href="#" class="ListItem">Home</a>
  <a href="#" class="ListItem">About Us</a>
  <a href="#" class="ListItem">Products</a>
  <a href="#" class="ListItem">Policy</a>
  <a href="#" class="LastItem">Contact Us</a>
</div>
```

And here is the CSS:

```
.MenuWrap {
  background-color: indigo;
  font-family: 'Oswald', sans-serif;
  font-size: 1rem;
  min-height: 2.75rem;
  display: flex;
  align-items: center;
  padding: 0 1rem;
}

.ListItem,
.LastItem {
  color: #ebebeb;
  text-decoration: none;
}

.ListItem {
  margin-right: 1rem;
}

.LastItem {
  margin-left: auto;
}
```

When you set `display: flex;` on a wrapping element, the children of that element become flex items, which then get laid out using the flex layout model. The magical property here is `margin-left: auto`, which makes that item use all of the available margin on that side.

Reverse the order of items

Want to reverse the order of the items?

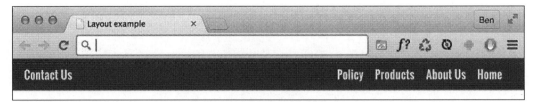

Figure 4.4: Reversing the visual order with Flexbox

It's as easy as adding `flex-direction: row-reverse;` to the wrapping element and changing `margin-left: auto` to `margin-right: auto` on the offset item:

```css
.MenuWrap {
  background-color: indigo;
  font-family: 'Oswald', sans-serif;
  font-size: 1rem;
  min-height: 2.75rem;
  display: flex;
  flex-direction: row-reverse;
  align-items: center;
  padding: 0 1rem;
}

.ListItem,
.LastItem {
  color: #ebebeb;
  text-decoration: none;
}

.ListItem {
  margin-right: 1rem;
}

.LastItem {
  margin-right: auto;
}
```

How about if we want them laid out vertically instead?

Simple. Change to `flex-direction: column;` on the wrapping element and remove the auto margin:

```css
.MenuWrap {
  background-color: indigo;
  font-family: 'Oswald', sans-serif;
  font-size: 1rem;
  min-height: 2.75rem;
  display: flex;
  flex-direction: column;
  align-items: center;
  padding: 0 1rem;
}

.ListItem,
.LastItem {
  color: #ebebeb;
  text-decoration: none;
}
```

Column reverse

Want them stacked in the opposite direction? Just change to `flex-direction: column-reverse;` and you're done.

 There is a `flex-flow` property that is shorthand for setting `flex-direction` and `flex-wrap` in one go. For example, `flex-flow: row wrap;` would set the direction to a row and set the wrapping on. However, at least initially, I find it easier to specify the two settings separately. The `flex-wrap` property is also absent from the oldest Flexbox implementations, so it can render the whole declaration void in certain browsers.

Different Flexbox layouts with media queries

As the name suggests, Flexbox is inherently flexible, so how about we go for a column list of items at smaller viewports and a row style layout when space allows? It's a piece of cake with Flexbox. In fact, we have already used that technique in the last chapter. Do you remember the header of the `https://rwd.education` website we started?

Here is the relevant section again:

```
.rwd-MastHead {
  display: flex;
  flex-direction: column;
}

@media (min-width: 1200px) {
  .rwd-MastHead {
    flex-direction: row;
    justify-content: space-between;
    max-width: 1000px;
    margin: 0 auto;
  }
}
```

At the outset, we set the content to flow in a column down the page, with the logo and navigation links one below the other. Then, at a minimum width of 1200px, we make those elements display as a row, one at either side. The space between them is provided by the `justify-content` property. We will look at this in more detail very shortly.

Inline-flex

Flexbox has an inline variant to complement `inline-block` and `inline-table`. As you might have guessed, it is `display: inline-flex;`. Thanks to its beautiful centering abilities, you can do some wacky things with very little effort:

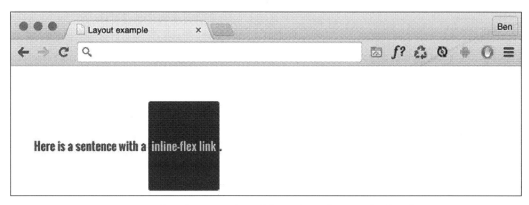

Figure 4.5: The inline equivalent of flex is the aptly named "inline-flex"

Here's the markup:

```
<p>
  Here is a sentence with a
  <a
    href="http://www.w3.org/TR/css-flexbox-1/#flex-containers"
    class="InlineFlex"
    >inline-flex link</a
  >.
</p>
```

And, using the same basic styles as the previous examples for the fonts, font size and colors, here is the CSS needed:

```
.InlineFlex {
  display: inline-flex;
  align-items: center;
  height: 120px;
  padding: 0 4px;
  background-color: indigo;
  text-decoration: none;
  border-radius: 3px;
  color: #ddd;
}
```

When items are set as `inline-flex` anonymously, which happens if their parent element is not set to `display: flex`, then they retain whitespace between elements, just like `inline-block` or `inline-table` do. However, if they are within a flex container, then whitespace is removed, much as it is with CSS table-cell items within a CSS table. Of course, you don't always have to center items within a Flexbox. There are a number of different options. Let's look at those now.

Flexbox alignment properties

If you want to play with this example, you can find it at `example_04-07`. Remember, the example code you download will be at the point where we finish this section, so if you want to "work along," you may prefer to delete all the HTML inside the `<body>` tag, and all the class based CSS rules in the example file, and start again.

The important thing to understand with Flexbox alignment is the concept of the axis. There are two axes to consider, the "main axis" and the "cross axis." What each of these represents depends on the direction the Flexbox is set to. For example, if the direction of your Flexbox is set to row, the main axis will be the horizontal axis and the cross axis will be the vertical axis.

Conversely, if your Flexbox direction is set to column, the main axis will be the vertical axis and the cross axis will be the horizontal axis.

The specification (`http://www.w3.org/TR/css-flexbox-1/#justify-content-property`) provides the following illustration to aid authors:

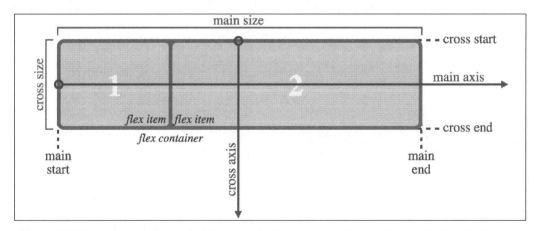

Figure 4.6: This image from the specification shows that the main axis always relates to the direction the flex container is heading

Here's the basic markup of our example:

```
<div class="FlexWrapper">
  <div class="FlexItem">I am content in the inner Flexbox.</div>
</div>
```

Let's set a few basic Flexbox-related styles:

```
.FlexWrapper {
  background-color: indigo;
  display: flex;
  height: 200px;
  width: 400px;
}

.FlexItem {
  background-color: #34005b;
  display: flex;
  height: 100px;
  width: 200px;
}
```

In the browser, that produces this:

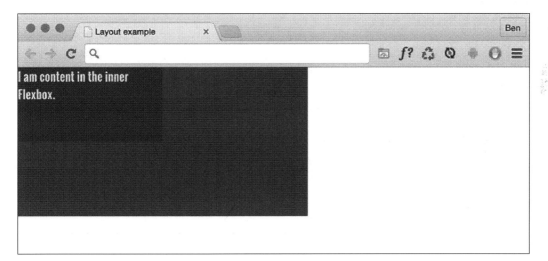

Figure 4.7: With no alignment properties set, child elements default to the top left

Right, let's test drive the effects of some of these properties.

The align-items property

The `align-items` property positions items in the cross axis. If we apply this property to our wrapping element, like so:

```
.FlexWrapper {
  background-color: indigo;
  display: flex;
  height: 200px;
  width: 400px;
  align-items: center;
}
```

As you would imagine, the item within that box gets centered vertically:

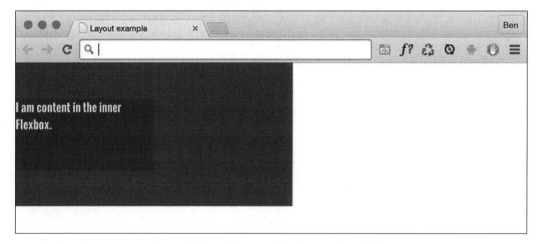

Figure 4.8: A one-liner provides cross-axis centering

The same effect would be applied to any number of children within.

The align-self property

Sometimes, you may want to pull just one item into a different alignment. Individual flex items can use the `align-self` property to align themselves. At this point, I'll remove the previous alignment properties in the CSS. I'll also add another two `div` elements to the markup, both also with a class of `FlexItem`. In the middle of these three items, I'll add an additional HTML class of `AlignSelf`. We'll use that class in the CSS to add the `align-self` property.

So, here's the HTML:

```
<div class="FlexWrapper">
```

```
<div class="FlexItem">I am content in the inner Flexbox 1</div>
<div class="FlexItem AlignSelf">I am content in the inner Flexbox
2</div>
<div class="FlexItem">I am content in the inner Flexbox 3</div>
</div>
```

And here is the CSS:

```css
.FlexWrapper {
  background-color: indigo;
  display: flex;
  height: 200px;
  width: 400px;
}
.FlexItem {
  background-color: #34005b;
  display: flex;
  height: 100px;
  width: 200px;
}

.AlignSelf {
  align-self: flex-end;
}
```

Here is the effect in the browser:

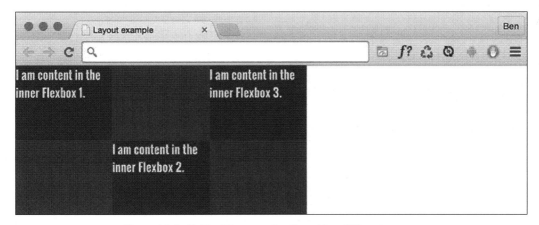

Figure 4.9: Individual items can be aligned in a different manner

Wow! Flexbox really makes these kinds of changes trivial. In that example, the value of `align-self` was set to `flex-end`. Let's consider the possible values we could use on the cross axis before looking at alignment in the main axis.

Possible alignment values

For cross-axis alignment, Flexbox has the following possible values:

- `flex-start`: Setting an element to `flex-start` would make it begin at the "starting" edge of its flex container.

- `flex-end`: Setting to `flex-end` would align the element at the end of the flex container.

- `center`: This puts it in the middle of the flex container.

- `baseline`: This sets all the flex items in the container so that their baselines align.

- `stretch`: This makes the items stretch to the size of their flex container (in the cross axis).

There are some particulars inherent to using these properties, so if something isn't playing happily, always refer to the specification for any edge case scenarios: http://www.w3.org/TR/css-flexbox-1/#align-items-property.

The justify-content property

Alignment in the main axis is controlled with `justify-content`. Possible values for `justify-content` are:

- `flex-start`
- `flex-end`
- `center`
- `space-between`
- `space-around`

The first three do exactly what you would now expect. However, let's take a look at what `space-between` and `space-around` do. Consider this markup:

```
<div class="FlexWrapper">
  <div class="FlexItem">I am content in the inner Flexbox 1.</div>
```

```
      <div class="FlexItem">I am content in the inner Flexbox 2.</div>
      <div class="FlexItem">I am content in the inner Flexbox 3.</div>
   </div>
```

And then consider this CSS. We are setting the three `div` elements with a class of `FlexItem` to each be 25% width, wrapped by a flex container, with a class of `FlexWrapper`, set to be 100% width:

```css
.FlexWrapper {
   background-color: indigo;
   display: flex;
   justify-content: space-between;
   height: 200px;
   width: 100%;
}
.FlexItem {
   background-color: #34005b;
   display: flex;
   height: 100px;
   width: 25%;
}
```

As the three items will only take up 75% of the available space, `justify-content` explains what we would like the browser to do with the remaining space. A value of `space-between` puts an equal amount of space between the items, and `space-around` puts it around the items. Perhaps a screenshot here will help – this is `space-between`:

Figure 4.10: Main axis alignment is carried out with the justify-content property

And here is what happens if we switch to `space-around`:

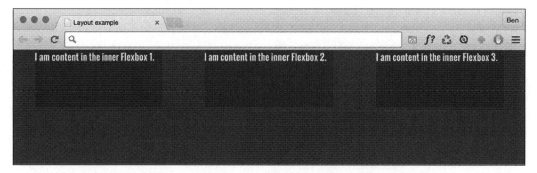

Figure 4.11: Subtly different but notice the space around, not just between items

The other alignment property I find myself using from time to time is `space-evenly`. This takes the available space and adds an equal amount to every gap.

 The various alignment properties of Flexbox are currently being specified in CSS Box Alignment Module Level 3. This should give the same fundamental alignment powers to other display properties, such as `display: block;` and `display: table`. The specification is still being worked on, so you can keep checking the status at `http://www.w3.org/TR/css3-align/`.

The flex property

We've used the `width` property on those flex items, but it's also possible to define the width, or "flexiness," if you will, with the `flex` property. To illustrate, consider another example with the same markup, but an amended CSS for the items:

```
.FlexItem {
  border: 1px solid #ebebeb;
  background-color: #34005b;
  display: flex;
  height: 100px;
  flex: 1;
}
```

The `flex` property is actually a shorthand way of specifying three separate properties: `flex-grow`, `flex-shrink`, and `flex-basis`. The specification covers these individual properties in more detail here: `http://www.w3.org/TR/css-flexbox-1/#flex-components`. However, the specification recommends that authors use the `flex` shorthand property, so that's what we will be learning here, capiche?

flex: 1 1 100px
| | |
grow shrink basis

Figure 4.12: Understanding the three possible values of the flex property

For items within a flex container, if a `flex` property is present, it is used to size the item rather than a width or height value (if also present). Even if the width or height value is specified after the `flex` property, it will still have no effect.

However, it is important to note that if the item you are adding the `flex` property to is not a flex item, the `flex` property will have no effect.

Now, let's look at what each of these flex properties actually does:

- `flex-grow` (the first value you can pass to flex) is the amount, in relation to the other flex items, the flex item can grow when free space is available.
- `flex-shrink` is the amount the flex item can shrink, in relation to the other flex items, when there is not enough space available.
- `flex-basis` (the final value you can pass to flex) is the basis size the flex item is sized to.

Although it's possible to just write `flex: 1`, and have that interpreted to mean `flex: 1 1 0`, I recommend writing all the values into a flex shorthand property yourself. I think it's clearer to understand what you intend to happen that way. For example, `flex: 1 1 auto` means that the item will grow into one part of the available space. It will also shrink one part when space is lacking and the basis size for the flexing is the intrinsic width of the content (that is, the size the content would be if flex wasn't involved).

Let's try another: `flex: 0 0 50px` means this item will neither grow nor shrink, and its basis is 50px (so it will be 50px regardless of any free space). What about `flex: 2 0 50%`? That's going to take two "lots" of available space, it won't shrink, and its basis size is 50%. Hopefully, these brief examples have demystified the `flex` property a little.

If you set the `flex-shrink` value to zero, then the `flex-basis` value effectively behaves like a minimum width. You can think of the `flex` property as a way to set ratios. With each flex item set to 1, they each take up an equal amount of space:

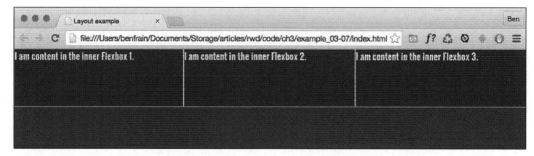

Figure 4.13: With the same flex values, all boxes are sized equally

Right, so to test the theory, let's amend the HTML classes in the markup. We're adding `FlexOne`, `FlexTwo`, and `FlexThree` to each item in turn:

```
<div class="FlexWrapper">
  <div class="FlexItem FlexOne">I am content in the inner Flexbox
1.</div>
  <div class="FlexItem FlexTwo">I am content in the inner Flexbox
2.</div>
  <div class="FlexItem FlexThree">I am content in the inner Flexbox
3.</div>
</div>
```

Now, let's remove the previous styles related to `FlexItem` and instead add this:

```
.FlexItem {
  border: 1px solid #ebebeb;
  background-color: #34005b;
  display: flex;
  height: 100px;
}

.FlexOne {
  flex: 1.5 0 auto;
}

.FlexTwo,
.FlexThree {
  flex: 1 0 auto;
}
```

In this instance, `FlexOne` takes up 1.5 times the amount of space that `FlexTwo` and `FlexThree` take up.

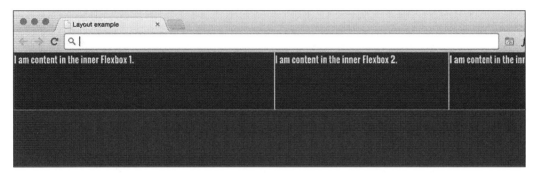

Figure 4.14: Alter the amount of free space elements take up with flex-grow

This shorthand syntax really becomes useful for quickly bashing out relationships between items. For example, if a request comes in, such as "that needs to be 1.8 times wider than the others," you could easily facilitate that request with the `flex` property.

Hopefully, the incredibly powerful `flex` property is starting to make a little sense now.

I could write chapters and chapters on Flexbox! There are so many examples we could look at. However, before we move on to the other main topic of this chapter (responsive images), there are just two more things I would like to share with you.

Simple sticky footer

Suppose you want a footer to sit at the bottom of the viewport when there is not enough content to push it there. This has always been a pain to achieve, but with Flexbox it's simple. Consider this markup:

```
<body>
  <div class="MainContent">
    Here is a bunch of text up at the top. But there isn't enough
content to
    push the footer to the bottom of the page.
  </div>
  <div class="Footer">
    However, thanks to flexbox, I've been put in my place.
  </div>
</body>
```

And here's the CSS:

```css
html,
body {
  margin: 0;
  padding: 0;
}

html {
  height: 100%;
}

body {
  font-family: 'Oswald', sans-serif;
  color: #ebebeb;
  display: flex;
  flex-direction: column;
  min-height: 100%;
}

.MainContent {
  flex: 1 0 auto;
  color: #333;
  padding: 0.5rem;
}

.Footer {
  background-color: violet;
  padding: 0.5rem;
}
```

Take a look at that in the browser and test by adding more content into `MainContent` `div`. You'll see that when there is not enough content, the footer is stuck to the bottom of the viewport. When there is enough, it sits below the content.

This works because our `flex` property is set to grow where space is available. As our body is a flex container of 100% minimum height, the main content can grow into all of that available space. Beautiful!

Changing the source order

Flexbox has visual source reordering built-in. Let's have a look at how it works.

Consider this markup:

```
<div class="FlexWrapper">
  <div class="FlexItem FlexHeader">I am content in the Header.</div>
  <div class="FlexItem FlexSideOne">I am content in the SideOne.</
div>
  <div class="FlexItem FlexContent">I am content in the Content.</
div>
  <div class="FlexItem FlexSideTwo">I am content in the SideTwo.</
div>
  <div class="FlexItem FlexFooter">I am content in the Footer.</div>
</div>
```

You can see here that the third item within the wrapper has an HTML class of FlexContent—imagine that this div is going to hold the main content for the page.

OK, let's keep things simple. We will add some simple colors to more easily differentiate the sections, and just get these items one under another in the same order they appear in the markup:

```
.FlexWrapper {
  background-color: indigo;
  display: flex;
  flex-direction: column;
}

.FlexItem {
  display: flex;
  align-items: center;
  min-height: 6.25rem;
  padding: 1rem;
}

.FlexHeader {
  background-color: #105b63;
}

.FlexContent {
  background-color: #fffad5;
```

```
  }

  .FlexSideOne {
    background-color: #ffd34e;
  }

  .FlexSideTwo {
    background-color: #db9e36;
  }

  .FlexFooter {
    background-color: #bd4932;
  }
```

That renders in the browser like this:

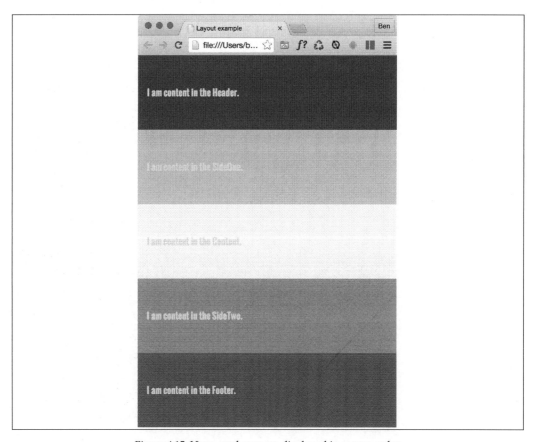

Figure 4.15: Here, our boxes are displayed in source order

Now, suppose we want to switch the order of `FlexContent` to be the first item, without touching the markup. With Flexbox, it's as simple as adding a single property/value pair:

```
.FlexContent {
  background-color: #fffad5;
  order: -1;
}
```

The `order` property lets us revise the order of items within a Flexbox simply and sanely. In this example, a value of `-1` means that we want it to be before all the others.

If you want to switch items around quite a bit, I'd recommend being a little more declarative and add an order number for each item. This makes things a little easier to understand when you combine them with media queries.

Let's combine our new source order changing powers with some media queries to produce not just a different layout at different sizes but different ordering.

Note: you can view this finished example at `example_04-09`.

Let's suppose we want our main content at the beginning of a document. In this example, our markup looks like this:

```
<div class="FlexWrapper">
  <div class="FlexItem FlexContent">I am content in the Content.</
div>
  <div class="FlexItem FlexSideOne">I am content in the SideOne.</
div>
  <div class="FlexItem FlexSideTwo">I am content in the SideTwo.</
div>
  <div class="FlexItem FlexHeader">I am content in the Header.</div>
  <div class="FlexItem FlexFooter">I am content in the Footer.</div>
</div>
```

First is the page content, then our two sidebar areas, then the header, and finally the footer. As I'll be using Flexbox, we can structure the HTML in the order that makes sense for the document, regardless of how things need to be laid out visually.

After some basic styling for each `FlexItem`, for the smallest screens (outside of any media query), I'll go with the following order:

```css
.FlexHeader {
  background-color: #105b63;
  order: 1;
}

.FlexContent {
  background-color: #fffad5;
  order: 2;
}

.FlexSideOne {
  background-color: #ffd34e;
  order: 3;
}

.FlexSideTwo {
  background-color: #db9e36;
  order: 4;
}

.FlexFooter {
  background-color: #bd4932;
  order: 5;
}
```

That gives us this in the browser:

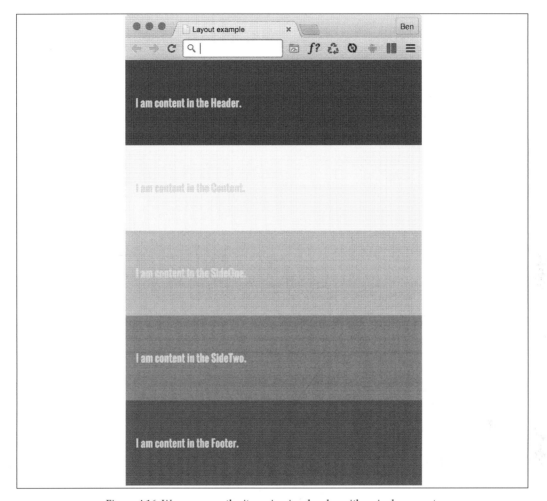

Figure 4.16: We can move the items in visual order with a single property

And then, at a breakpoint, I'm switching to this:

```
@media (min-width: 30rem) {
  .FlexWrapper {
    flex-flow: row wrap;
  }
  .FlexHeader {
    width: 100%;
  }
  .FlexContent {
    flex: 1 0 auto;
    order: 3;
  }
  .FlexSideOne {
    width: 150px;
    order: 2;
  }
  .FlexSideTwo {
    width: 150px;
    order: 4;
  }
  .FlexFooter {
    width: 100%;
  }
}
```

That gives us this in the browser:

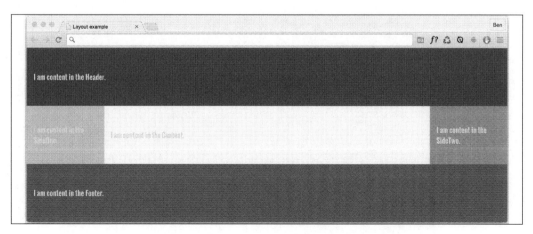

Figure 4.17: With a media query, we can change the visual order again

In that example, the shortcut `flex-flow: row wrap` has been used. `flex-flow` is actually a shorthand property of sorts that lets you set two properties in one: `flex-direction` and `flex-wrap`.

We've used `flex-direction` already to switch between rows and columns and to reverse elements. However, we haven't looked at `flex-wrap` yet.

Wrapping with flex

By default, items in a flex container will shrink to fit and, if they can't, they will overflow the container. For example, consider this markup:

```
<div class="container">
   <div class="items">Item 1</div>
   <div class="items">Item 2</div>
   <div class="items">Item 3</div>
   <div class="items">Item 4</div>
</div>
```

And this CSS:

```
.container {
  display: flex;
  width: 500px;
  background-color: #bbb;
  align-items: center;
  border: 1px solid #111;
}

.items {
  color: #111;
  display: inline-flex;
  align-items: center;
  justify-content: center;
  font-size: 23px;
  flex: 0 0 160px;
  height: 40px;
  border: 1px dashed #545454;
}
```

You may be wondering why the outer container is set with a `width` and not the `flex` shorthand property we looked at before. Remember, this is because unless the element is a flex item (inside a Flexbox itself), `flex` has no effect.

Because there is a width of only 500px on the flex container, those four elements don't fit:

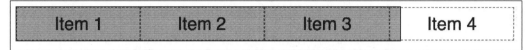

Figure 4.18: By default Flexbox will always keep child elements from wrapping

However, those items can be set to wrap with `flex-wrap: wrap`. This wraps the items once they hit the edge of the container.

The likelihood is that there will be times when you want flex items to wrap and other times when you don't. Remember that the default is to not wrap, but you can easily make the change with a single line.

Also, remember that you can set the wrapping by itself with `flex-wrap`, or as part of the `flex-flow` direction and wrap shorthand.

Let's solve a real-world problem with `flex-wrap`. Consider this list of paragraphs in the following image. At this width, they are not easy to read.

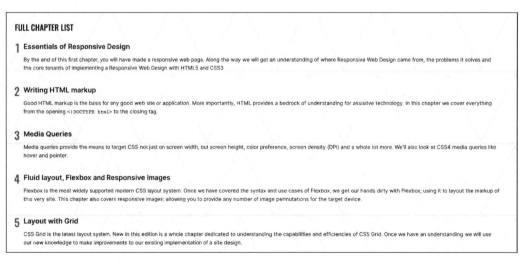

Figure 4.19: This content is overstretched at this viewport width

Let's amend that layout with a media query and a few choice flex properties. I'm consolidating all of these changes into one media query here for brevity, but remember that you can use as many as you like to organize your code however you see fit. We covered the options extensively in *Chapter 3, Media Queries – Supporting Differing Viewports*:

```css
@media (min-width: 1000px) {
  .rwd-Chapters_List {
    display: flex;
    flex-wrap: wrap;
  }
  .rwd-Chapter {
    flex: 0 0 33.33%;
    padding: 0 20px;
  }
  .rwd-Chapter::before {
    left: -20px;
  }
}
```

And that produces this effect in the browser:

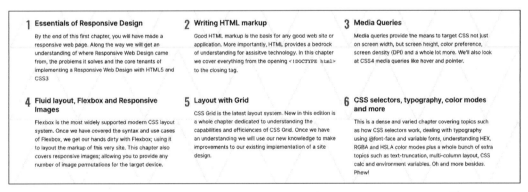

Figure 4.20: Setting the flex container to wrap means the content can space out equally

We made the container of the chapters into a flex container. Then, to stop the elements scrunching up into one another, we set the container to wrap. To limit the chapter section widths to a third of the container, we used the flex shorthand to set 33.33% as the `flex-basis` and prevented the element from growing or shrinking. Padding was used to provide a little space between them. The final small tweak was to bring in the chapter numbers a little.

Wrapping up Flexbox

There are near endless possibilities when using the Flexbox layout system and, due to its inherent "flexiness," it's a perfect match for responsive design. If you've never built anything with Flexbox before, all the new properties and values can seem a little odd, and it's sometimes disconcertingly easy to achieve layouts that have previously taken far more work.

The other modern layout system we have in CSS is Grid, but that's a topic for *Chapter 5, Layout with CSS Grid*. Before we get there, let's tackle responsive images and media.

Responsive images

Serving the appropriate image to users based on the particulars of their device and environment has always been a tricky problem. This problem was accentuated with the advent of responsive web design, the very nature of which is to serve a single code base to each and every device.

The inherent problem of responsive images

As an author, you cannot know about every possible device that may visit your site now or in the future. Only a browser knows the particulars of the device viewing a website: its screen size and device capabilities, for example.

Conversely, only the people making the website know what versions of an image we have at our disposal. For example, we may have three versions of the same image: small, medium, and large; each with increasing dimensions to cover off the anticipated screen size and screen density eventualities. The browser does not know this. We have to tell it.

To summarize the conundrum, we, as the website authors, have only half of the solution, in that we know what images we have. The browser has the other half of the solution in that it knows what device is visiting the site and what the most appropriate image dimensions and resolution would be.

How can we tell the browser what images we have at our disposal so that it may choose the most appropriate one for the user?

In the first few years of responsive web design, there was no specified way. Thankfully, now we have the Embedded content specification: `https://html.spec. whatwg.org/multipage/embedded-content.html`.

The Embedded content specification describes ways to deal with the simple resolution switching of images — to facilitate a user on a higher resolution screen receiving a higher resolution version of images. It also facilitates "art direction" situations for when authors want users to see a totally different image, depending on a number of device characteristics (think media queries). For example, a close-up image of something on smaller viewports and then a wide-angle image of the same thing for larger viewports.

Demonstrating responsive image examples is tricky. It's not possible to appreciate on a single screen the different images that could be loaded with a particular syntax or technique. Therefore, the examples that follow will be mainly code, and you'll just have to trust me that's it's going to produce the result you need in supporting browsers.

Let's look at the two most common scenarios you're likely to need responsive images for. These are switching one image for another when a different resolution is needed and changing an image entirely depending on the available viewport space.

Simple resolution switching with srcset

Let's suppose you have three versions of the same image. One is a smaller size for smaller viewports, another caters for medium-sized viewports, and, finally, a larger version covers off every other viewport. Here is how we can let the browser know that we have these three versions available:

```
<img
  src="scones_small.jpg"
  srcset="scones_medium.jpg 1.5x, scones_large.jpg 2x"
  alt="a delicious looking baked scone"
/>
```

This is about as simple as things get with responsive images, so let's ensure that the syntax makes perfect sense.

First of all, the `src` attribute, which you will already be familiar with, has a dual role here; it's specifying the small 1x version of the image, and it also acts as a fallback image if the browser doesn't support the `srcset` attribute. That's why we are using it for the small image. This way, older browsers that will ignore the `srcset` information will get the smallest and best-performing image possible.

For browsers that understand `srcset`, with that attribute, we provide a comma-separated list of images that the browser can choose from. After the image name (such as `scones_medium.jpg`), we issue a simple resolution hint.

I've specifically called it a hint rather than an instruction or a command, and you will see why in a moment. In this example, 1.5x and 2x have been used but any integer would be valid. For example, 3x or 4x would work too (providing you can find a suitably high-resolution screen).

However, there is an issue here; a device with a 1440px wide, 1x screen will get the same image as a 480px wide, 3x screen. That may or may not be the desired effect.

Advanced switching with srcset and sizes

Let's consider another situation. In a responsive web design, it wouldn't be uncommon for an image to be the full viewport width on smaller viewports, but only half the width of the viewport at larger sizes. The main example in *Chapter 1, The Essentials of Responsive Web Design*, was a typical example of this. Here's how we can communicate these intentions to the browser:

```
<img
  srcset="scones-small.jpg 450w, scones-medium.jpg 900w"
  sizes="(min-width: 280px) 100vw, (min-width: 640px) 50vw"
  src="scones-small.jpg"
  alt="Lots of delicious scones"
/>
```

Inside the image tag, we are utilizing srcset again. However, this time, after specifying the images, we are adding a value with a w suffix. This tells the browser how wide the image is. In our example, we have a 450px wide image (called scones-small.jpg) and a 900px wide image (called scones-medium.jpg). It's important to note this w-suffixed value isn't a "real" size. It's merely an indication to the browser, roughly equivalent to the width in "CSS pixels."

 What exactly defines a pixel in CSS? I wondered that myself. Then, I found the explanation at http://www.w3.org/TR/css3-values/#reference-pixel and wished I hadn't wondered.

This w-suffixed value makes more sense when we factor in the sizes attribute. The sizes attribute allows us to communicate the intentions for our images to the browser. In our preceding example, the first value is equivalent to "for devices that are at least 280px wide, I intend the image to be around 100vw wide."

If some of the units used, such as vh (where 1vh is equal to 1% of the viewport height) and vw (where 1vw is equal to 1% of the viewport width), don't make sense, be sure to read *Chapter 6, CSS Selectors, Typography, Color Modes, and More.*

The second part is, effectively, "Hi browser, for devices that are at least 640px wide, I only intend the image to be shown at 50vw." That may seem a little redundant until you factor in DPI (or DPR for device pixel ratio). For example, on a 320px wide device with a 2x resolution (effectively requiring a 640px wide image, if shown at full width), the browser might decide the 900px wide image is actually a better match as it's the first option it has for an image that would be big enough to fulfill the required size.

Did you say the browser "might" pick one image over another?

An important thing to remember is that the values given in the `sizes` attribute are merely hints to the browser. That doesn't necessarily ensure that the browser will always obey. This is a good thing. Trust me, it really is. It means that, in the future, if there is a reliable way for browsers to ascertain network conditions, it may choose to serve one image over another because it knows things at that point that we can't possibly know at this point as the author. Perhaps a user has a setting on their device to "only download 1x images" or "only download 2x images." In these scenarios, the browser can make the best call.

The alternative to the browser deciding is to use the `picture` element. Using this element ensures that the browser serves up the exact image you asked for. Let's take a look at how it works.

Art direction with the picture element

The final scenario you may find yourself in is one in which you have different images that are applicable at different viewport sizes. For example, consider our cake-based example again from *Chapter 1*. Maybe on the smallest screens we would like a close-up of the scone with a generous helping of jam and cream on top. For larger screens, perhaps we have a wider image we would like to use. Perhaps it's a wide shot of a table loaded up with all manner of cakes. Finally, for larger viewports still, perhaps we want to see the exterior of a cake shop on a village street with people sat outside eating cakes and drinking tea (I know, sounds like nirvana, right?).

We need three different images that are most appropriate at different viewport ranges. Here is how we could solve this with `picture`:

```
<picture>
  <source media="(min-width: 480px)" srcset="cake-table.jpg" />
  <source media="(min-width: 960px)" srcset="cake-shop.jpg" />
  <img src="scones.jpg" alt="Lots of cakes" />
</picture>
```

First of all, be aware that when you use the `picture` element, it is merely a wrapper to facilitate other images making their way to the `img` tag within. If you want to style the images in any way, it's the `img` tag that should get your attention.

Secondly, the `srcset` attribute here works exactly the same as the previous example.

Thirdly, the `img` tag provides your fallback image and also the image that will be displayed if a browser understands `picture` but none of the media definitions match. Just to be crystal clear, do not omit the `img` tag from within a `picture` element or things won't end well.

The key difference with `picture` is that we have a `source` tag. Here, we can use media query-style expressions to explicitly tell the browser which asset to use in a matching situation. For example, our first one in the preceding example is telling the browser, "Hey you, if the screen is at least 480px wide, load in the cake-table.jpg image instead." As long as the conditions match, the browser will dutifully obey.

Facilitate new image formats

As a bonus, `picture` also facilitates us providing alternate formats of an image. "WebP" is a newer image format, pushed by Google that Apple's Safari browser lacks support for (check whether that is still the case at http://caniuse. com/#search=WebP). It provides a comparable quality as a JPG, but in a far smaller payload. So, if a browser supports it, it makes sense to let them have that version of the image instead. For browsers that support it, we can offer a file in that format and a more common format for those that don't:

```
<picture>
  <source type="image/webp" srcset="scones-baby-yeah.webp" />
  <img src="scones-baby-yeah.jpg" alt="delicious cakes" />
</picture>
```

Hopefully, this is now a little more straightforward. Instead of the `media` attribute, we are using `type`, which, although more typically used to specify video sources (possible video source types can be found here: `https://html.spec.whatwg.org/multipage/embedded-content.html#attr-source-type`), allows us here to define WebP as the preferred image format. If the browser can display it, it will; otherwise, it will grab the default one in the `img` tag.

Summary

We've covered a lot of ground in this chapter. We started by understanding how to create fluid layouts that can flex between the media queries we set. We then spent considerable time getting acquainted with Flexbox, learning how to solve common layout problems with relative ease.

We have also covered how we can serve up any number of alternative images to our users depending on the problems we need to solve. By making use of `srcset`, `sizes`, and `picture`, our users should always get the most appropriate image for their needs—both now and in the future.

As luck would have it, two great layout mechanisms arrived in CSS in relatively quick succession. Hot on the heels of the Flexible Box Layout Module was Grid Layout Module Level 1: `http://www.w3.org/TR/css3-grid-layout/`.

Like Flexbox, CSS Grid means learning quite a bit of alien syntax. But don't let that put you off. The next chapter is completely dedicated to Grid: what it can do, how it does it, and how we can bend it to our will.

5
Layout with CSS Grid

Without a doubt, the biggest "game-changer" to CSS layout has been Grid.

We now have a layout system capable of achieving everything we have done before with less code and more predictability, as well as enabling things we simply couldn't do before!

I'd go as far as saying Grid is revolutionary rather than evolutionary. There are entirely new concepts to understand that have no real forebears in past CSS. As such, expect to take some time getting comfortable using it.

But trust me, it is worth it. Let's go!

In this chapter, we will learn the following:

- What CSS Grid is and the problems it solves
- The essential concepts to understand when dealing with Grid layout
- Grid-specific terminology
- How to set up a grid
- How to position items in a grid
- How to create powerful responsive patterns with minimal code
- How to understand and write the grid shorthand syntax

Toward the end of the chapter, you will also be tasked with a small exercise to use some of the techniques we have learned to refactor the layout of a portion of the `https://rwd.education` website we have been looking at in previous chapters.

What CSS Grid is and the problems it solves

CSS Grid is a two-dimensional layout system. Flexbox, which we covered in the last chapter, concerns itself with items being laid out in a single dimension/direction at a time. A Flexbox container either lays things out in a row, or it lays them out in a column. It cannot facilitate laying out items across and down at once; that is what Grid is for.

I should point out at the outset that you don't need to choose between Flexbox or Grid when building projects. They are not mutually exclusive. I commonly use both, even within a single visual component.

To be completely clear, when you adopt Grid, you don't have to forsake any other display methods. For example, a Grid will quite happily allow a Flexbox inside it. Equally, part of your interface coded with Grid can quite happily live inside a Flexbox, standard block, or inline-block.

So there are times when using Grid is the most appropriate option, and there are times when Flexbox, or another layout method, is the most appropriate.

The truth is, we've been creating grid layouts with CSS for years. We just haven't had a specific grid layout mechanism in CSS to do it. We have made use of blocks, floats, tables, and many other ingenious techniques to work around the fact we didn't have a proper grid layout system in CSS. Now, thankfully, we do.

Using CSS Grid, we can create grids of virtually infinite permutations and position child elements wherever we want them, regardless of their source order. What's more, Grid even makes provision for when additional items are added and adapts itself to the needs of the content. This might sound hyperbolic, so let's not waste any more text. Let's get to it.

Basic Grid syntax

In the most simple terms, to use Grid, we need to tell the browser:

- How many rows and columns our grid should have
- How those rows and columns should be sized
- Where we want to place the items of our grid
- What should happen when the size of the grid changes or more items are added to the grid

Relating that to the browser is, therefore, just a matter of understanding the terminology.

Grid-specific concepts and terminology

The first concept to understand is "explicit" and "implicit" item placement. The grid you define in your CSS with columns and rows is the explicit grid; it's the layout of the items you have explicitly defined. Meanwhile, the implicit grid is the grid placement of items that happens when additional items you didn't foresee also get added to the grid. The placement of these new items is implied by the layout of your explicit grid.

The next concept that commonly confuses people (it certainly did me) is that grid lines are on either side of the grid items. The bit in the middle, between the lines, is referred to as a grid "track." Where two tracks from different directions intersect is where a "grid area" is formed.

A key takeaway is that when you place items within a grid, you can do so referencing the grid lines (which, therefore, implies a grid area) or the grid areas themselves if named.

 There is no limit, theoretically, to the number of tracks a grid can have. However, browsers are at liberty to truncate grids. If you set a value beyond the browser's limit, the grid will be truncated to that limit. Practically, I can't imagine hitting a browser's limit being a likely scenario, but I'm mentioning it here for completeness.

Setting up a grid

Here is the introduction to the explicit grid section of the W3C specification (`https://www.w3.org/TR/css-grid-1/#explicit-grids`). It's worth rereading a few times as it is dense with essential information for understanding how the grid works:

> "*The three properties grid-template-rows, grid-template-columns, and grid-template-areas together define the explicit grid of a grid container. The final grid may end up larger due to grid items placed outside the explicit grid; in this case implicit tracks will be created, these implicit tracks will be sized by the grid-auto-rows and grid-auto-columns properties.*
>
> *The size of the explicit grid is determined by the larger of the number of rows/columns defined by grid-template-areas and the number of rows/columns sized by grid-template-rows/grid-template-columns.*

Any rows/columns defined by grid-template-areas but not sized by grid-template-rows/grid-template-columns take their size from the grid-auto-rows/grid-auto-columns properties. If these properties don't define any explicit tracks the explicit grid still contains one grid line in each axis.

Numeric indexes in the grid-placement properties count from the edges of the explicit grid. Positive indexes count from the start side (starting from 1 for the start-most explicit line), while negative indexes count from the end side (starting from -1 for the end-most explicit line).

The grid and grid-template are properties that allow a shorthand to be used to set all three explicit grid properties (grid-template-rows, grid-template-columns, and grid-template-areas) at the same time. The grid shorthand also resets properties controlling the implicit grid, whereas the grid-template property leaves them unchanged."

Now, I'm conscious that when you haven't worked at all with Grid it can be very intimidating, and that quoted section from the specification might seem completely opaque right now. Hopefully, when you have read this chapter through, and played with Grid yourself, it will make a little more sense.

Again, don't worry if little of that previous text made sense. Let's start our Grid journey in code with a very simple example. First, the world's easiest grid layout: four numbered boxes. It will look like this in the browser:

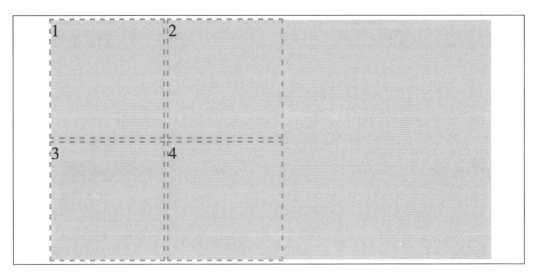

Figure 5.1: Our first grid; as simple as possible

Here is the markup:

```html
<div class="my-first-grid">
  <div class="grid-item-1">1</div>
  <div class="grid-item-2">2</div>
  <div class="grid-item-3">3</div>
  <div class="grid-item-4">4</div>
</div>
```

The first thing I want you to consider is that with Grid, the markup pattern is a containing element, which is the grid, and the elements of the grid are the direct children. Write the markup for grid child elements in the order that makes the most sense for the content; Grid can place them visually wherever you need it. Here is the related CSS:

```css
.my-first-grid {
  display: grid;
  grid-gap: 10px;
  grid-template-rows: 200px 200px;
  grid-template-columns: 200px 200px;
  background-color: #e4e4e4;
}

.grid-item-1 {
  grid-row: 1;
  grid-column: 1;
}
.grid-item-2 {
  grid-row: 1;
  grid-column: 2;
}
.grid-item-3 {
  grid-row: 2;
  grid-column: 1;
}
.grid-item-4 {
  grid-row: 2;
  grid-column: 2;
}

[class^='grid-item'] {
```

```
    outline: 3px dashed #f90;
    font-size: 30px;
    color: #333;
}
```

The parts to concentrate on in that CSS are the grid-specific properties. I've added some outlines and a background to make it easier to see where the grid is and the size and shape of the grid items.

We use `display: grid` to set our container as a grid and then use `grid-template-rows: 200px 200px` to set two rows, each 200px high, and `grid-template-columns: 200px 200px` to set the grid to have two 200px wide columns.

In terms of the child elements of the grid, we use `grid-row` with a number to tell Grid which row to place the item and `grid-column` to tell it which column to place it in.

By default, the child elements of a grid remain as their standard layout type. Although our grid items belong to our grid, in this example, as they are all `div` elements, they are still computed as `display: block`. This is important to understand when we start trying to align grid items.

 You can play about with this first example in the `example_05-01` code sample.

Let's use the alignment properties we learned about in the last chapter to try centering our grid items:

```
.my-first-grid {
  display: grid;
  grid-gap: 10px;
  grid-template-rows: 200px 200px;
  grid-template-columns: 200px 200px;
  background-color: #e4e4e4;
  align-items: center;
  justify-content: center;
}
```

When I first started with Grid and tried something like this, I expected to see the numbers perfectly centered in their respective grid tracks. However, that is not the case:

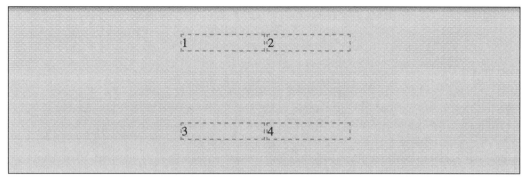

Figure 5.2: If you don't set a width, a Grid will consume the available space

If we think about what we have done, it does make sense. We made a grid, with two columns and two rows, each 200px, and asked for the items to be both vertically and horizontally centered. Because we have used `grid` and not `inline-grid`, the grid fills the entire width of the page, despite the fact that our grid items don't need all that space.

Let's tweak this so that the grid is only as wide as its content. Furthermore, let's center the items inside their respective grid items. To do that, we can make the items themselves either Flexbox or Grid. As this is a chapter about Grid, let's try using that:

```css
.my-first-grid {
  display: inline-grid;
  grid-gap: 10px;
  grid-template-rows: 200px 200px;
  grid-template-columns: 200px 200px;
  background-color: #e4e4e4;
}

[class^='grid-item'] {
  display: grid;
  align-items: center;
  justify-content: center;
  outline: 3px dashed #f90;
  font-size: 30px;
  color: #333;
}
```

If that selector with the hat symbol doesn't make sense, don't worry. We cover that in *Chapter 6, CSS Selectors, Typography, Color Modes, and More.*

We switched our container to be an `inline-grid`, set all the grid items to `display: grid`, and used the alignment properties `justify-content` and `align-items`.

That produces this result:

Figure 5.3: By making the child elements flex or grid we can center their contents

 This example is in the code examples as `example_05-02`. As an exercise, try moving the position of the grid elements to different rows and columns.

OK, a little progress has been made. Let's move on to the topic of explicit and implicit item placement.

Explicit and implicit

Earlier in the chapter, we discussed the difference between an explicit and implicit grid; an explicit grid being the structure you define in your CSS when setting up the grid. When more content is placed in that grid than you provisioned for, the "implicit" grid comes into effect.

Let's look at that again by extending our prior example.

Let's add in another item and see what happens:

```html
<div class="my-first-grid">
  <div class="grid-item-1">1</div>
  <div class="grid-item-2">2</div>
  <div class="grid-item-3">3</div>
  <div class="grid-item-4">4</div>
  <div class="grid-item-5">5</div>
</div>
```

With that added, this is what we get in the browser:

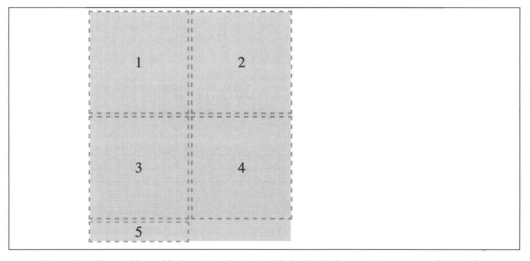

Figure 5.4: The grid has added our item but not with the kind of proportions we were hoping for

That's sort of useful; the grid has created implicit grid lines to create an implicit track for our new item. Now, we didn't tell it what to do with that extra item, so it made the best guess. However, we can control how Grid handles items implicitly with the following properties: `grid-auto-rows` and `grid-auto-columns`.

grid-auto-rows and grid-auto-columns

Let's use `grid-auto-rows` and `grid-auto-columns` to make any extra grid items the same size as the existing ones:

```css
.my-first-grid {
  display: inline-grid;
  grid-gap: 10px;
  grid-template-rows: 200px 200px;
  grid-template-columns: 200px 200px;
```

```
    grid-auto-rows: 200px;
    grid-auto-columns: 200px;
    background-color: #e4e4e4;
}
```

Now, without writing any extra CSS, when additional items are placed in our grid, they get the 200px × 200px sizing we have defined. Here we have added another item in the DOM for a total of six:

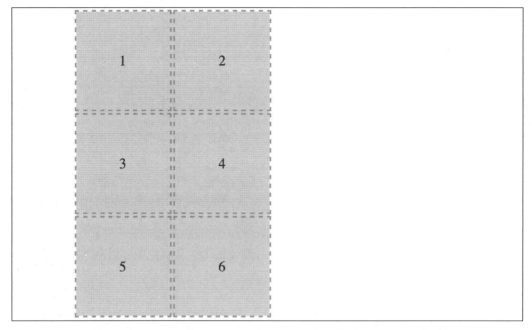

Figure 5.5: With some auto settings, extra elements can be added at a more preferable size

You can even make patterns so that the first extra item is one size and the next is another. The pattern gets repeated:

```
.my-first-grid {
    display: inline-grid;
    grid-gap: 10px;
    grid-template-rows: 200px 200px;
    grid-template-columns: 200px 200px;
    grid-auto-rows: 100px 150px;
    grid-auto-columns: 100px 150px;
    background-color: #e4e4e4;
}
```

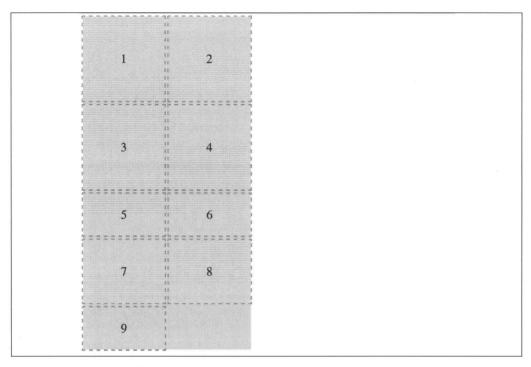

Figure 5.6: You can specify a sizing pattern for any auto added rows or columns

Can you see how item 5 onwards uses the pattern we defined in the value of the grid-auto-rows property? First, it is 100px tall, then 150px, and then back to 100px.

So far, you can see that the grid items are flowing vertically down the page. You can easily switch this to flow across the page instead! You can play about with this code in example_05-03.

grid-auto-flow

The grid-auto-flow property allows you to define the direction that any implicitly added items flow inside the grid. Use a value of column when you want the grid to add extra columns to accommodate extra items, and use a value of row when you want the grid to add extra rows.

Let's amend our example by adding `grid-auto-flow: column` to make the items flow across the page instead of down:

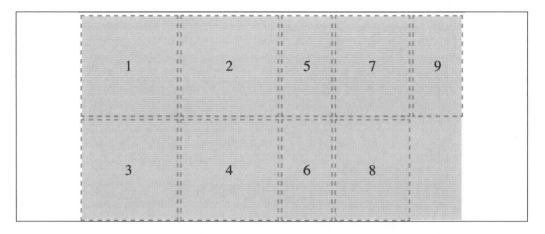

Figure 5.7: Switching the grid to add extra items horizontally

There is an additional `dense` keyword that can be added to `grid-auto-flow: column dense` or `grid-auto-flow: row dense` – we'll look at that shortly.

Placing and sizing grid items

So far, each item we have added to a grid has taken up a single grid area. We are going to start a new example now (you can find it in the code as `example_05-04`). This grid will have 20 grid items; these are just random food items and their source order within their container as a number. However, there are quite a few new things to go over in the CSS. Before we go through each new thing step by step, take a look at the code and the screenshot and see how much of it you can make sense of before reading on.

It's also worth mentioning that I've purposely mixed up the use of whitespace in the values. You can write `grid-row: 6 / span 2` or `grid-row: 6/span 2` — either is just as valid. Just pick which you prefer.

Here's the markup:

```
<div class="container">
  <div class="grid-item1">1. tofu</div>
  <div class="grid-item2">2. egg plant</div>
  <div class="grid-item3">3. onion</div>
  <div class="grid-item4">4. carrots</div>
  <div class="grid-item5">5. swede</div>
```

```html
    <div class="grid-item6">6. scones</div>
    <div class="grid-item7">7. cucumber</div>
    <div class="grid-item8">8. carrot</div>
    <div class="grid-item9">9. yam</div>
    <div class="grid-item10">10. sweet potato</div>
    <div class="grid-item11">11. peas</div>
    <div class="grid-item12">12. beans</div>
    <div class="grid-item13">13. lentil</div>
    <div class="grid-item14">14. tomato</div>
    <div class="grid-item15">15. butternut squash</div>
    <div class="grid-item16">16. ham</div>
    <div class="grid-item17">17. pizza</div>
    <div class="grid-item18">18. pasta</div>
    <div class="grid-item19">19. cheese</div>
    <div class="grid-item20">20. milk</div>
</div>
```

Here is the CSS:

```css
.container {
  font-size: 28px;
  font-family: sans-serif;
  display: grid;
  gap: 30px;
  background-color: #ddd;
  grid-template-columns: repeat(4, 1fr);
  grid-auto-rows: 100px;
  grid-auto-flow: row;
}

[class^='grid-item'] {
  outline: 1px #f90 dashed;
  display: grid;
  background-color: goldenrod;
  align-items: center;
  justify-content: center;
}

.grid-item3 {
  grid-column: 2/-1;
}

.grid-item6 {
```

```
    grid-row: 3/6;
    grid-column: 3 / 5;
}

.grid-item17 {
  grid-row: 6 / span 2;
  grid-column: 2/3;
}

.grid-item4 {
  grid-row: 4 / 7;
}
```

And here is what we get in the browser:

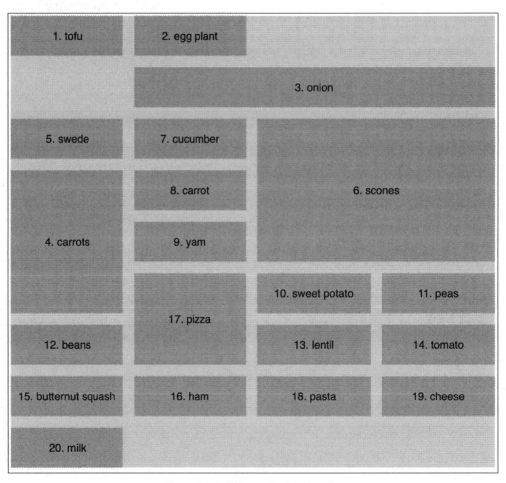

Figure 5.8: Grid items sized arbitrarily

We've introduced a few new things here. Let's cover each in turn.

gap

I've used `gap` in some of the prior code samples, but I've not explained it. Forgive me! The `gap` property lets you specify a gap between grid tracks. It is actually shorthand for both `row-gap` and `column-gap`. Just like when you specify a margin with two values, the first value applies to the top and bottom (row), and the second to the left and right (columns). If you specify a single value, as we have, it applies to both.

 You might see `grid-gap` used instead of `gap`. That's because, initially, the property was called `grid-gap` before being revised, and plenty of browsers only supported `grid-gap` initially. If you want the widest browser support, you can safely use `grid-gap` instead.

repeat

If you were making a grid with 30 identical columns, it would get a little tiring having to write `auto` 30 times, for instance, `grid-template-columns: auto auto auto auto auto auto...`; in fact, I got bored just writing that!

Thankfully, the grid specification writers have blessed us with `repeat()`. As you might have guessed, the `repeat()` function provides a convenient way of stamping out the needs of any number of items. In our example, we have used it to create four columns, all `1fr` in width:

```
repeat(4, 1fr);
```

The format of the syntax is that, inside the parentheses, the first value is the number of times you want something repeated, and the second value is the width of each item.

Don't worry, I'll explain `fr` units in a moment; for now, just know that you can create multiple columns/rows with ease. Do you want 15 columns, all 100px wide? It's as easy as `repeat(15, 100px)`.

fr units

The `fr` unit represents "flexible length" and stands for "flex fraction." It's used to communicate how much of any available free space we want something to gobble up, much like the `flex-grow` unit we covered for Flexbox in *Chapter 4, Fluid Layout, Flexbox, and Responsive Images*.

The specification doesn't say so, but I conceptualize `fr` as standing for "free room" when I'm thinking about a layout. In our example, we have made four columns, each taking up one portion of the available free room.

Placing items in the grid

Before this example, we have been positioning each grid item in a single grid area. However, here, we have certain grid items being assigned spans of columns or rows numerically.

Let's take the `grid-item3` example:

```css
.grid-item3 {
  grid-column: 2/-1;
}
```

Here, the `grid-column` property is being set to start at the second grid line and end at the -1 grid line. The `-1` looks pretty odd at first, but it is part of a very smart piece of syntax.

The first number is the start point, which is separated from the endpoint with a forward slash. Positive numbers count from the start side — the left-hand side in our column example, while negative numbers start from the end side — the right, in this instance. So, `-1` basically just means the last grid line. So, this nice terse syntax just reads: "Start at line 2 and go to the end."

I've purposely left some of the other examples with messy whitespace around the numbers to show that you can keep the space or omit it — no drama either way.

There's an example of spanning across rows in there too. Take a look at this one again:

```css
.grid-item4 {
  grid-row: 4 / 7;
}
```

This one says, "Start at grid row line 4 and end at grid row line 7."

span

Take a look at the CSS for `.grid-item17` now:

```
.grid-item17 {
  grid-row: 6 / span 2;
  grid-column: 2/3;
}
```

Can you see how we have done something a little different with the value for `grid-row`?

Rather than stipulating a definite start and end point when placing grid items, you can give one or the other and then tell the item to span a number of rows/columns from that point either forward or backward. In our example, we told the item to start at grid line 6 and span 2 rows.

I find going backward a little more confusing, but that might just be me! But to illustrate, we could achieve the same visual effect for our example by changing that line to `grid-row: span 2 / 8`. In this instance, the definite point we have is the endpoint, so we are telling the grid to make the item start at grid row 8 and span 2 back from there.

dense

Remember when we looked at `grid-auto-flow`, I mentioned the `dense` keyword? Well, this is the perfect opportunity to show you what that does. I'll amend the value of the `grid-auto-flow` property to this: `grid-auto-flow: row dense;`. And here is what it does in the browser:

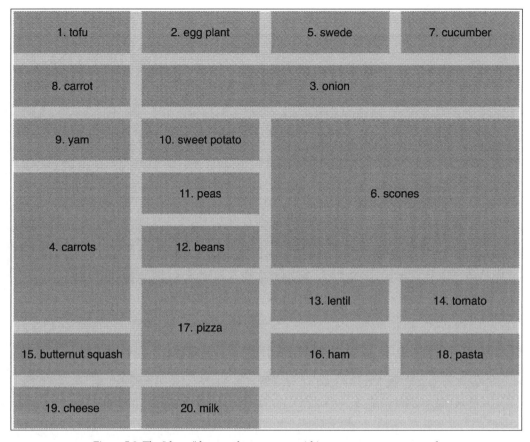

Figure 5.9: The "dense" keyword rearranges grid items so gaps are removed

Can you see how the gaps have been filled? That's what dense does for you. However, while this might seem more aesthetically pleasing, there is a cost. The reason the items are numbered is that I wanted to highlight to you that using dense tells the grid algorithm to move things, visually, from their source order to any available space.

Named grid lines

Grid allows authors to work with grids in a number of ways. For example, if you'd rather work with words than numbers, it's possible to name grid lines. Consider a 3-column by 3-row grid.

You can find this example in the book's code as `example_05-05`.

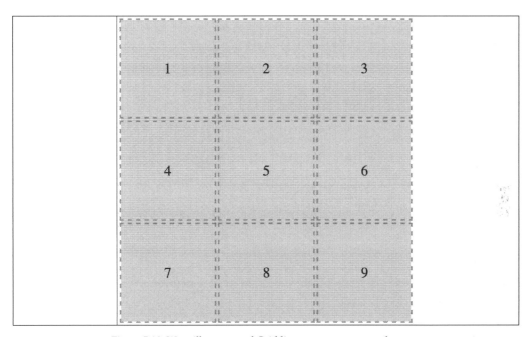

Figure 5.10: We will use named Grid lines to rearrange our elements

Here's our markup:

```
<div class="my-first-grid">
  <div class="grid-item-1">1</div>
  <div class="grid-item-2">2</div>
  <div class="grid-item-3">3</div>
  <div class="grid-item-4">4</div>
  <div class="grid-item-5">5</div>
  <div class="grid-item-6">6</div>
  <div class="grid-item-7">7</div>
  <div class="grid-item-8">8</div>
  <div class="grid-item-9">9</div>
</div>
```

We set the grid up with this rule. Note the words in square brackets:

```css
.my-first-grid {
  display: inline-grid;
  grid-gap: 10px;
  grid-template-columns: [left-start] 200px [left-end center-start]
200px [center-end right-start] 200px [right-end];
  grid-template-rows: 200px 200px 200px;
  background-color: #e4e4e4;
}
```

What we are doing inside the square brackets is giving a name to the grid line. In this instance, the first column grid line we have named `left-start`, and the one after the first column we have named `left-end`. Notice that, in the center grid line, we have assigned two names: `left-end` and `center-start`. We can do this by space-separating the names. In this situation, it makes sense because that grid line is both the end of the left column and the beginning of the center one.

Let's amend our `grid-template-row` and add some named grid lines there too:

```css
grid-template-rows: [top-start] 200px [top-end middle-start] 200px
[middle-end bottom-start] 200px [bottom-end];
```

Here's an example of how we can use these names to position grid items instead of numerical values. This is just the first three of the items we will see in the following diagram:

```css
.grid-item-1 {
  grid-column: center-start / center-end;
  grid-row: middle-start / middle-end;
}

.grid-item-2 {
  grid-column: right-start / right-end;
  grid-row: bottom-start / bottom-end;
}

.grid-item-3 {
  grid-column: left-start / left-end;
  grid-row: top-start / middle-start;
}
```

In the example code, I have set each grid item to a random position using this technique. You can see how the three above are placed in this diagram:

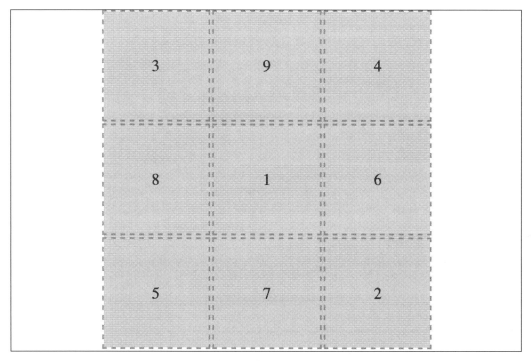

Figure 5.11: You can move things around just as easily with named grid lines

In specification terms, the names we assign to grid lines are known as a "custom ident." Because they are just words, avoid using terminology that might interfere with grid keywords. For example, don't start naming grid lines "dense," "auto-fit," or "span," for example!

Grid has an extra nicety you can make use of when you use named grid lines. If you append your names with "-start" and "-end," as we have in our example, then grid automagically (yes, I know, that's not a real word) makes you a named grid area. Wait, what? Yep, that means that once you have named your grid lines, you can place items in your grid with a one-line `grid-area`. To prove that point, here are just the first three grid-item rules from earlier rewritten this way:

```
.grid-item-1 {
  grid-area: middle / center;
}

.grid-item-2 {
  grid-area: bottom / right;
```

```
}

.grid-item-3 {
  grid-area: top / left;
}
```

I've gotten a little bit ahead of myself now, as I have introduced `grid-area` without any explanation. Let's cover that now.

grid-template-areas

Yet another way you can work with Grid is to create grid template areas to establish the areas of your grid. Let's rework our prior example and we will remove the named grid lines entirely, starting again with this basic CSS for the grid.

This is `example_05-06` in the code:

```
.my-first-grid {
  display: inline-grid;
  grid-gap: 10px;
  grid-template-columns: 200px 200px 200px;
  grid-template-rows: 200px 200px 200px;
  background-color: #e4e4e4;
}

[class^='grid-item'] {
  display: grid;
  align-items: center;
  justify-content: center;
  outline: 3px dashed #f90;
  font-size: 30px;
  color: #333;
}
```

Now, we will define our grid template areas like this, which we will add to the `.my-first-grid` rule:

```
grid-template-areas:
  'one two three'
  'four five six'
  'seven eight nine';
```

With `grid-template-areas`, we can define rows and columns very simply. A row is defined with quotes (double or single), with the names of each column space-separated inside. Each row in the grid is just another pair of quotes with custom idents inside.

You can use numbers for the start of each grid area but you then need to "escape" them when you reference them. For example, if one of our areas was named "9," it would have to be referenced like this: `grid-area: "\39;"`. I find that too burdensome, so I suggest using a string for each area or, at least, starting each custom ident with an alpha character.

And that means we can position our items with `grid-area` like this:

```
.grid-item-1 {
  grid-area: five;
}

.grid-item-2 {
  grid-area: nine;
}

.grid-item-3 {
  grid-area: one;
}
```

Admittedly, this is a simplistic example, but hopefully, you can imagine a more useful scenario: perhaps a blog layout with a header, left-hand sidebar area, main content area, and footer. You might define the necessary `grid-template-areas` like this:

```
grid-template-areas:
  'header header header header header header'
  'side side main main main main'
  'side side footer footer footer footer';
```

As the specification (the link for the relevant section follows) states that any whitespace character fails to produce a token, you could opt to separate columns with tab characters if you would rather, to aid visually lining up the columns:

https://www.w3.org/TR/css-grid-1/#valdef-grid-template-areas-string.

When you write the grid template areas, the indentation is not important, nor are the carriage returns; you could lay each row out in a long space-separated list if you liked. As long as the names for each area are inside quotes, with a whitespace character between each, and there is a space between each set of quotes, all is well.

Applying what you have learned so far

As an exercise, consider this section of the `https://rwd.education` website:

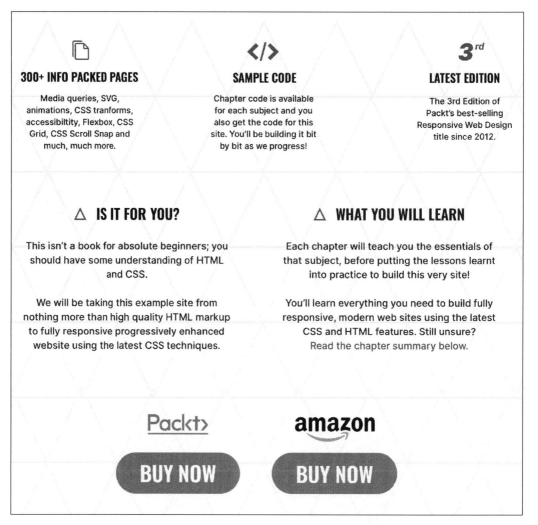

Figure 5.12: Can you use your grid knowledge to lay out this section?

If you look in the `Start` folder for this chapter's code, you will see that, currently, those sections are just one under the other. Try to amend the code for that section with Grid. Perhaps think about how you could easily have it showing one or two of those sections when screen space is limited, and the layout that is shown in the preceding screenshot when space allows.

There's already a working draft for CSS Grid Layout Module Level 2. The principle benefit it brings with it is the ability to have subgrids: grids within grids that can inherit the track sizing of their parents. You can read the current specification here: https:// www.w3.org/TR/css-grid-2/.

Let's move on to some even more advanced Grid techniques now.

auto-fit and auto-fill

`auto-fit` and `auto-fill` are "repeat-to-fill" keywords used to describe repetition to Grid.

Thanks to the similarity of their names, I can't help but feel that the `auto-fit` and `auto-fill` keywords are almost guaranteed to confuse—just like `cover` and `contain` do for background-image sizing (we cover them in *Chapter 7, Stunning Aesthetics with CSS*).

The upshot of this is that I frequently have to check which one is which. Thankfully, for both our benefits, we're going to clarify what each of these does now, and why you might want to use them.

Let me start with the why, as that covers both keywords. What if I told you that with the help of `auto-fill` or `auto-fit`, we can create a fully responsive grid that adds/removes columns based upon the available size of the viewport, with no media queries needed?

Compelling, right?

Consider a 9-column grid, where each column is at least 300px wide. In a slightly back-to-front way, I want to start this by showing you the solution:

```
grid-template-columns: repeat(auto-fit, minmax(300px, 1fr));
```

And here is what that gives you in the browser in a smaller viewport:

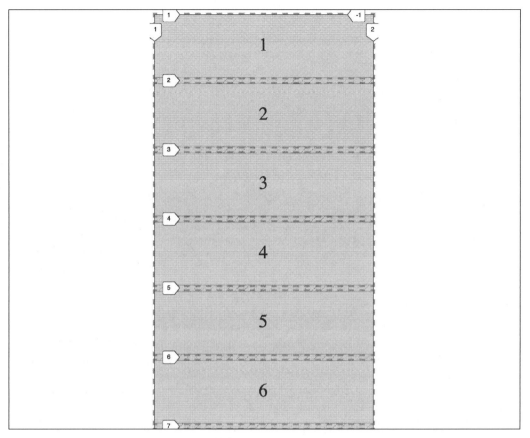

Figure 5.13: One line with Grid gives you a mobile layout…

And the same thing on a wider screen:

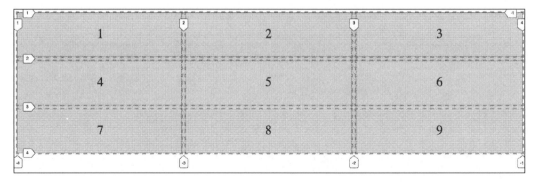

Figure 5.14: …and also a layout for wider viewports!

Pretty handy, right?

Let's break down all the magic in that one-liner.

We are using `grid-template-columns`, as we have done before, to set up the columns of our grid. We are using the `repeat()` function to set up a repeating pattern of columns; however, instead of passing in a number of columns, we tell the grid to `auto-fit`. We may have used `auto-fill` there too, but we'll get to the differences between them in a moment. For now, we have told the browser to repeatedly create auto-fit columns, and we define the width of those columns using the `minmax` function.

The minmax() function

Now, if you are new to Grid, it's likely you haven't used `minmax()` before. It's a CSS function that allows you to set up a range for the browser. You specify a minimum size and a maximum size, and it computes something in between based on the available space. In our example, we are passing `minmax()` a minimum size of 300px and a maximum size of one `fr` (remember, it might help to think of `fr` as "free room").

> When dealing with `minmax()`, if you specify a maximum size that is smaller than the minimum, the maximum will be ignored and the minimum will be the computed value.

With that set, the grid "auto-fits" columns that are at least 300px wide and no more than the size of its content plus a 1fr share of any remaining space.

In practical terms, this provides a responsive layout that lets our grid resize itself based on the available viewport width.

To more easily show you the difference between `auto-fit` and `auto-fill`, let's revise our one-liner to a minimum of 100px:

```
grid-template-columns: repeat(auto-fit, minmax(100px, 1fr));
```

That gives us this layout on a wide viewport:

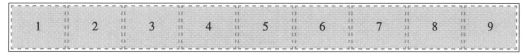

Figure 5.15: Using auto-fit will fit our content into the available space

Note how the columns span the entire width of the page. Now we will change to `auto-fill`:

```
grid-template-columns: repeat(auto-fill, minmax(100px, 1fr));
```

Here is what that produces:

Figure 5.16: Using auto-fill, any spare space is filled up with invisible columns

Notice the space at the end? What happened there?

The key to understanding the difference comes down to whether spare columns are collapsed or not.

When the browser creates the grid in both `auto-fit` and `auto-fill`, it initially lays them out the same. However, when using `auto-fit`, any extra columns left, having laid out the content, are collapsed, leaving that space free to be distributed evenly between the items in the row. In our example, because each item also has a maximum size of 1fr unit, each takes up an equal portion of that free space. This results in columns that span the entire width of the space.

However, with `auto-fill`, once the items (in our example, 100px wide) are laid out, if there is any extra space, the extra empty columns are not collapsed. They remain in situ, filled up, and subsequently the space is not free for the grid items to gobble up. The result is that we get space at the end.

There will be instances where one is more appropriate than the other; just be aware that you can achieve either.

> You can see, in some of the screenshots, indicators for where the grid lines are. These are grabs from the Firefox Grid tool, which is part of its developer tools. As I write this, in early 2020, I think Firefox has, by far, the best developer tools for dealing with Grid.

Shorthand syntax

There are a couple of shorthand syntaxes you can use with Grid: one relatively straightforward, one less so. The first one that you'll probably find most utility for is `grid-template`.

While shorthand syntaxes can be great, my advice would be to write your grids one property at a time, at least to begin with. When you get confident enough that writing each property and value out individually becomes a chore, take the time to learn the shorthand variant.

With that advice dispensed, let's look at these two shorthand methods.

grid-template shorthand

This allows you to set `grid-template-rows`, `grid-template-columns`, and `grid-template-areas` in one line.

So, for example, for a grid with two 200px rows and three 300px columns, we could write:

```
grid-template: 200px 200px / 300px 300px 300px;
```

Or, if you'd rather do it with the `repeat` function, you could write:

```
grid-template: repeat(2, 200px) / repeat(3, 300px);
```

The part before the forward slash deals with the rows and the bit after the columns. You can add `grid-template-areas` in there too if you like:

```
grid-template:
    [rows-top] 'a a a' 200px
    'b b b' 200px [rows-bottom]
    / 300px 300px 300px;
```

That computes to this in the browser:

```
grid-template-rows: [rows-top] 200px 200px [rows-bottom];
grid-template-columns: 300px 300px 300px;
grid-template-areas: 'a a a' 'b b b';
```

Personally, I find that once you start throwing template areas into the values, it starts getting a bit too much to reason about. Regardless, some people love the shorthand and you should be aware it's possible.

However, we're going to take it up another notch now and deal with the `grid` shorthand.

grid shorthand

The other shorthand syntax, `grid`, lets you define a grid all in one line.

Using this one property, you can set the properties controlling the explicit portion of a grid: `grid-template-rows`, `grid-template-columns`, and `grid-template-areas`, as well as the properties controlling the implicit part of a grid: `grid-auto-rows`, `grid-auto-columns`, and `grid-auto-flow`.

An essential concept to hold onto when writing the `grid` shorthand is that a grid can only grow implicitly with either rows or columns, not both. At first, that might seem odd, but if you think about it, how would a grid that could add both rows and columns implicitly lay items out? How would it decide whether to add rows or columns?

So, with that in mind, we can endeavor to wrap our heads around the `grid` shorthand.

The `grid` shorthand is not for the faint-hearted, so don't be discouraged if it spits you back out a few times before you get to grips with it. I consider myself pretty familiar with CSS (I know, you'd hope so, right?), but it took me hours rather than minutes to feel confident with what the `grid` shorthand syntax was doing.

I hope you know your Backus-Naur form, because here is how the property is described in the specification:

```
<'grid-template-rows'> / [ auto-flow && dense? ] <'grid-auto-
columns'>? [ auto-flow && dense? ] <'grid-auto-rows'>? / <'grid-
template-columns'>
```

Simple, right?

I kid, of course. At this point, when trying to understand a specification, I tend to search out this piece on understanding CSS specifications: `https://www.smashingmagazine.com/2016/05/understanding-the-css-property-value-syntax/`.

After rereading that, I'll now do my best to distill that piece of the specification into something more human friendly. What that means is, the `grid` shorthand can accept any one of three different sets of syntax as its value.

grid shorthand value – option one

This is the same value that you would use if you were using `grid-template`. For example, here is a grid with two 100px rows and three 200px columns:

```
grid: 100px 100px / 200px 200px 200px;
```

Just like with our `grid-template` examples from earlier, you can also use `grid-template-areas` if you like.

grid shorthand value – option two

A set of lengths for explicit grid rows, then, separated by the slash, a definition for how you want to handle implicit columns. This can be `auto-flow` to set `grid-auto-rows`, with the option of setting `grid-auto-flow` by adding `dense` too. Or, alternatively, you could add a length value for the width of the columns if you want to set `grid-template-columns` instead.

Phew, that's a lot to compute. Take a look at some examples.

So, for a grid with two explicit 100px rows and any number of explicit columns that are 75px wide:

```
grid: 100px 100px / repeat(auto-fill, 75px);
```

With this grid, should you have too many items, they will spill over into the implicit rows with a default size of `auto`.

In the browser, that shorthand will compute to the following:

```
grid-template-rows: 100px 100px;
grid-template-columns: repeat(auto-fill, 75px);
grid-template-areas: none;
grid-auto-flow: initial;
grid-auto-rows: initial;
grid-auto-columns: initial;
```

Let's try another. Say we want to lay out a grid that has only one row, 100px high, but any number of columns, potentially running off the side of the container:

```
grid: 100px / auto-flow;
```

That rule computes to the following:

```
grid-template-rows: 100px;
grid-template-columns: initial;
grid-template-areas: initial;
grid-auto-flow: column;
grid-auto-rows: initial;
grid-auto-columns: initial;
```

It's also worth knowing that, when you use the grid shorthand, you are resetting all of the values it deals with back to their initial state. You can see that if you look at the computed values of styles in the developer tools of your browser.

grid shorthand value – option three

The final syntax you can pass to grid is effectively the opposite of option two. This time, you set grid-auto-flow to handle implicit rows (with an optional dense) with an optional grid-auto-rows value for the size of the rows. Then, after the slash, we handle grid-template-columns.

With this kind of value, we are getting our grid to lay out in rows when needed, rather than in columns, as in the previous option. Here are some examples.

How about a grid that creates as many 100px rows as needed and 5 columns that occupy 1fr each?

```
grid: auto-flow 100px / repeat(5, 1fr);
```

That computes to this:

```
grid-template-rows: initial;
grid-template-columns: repeat(5, 1fr);
grid-template-areas: initial;
grid-auto-flow: row;
grid-auto-rows: 100px;
grid-auto-columns: initial;
```

Or, what about a grid that creates a single column with as many 100px rows as needed for the content?

```
grid: auto-flow 100px / auto;
```

That computes to this:

```
grid-template-rows: initial;
grid-template-columns: auto;
grid-template-areas: initial;
grid-auto-flow: row;
grid-auto-rows: 100px;
grid-auto-columns: initial;
```

You can see that the grid shorthand is very powerful but, arguably, not particularly intuitive. For some people, the shorthand is preferable. For some, it is maddening. There is no right or wrong—just what is right or wrong for you.

Summary

If you are fairly new to building on the web, you almost have an advantage when it comes to learning CSS Grid; a "beginner's mind" if you like. For people that have been laying things out with other techniques over the years, the difficulty, in some ways, is undoing what you already know about layout with CSS.

Having read this chapter, you should have some understanding of what is possible with Grid and how you might employ it.

Furthermore, if you were in any way successful with the exercises, you should congratulate yourself; there's a lot to consider when you first start using Grid. If you accomplished something with your first effort, you did admirably.

At this point, I'll also reiterate that Grid is tricky at first. It comes with a lot of possibilities but also quite a few new pieces of terminology and concepts. Expect to take a few runs at it the first time you use it. But I promise that, once you get competent, it will pay you back handsomely for your investment.

The last two chapters have covered fairly broad topics: how to do layouts with the most modern techniques and how to deal with responsive images. The next chapter is going to be more detail-orientated. Lots of lovely little tricks and techniques are made possible with CSS; it is a veritable grab-bag of CSS goodies. Turn that page, and let's move on to *Chapter 6, CSS Selectors, Typography, Color Modes, and More*.

6

CSS Selectors, Typography, Color Modes, and More

In the last few years, CSS has enjoyed a raft of new features. Some enable us to animate and transform elements. Others allow us to create multiple background images, gradients, and mask and filter effects, and others allow us to bring SVG elements to life.

We will get to all those capabilities in the next few chapters. Firstly, I think it will be useful to look at more recent improvements to some of the fundamentals of CSS.

No one can know every nuance, capability, and syntax in the CSS language. I've been working with CSS for two decades and on a weekly basis I still discover something new (or just as likely rediscover something I'd forgotten). As such, I don't feel that trying to know every possible CSS property and value permutation is actually a worthy pursuit. Instead, I think it's more sensible to develop a good grasp of what's possible and what capabilities exist that solve the most common problems.

As such, we are going to concentrate in this chapter on some of the techniques, units, and selectors I have found most useful when building responsive web designs. I'm hoping you'll then have the requisite knowledge to solve most problems that come your way when developing a responsive web design.

As there are quite a few topics to cover they have been grouped:

Selectors, units, and capabilities:

- `::before` and `::after` pseudo-elements
- Attribute selectors and substring matching
- Structural pseudo-classes, including `:last-child`, `:nth-child`, `:empty`, and `:not`
- Combinator selectors, including child, next sibling, and subsequent sibling
- Viewport related length units: vh, vw, vmax, and vmin
- The `calc()` function
- CSS custom properties and environment variables
- Using `@supports` to fork CSS

Web typography:

- `@font-face` rule
- Font formats, including `.woff` and `.woff2`
- Font loading control with the `font-display` property
- Variable fonts and font features

Color:

- RGB
- HSL
- RGBA and HSLA

As you can see, we have a lot to get through. Let's begin.

Selectors, units, and capabilities

Although they may not seem like the most exciting of subjects, selectors, units, and capabilities are the "meat and potatoes" of CSS. Master these and your power to solve problems with CSS will increase substantially. So, skip this section at your peril!

Anatomy of a CSS rule

Before exploring some of the recent additions to CSS, to prevent confusion, let's establish the terminology we use to describe a CSS rule. Consider the following example:

```
.round {
  /* selector */
  border-radius: 10px; /* declaration */
}
```

This rule is made up of the selector (`.round`) and then the declaration (`border-radius: 10px`). The declaration is further defined by the property (`border-radius`) and the value (`10px`). Happy we're on the same page? Great, let's press on.

 At the time of writing this, the Selectors Level 4 working draft details a host of new selectors such as `is()`, `has()`, and `nth-col`. Sadly, there is not a single implementation in any of the common browsers available. However, if you want to see how things are shaping up for the future, head to the draft at `https://www.w3.org/TR/selectors-4/`.

Pseudo-elements and pseudo-classes

There is potential for some confusion when we go on shortly to talk about "pseudo" selectors. The reason being is that, in CSS, there are both pseudo-selectors and pseudo-elements. Let's therefore take a moment to establish the difference.

The word "pseudo" in this context means something that is like something but not really it. So, a pseudo-element is something that is like an element but not really one, and a pseudo-selector is something that selects something that isn't really something. Wow, I'm sounding like the Riddler now from Batman! Let's clarify with some code. Here is how you create a pseudo-element in CSS:

```
.thing::before {
    content: "Spooky";
}
```

That inserts a `::before` pseudo-element into the `.thing` element with the content "Spooky." A `::before` behaves like a first child of the element and an `::after` behaves like a last child.

The following image might help. It's showing a single element represented in the Firefox developer tools, containing text with both a `::before` and an `::after` pseudo-element added in CSS:

```
<!DOCTYPE html>
▼ <html class="" lang="en"> event
  ▶ <head> ⬤ </head>
  ▼ <body>
    ▼ <div class="thing">
        ::before
        Here is text in the element
        ::after
      </div>
    </body>
  </html>
```

Figure 6.1: The Firefox developer tools will show you where pseudo-elements are in the DOM

The key thing to remember with pseudo-elements is that if you don't provide a value for `content`, nothing will show on the page. Notice the double colon before `before`? Officially, that is how you should code pseudo-elements as it helps differentiate them from pseudo-selectors, which only use one. However, a single colon worked with the first implementations of `::before` and `::after` and so you can still write them that way too.

You can't do the same with pseudo-selectors; they always have a single colon. For example, `:hover`, `:active`, and `:focus` are all pseudo-selectors and are written with a single colon.

At the risk of oversimplification, it might be useful to think of a pseudo-selector as one that selects a subpart of the original thing it is selecting.

Hopefully, the difference between pseudo-selectors and elements is now clear.

With that distinction made, let's move on and look at some of the powerful selectors available to us today in CSS.

CSS Level 3 selectors and how to use them

CSS now provides incredible power for selecting elements within a page. You may not think this sounds very glitzy but trust me, it will make your life easier and you'll love CSS for it! I'd better qualify that bold claim.

CSS attribute selectors

You've probably used CSS attribute selectors to create rules. For example, consider the following markup:

```
<img src="https://placeimg.com/640/480/any" alt="an inquisitive
cat">
```

And this CSS:

```
img[alt] {
   border: 3px dashed #e15f5f;
}
```

This would select the `img` element in the preceding code, and any others on the page provided that they have an `alt` attribute.

In fact, to make something a little more useful, we could combine this with the `:not` negation selector (we will look at that in detail later in this chapter) to add a red border around any images that have no `alt` attribute or an `alt` attribute with no value:

```
img:not([alt]),
img[alt=""] {
      border: 3px solid red;
}
```

That would be useful from an accessibility point of view as it would visually highlight any images that didn't have alternate text included for assistive technology.

As another example, let's say we wanted to select all elements with a `data-sausage` attribute:

```
[data-sausage] {
   /* styles */
}
```

The key thing here is to use square brackets to specify the attribute you want to select.

The data-* type attribute was introduced in HTML5 to provide a place for custom data that can't be stored sensibly by any other existing mechanism. The specification description for these can be found here: http://www.w3.org/TR/2010/WD-html5-20101019/elements.html#embedding-custom-non-visible-data-with-the-data-attributes.

You can also narrow things down by specifying what the attribute value is. For example, consider the following rule:

```
img[alt="Sausages cooking"] {
  /* Styles */
}
```

This would only target images that have an `alt` attribute of "Sausages cooking"; for example:

```
<img src="img/sausages.png" alt="Sausages cooking" />
```

So far, so "big deal, we could do that in CSS2." What do CSS Level 3 selectors bring to the party?

CSS substring matching attribute selectors

CSS3 added the ability to select elements based upon the substring of their attribute selector. That sounds complicated. It isn't! The three options are whether the attribute:

- Begins with a certain substring
- Contains an instance of a certain substring
- Ends with a certain substring

Let's see what they look like.

The "beginning with" substring matching attribute selector

Consider the following markup:

```
<li data-type="todo-chore">Empty the bins</li>
<li data-type="todo-exercise">Play football</li>
```

Suppose that markup represents two items in a "todo" list application we are building. Even though they both have different `data-type` attribute values, we can select them both with the "beginning with" substring matching attribute selector, like this:

```
[data-type^="todo"] {
/* Styles */
}
```

The key character in all this is the ^ symbol. That symbol is called the "caret," although it is often referred to as the "hat" symbol too. In this instance, it signifies "begins with." Because both `data-type` attributes have values that begin with "todo," our selector selects them.

The "contains an instance of" substring matching attribute selector

The "contains an instance of" substring matching attribute selector has the following syntax:

```
[attribute*="value"] {
/* Styles */
}
```

Like all attribute selectors, you can combine them with a `type` selector (one that references the actual HTML element used) if needed, although I would only do that if I had to—in case you want to change the type of element used.

Let's try an example. Consider this markup:

```
<p data-ingredients="scones cream jam">Will I get selected?</p>
```

We can select that element like this:

```
[data-ingredients*="cream"] {
    color: red;
}
```

The key character in all this is the * symbol, which in this context means "contains."

The "begins with" selector would not have worked in this markup as the string inside the attribute didn't begin with "cream." It did, however, contain "cream," so the "contains an instance of" substring attribute selector finds it.

The "ends with" substring matching attribute selector

The "ends with" substring matching attribute selector has the following syntax:

```
[attribute$="value"] {
/* Styles */
}
```

An example should help. Consider this markup:

```
<p data-ingredients="scones cream jam">Will I get selected?</p>
<p data-ingredients="toast jam butter">Will I get selected?</p>
<p data-ingredients="jam toast butter">Will I get selected?</p>
```

Suppose we only want to select the element with scones, cream, and jam in the `data-ingredients` attribute (the first element). We can't use the "contains an instance of" (it will select all three) or "begins with" (it will only select the last one) substring attribute selector. However, we can use the "ends with" substring attribute selector:

```
[data-ingredients$="jam"] {
    color: red;
}
```

The key character in all this is the $ (dollar) symbol, which means "ends with."

Right, we have some pretty handy attribute related selectors now. It's also worth knowing that you can chain attribute selectors, just like you can class selectors.

Chaining attribute selectors

You can have even more possibilities for selecting items by grouping attribute selectors.

Suppose we had this markup:

```
<li
  data-todo-type="exercise"
  data-activity-name="running"
  data-location="indoor"
>
  Running
</li>
<li
  data-todo-type="exercise"
  data-activity-name="swimming"
  data-location="indoor"
>
  Swimming
</li>
<li
  data-todo-type="exercise"
```

```
    data-activity-name="cycling"
    data-location="outdoor"
  >
    Cycling
</li>
<li
    data-todo-type="exercise"
    data-activity-name="swimming"
    data-location="outdoor"
  >
    Swimming
</li>
```

Let's suppose I only wanted to select "indoor swimming." I can't use just `data-location="indoor"` as that would get the first element too. I can't use `data-activity-name="swimming"` as that would get me the first and the third, but I can do this:

```
[data-activity-name="swimming"][data-location="indoor"] {
    /* Styles */
}
```

This selects elements that have "swimming" as the activity name, as long as they also have "indoor" as the location.

 Attribute selectors allow you to select IDs and classes that start with numbers. Before HTML5, it wasn't valid markup to start IDs or class names with a number. HTML5 removes that restriction. When it comes to IDs, there are still some things to remember. There should be no spaces in the ID name, and it must be unique on the page. For more information, visit `http://www.w3.org/html/wg/drafts/html/master/dom.html#the-id-attribute`. Now, although you can start ID and class values with numbers in HTML5, CSS still restricts you from using ID and class selectors that start with a number (`http://www.w3.org/TR/CSS21/syndata.html#characters`). Luckily for us, we can easily work around this by using an attribute selector; for example, `[id="10"]`.

Right, I think our attribute selecting skills are now pretty tight. Let's move on to how we can deal with selecting elements based upon where they are in the document.

CSS structural pseudo-classes

CSS gives us more power to select elements based upon where they sit in the structure of the DOM. Let's consider a common design treatment; we're working on the navigation bar for a larger viewport and we want to have all but the last link over on the left. Historically, we would have needed to solve this problem by adding a class name to the last link so we could select it, like this:

```
<nav class="nav-Wrapper">
  <a href="/home" class="nav-Link">Home</a>
  <a href="/About" class="nav-Link">About</a>
  <a href="/Films" class="nav-Link">Films</a>
  <a href="/Forum" class="nav-Link">Forum</a>
  <a href="/Contact-Us" class="nav-Link nav-LinkLast">Contact Us</a>
</nav>
```

This in itself can be problematic. For example, sometimes, just getting a content management system to add a class to a final list item can be frustratingly difficult. Thankfully, in those eventualities, it's no longer a concern. We can solve this problem and many more with CSS structural pseudo-classes.

The :last-child selector

CSS 2.1 already had a selector applicable for the first item in a list; the `:first-child` selector:

```
div:first-child {
  /* Styles */
}
```

However, CSS Level 3 added a selector that can also match the last:

```
div:last-child {
  /* Styles */
}
```

Let's look how that selector could fix our prior problem if we didn't want to, or couldn't add, another class at the desired point in the markup:

```
.nav-Wrapper {
  display: flex;
}
.nav-Link:last-child {
  margin-left: auto;
}
```

There are also useful selectors for when something is the only item: `:only-child` and the only item of a type: `:only-of-type`.

The nth-child selectors

The `nth-child` selectors let us solve even more difficult problems. With the same markup as before, let's consider how `nth-child` selectors allow us to select any arbitrary link(s) we want within the list.

Firstly, what about selecting every other list item? We could select the odd ones like this:

```
.nav-Link:nth-child(odd) {
   /* Styles */
}
```

Or, if you wanted to select the even ones, you could do this:

```
.nav-Link:nth-child(even) {
   /* Styles */
}
```

Understanding what nth rules do

For the uninitiated, nth-based selectors can look pretty intimidating. However, once you've mastered the logic and syntax, you'll be amazed what you can do with them. Let's take a look.

Here are the nth-based selectors at our disposal:

- `nth-child(n)`
- `nth-last-child(n)`
- `nth-of-type(n)`
- `nth-last-of-type(n)`

We've seen that we can use (odd) or (even) values already in an nth-based expression, but the (n) parameter can be used in another couple of ways:

- As an integer; for example, `:nth-child(2)` would select the second item. Passing a number/integer into the nth selector is easy enough to understand; just enter the element number you want to select.

- However, you can also pass a numeric expression. For example, `:nth-child(3n+1)` would start at the first element, and then select every third element.

The numeric expression version of the selector is the part that can be a little baffling at first. Let's break it down.

Breaking down the math

Let's consider 10 spans on a page (you can play about with these by looking at `example_06-05`):

```
<span></span>
<span></span>
<span></span>
<span></span>
<span></span>
<span></span>
<span></span>
<span></span>
<span></span>
<span></span>
```

We will style them like this:

```
span {
    height: 2rem;
    width: 2rem;
    background-color: blue;
    display: inline-block;
}
```

As you might imagine, this gives us 10 squares in a line:

Figure 6.2: We will test our nth-child selection skills on these ten identical elements

OK, let's look at how we can select different ones with nth-based selections.

For practicality, when considering the expression within the parentheses, I start from the right. So, for example, if I want to figure out what (2n+3) will select, I start with the right-most number (the "3" here indicates the third item from the left) and know it will select every second element from that point on. So, adding this rule:

```
span:nth-child(2n + 3) {
    background-color: #f90;
```

```
    border-radius: 50%;
}
```

Results in this in the browser:

Figure 6.3: Anything that matches our nth-child selector gets turned round and orange

As you can see, our nth selector targets the third list item and then every subsequent second one after that too. If there were 100 list items, it would continue selecting every second one.

How about selecting everything from the second item onwards? Well, although you could write :nth-child(1n+2), you don't actually need the first number 1 as, unless otherwise stated, n is equal to 1. We can, therefore, just write :nth-child(n+2). Likewise, if we wanted to select every third element, rather than write :nth-child(3n+3), we could just write :nth-child(3n) as every third item would begin at the third item anyway, without needing to state it explicitly.

The expression can also use negative numbers; for example, :nth-child(3n-2) starts at minus 2 and then selects every third item.

You can also change the direction. By default, once the first part of the selection is found, the subsequent ones go down the elements in the DOM (and therefore from left to right in our example). However, you can reverse that with a minus; for example:

```
span:nth-child(-2n+3) {
    background-color: #f90;
    border-radius: 50%;
}
```

This example finds the third item again, but then goes in the opposite direction to select every two elements (up the DOM tree and therefore from right to left in our example):

Figure 6.4: With a minus symbol we can select in the opposite direction

Hopefully, the nth-based expressions are making more sense now. `nth-child` and `nth-last-child` differ in that the `nth-last-child` variant works from the opposite end of the document tree. For example, `:nth-last-child(-n+3)` starts at 3 from the end and then selects all the items after it. Here's what that rule gives us in the browser:

Figure 6.5: nth-last-child lets you start from the opposite end of the elements

Finally, let's consider `:nth-of-type` and `:nth-last-of-type`. While the previous examples count any children, regardless of type (always remember the `nth-child` selector targets all children at the same DOM level, regardless of classes), `:nth-of-type` and `:nth-last-of-type` let you be specific about the type of item you want to select. Consider the following markup (`example_06-06`), which is a mixture of `div` and `span` elements, albeit with the same class:

```
<span class="span-class"></span>
<span class="span-class"></span>
<span class="span-class"></span>
<span class="span-class"></span>
<span class="span-class"></span>

<div class="span-class"></div>
<div class="span-class"></div>
<div class="span-class"></div>
<div class="span-class"></div>
<div class="span-class"></div>
```

If we used the selector:

```
.span-class:nth-of-type(-2n+3) {
  background-color: #f90;
  border-radius: 50%;
}
```

Even though all the elements have the same `span-class` class, they don't get seen as one group. The selector applies once to the `span` elements, and then to the `div` elements. Here is what gets selected:

Figure 6.6: nth-of-type selectors work on each type of element they find

CSS doesn't count like JavaScript and jQuery! If you're used to using JavaScript and jQuery, you'll know that it counts from 0 upward (zero index-based). For example, if selecting an element in JavaScript or jQuery, an integer value of 1 would actually be the second element. CSS, however, starts at 1 so that a value of 1 is the first item it matches.

nth-based selection in responsive web designs

Just to close out this little section, I want to illustrate a real-life responsive web design problem and how we can use nth-based selection to solve it. Imagine we are building a page where we want to list the top grossing movies from a given year. Our content management system simply spits all the items out in a list, but we want to show them in a grid of sorts.

For some viewports, we will only be able to fit two items wide. However, as the viewport increases in width, we can show three items and at larger sizes still, we can show four. Here is the problem, though. Regardless of the viewport size, we want to prevent any items on the bottom row from having a border on the bottom.

You can view this code at `example_06-09`. Here is how it looks with four items wide:

Figure 6.7: Our task here is to remove the border on the bottom row, regardless of how many are showing

See that pesky border below the bottom two items? That's what we need to remove. However, I want a robust solution so that if there was another item on the bottom row (we want to go one better than other sites and show the top 11 top grossing films!), the border would also be removed from that too.

Now, because there are a different number of items on each row at different viewports, we will also need to change the nth-based selection at different viewport widths. But we can use media queries for that. For the sake of brevity, I'm not going to show you the selection for each media query. I'll just show you the selection that matches four items per row, as you can see in the preceding screenshot. However, you can open the code sample to see the selections for each different viewport:

```
@media (min-width: 55rem) {
  .Item {
    width: 25%;
  }
  /* Get me every fourth item and of those, only ones that are in
the last four items */
  .Item:nth-child(4n+1):nth-last-child(-n+4),
  /* Now get me every one after that same collection too. */
```

```
    .Item:nth-child(4n+1):nth-last-child(-n+4) ~ .Item {
        border-bottom: 0;
    }
}
```

You'll notice here that we are chaining the nth-based pseudo-class selectors, much like we chained attribute selectors earlier in this chapter. It's important to understand when you chain nth selectors like this that the first selector doesn't "filter" the selection for the next selector; rather, the element has to match each of the selections.

So, for the line like this:

```
    .Item:nth-child(4n+1):nth-last-child(-n+4),
```

`.Item` has to be the first item of four and also be one of the last four:

Figure 6.8: Achievement unlocked—using nth-child selectors like some kind of nth-child wizard!

Nice! Thanks to nth-based selections, we have a defensive set of rules to remove the bottom border, regardless of the viewport size or number of items we are showing.

Now, one nifty bit of selection we are doing in that prior example is using the "subsequent sibling" selector. We haven't looked at that, so we will cover that next.

Combinator selectors – child, next sibling, and subsequent sibling

I'm making the assumption at this point that you understand the basic selector pattern where one class followed by another selects any descendant that matches. For example, `.parent .descendant {}` would select any element that was a descendant of the `.parent` element with a class of `.descendant`, no matter how many levels deep.

The child combinator

The child combinator only selects direct descendants. Consider this markup:

```
<div class="parent">
  <div class="descendant child">
    <div class="descendant grandchild"></div>
  </div>
</div>
```

We can select only the direct "child" of the parent element, like this:

```
.parent > .descendant {
  /* Styles */
}
```

Notice the right angle bracket between the two class names in the selector; that's the child combinator symbol.

The next sibling

Consider another example:

```
<div class="item one">one</div>
<div class="item">two</div>
<div class="item">three</div>
<div class="item">four</div>
<div class="item">five</div>
<div class="item">six</div>
```

Let's suppose we wanted to select an item, but only if it is the next sibling of `.one`. With that markup, we could select the two elements like this:

```
.one + .item {
  border: 3px dashed #f90;
}
```

The + symbol there means "next sibling," so select the next sibling element of .one.

The subsequent sibling

With the same markup from the previous example, if we wanted to select all items after the third, we could do this:

```
.item:nth-child(3) ~ .item {
    border: 3px dashed #f90;
}
```

The ~ symbol, called "tilde," says "every subsequent sibling."

The negation (:not) selector

Another handy selector is the negation pseudo-class selector. This is used to select everything that isn't something else. Consider this:

```
<div class="a-div"></div>
<div class="a-div"></div>
<div class="a-div"></div>
<div class="a-div not-me"></div>
<div class="a-div"></div>
```

And then these styles:

```
div {
    display: inline-block;
    height: 2rem;
    width: 2rem;
    background-color: blue;
}

.a-div:not(.not-me) {
    background-color: orange;
    border-radius: 50%;
}
```

Our final rule will make every element with a class of `.a-div` orange and round, with the exception of the `div` that also has the `.not-me` class. You can find that code in the `example_06-07` folder of the code samples (remember, you can grab them all at `https://rwd.education`):

Figure 6.9: The negation selector allows you to exclude elements from selection

So far, we have looked primarily at what's known as structural pseudo-classes (full information on this is available at `http://www.w3.org/TR/selectors/#structural-pseudos`). However, CSS has many more selectors. If you're working on a web application, it's worth looking at the full list of UI element states pseudo-classes (`http://www.w3.org/TR/selectors/#UIstates`) as they can, for example, help you target rules based on whether something is selected or not.

The empty (:empty) selector

I've encountered situations where I have an element that includes some padding on the inside and gets content dynamically inserted. Sometimes, it gets content inserted, while sometimes, it doesn't. The trouble is, when it doesn't include content, I still see the padding. Consider the HTML in `example_06-08`:

```
<div class="thing"></div>
```

And here's the CSS:

```
.thing {
  padding: 1rem;
  background-color: violet;
}
```

Without any content in that element, I still see the background color. Thankfully, we can easily hide it, like this:

```
.thing:empty {
  display: none;
}
```

However, just be careful with the `:empty` selector. For example, you might think this is empty:

```
<div class="thing"> </div>
```

It isn't! Look at the whitespace in there. Whitespace is not "no" space! And nor would something like a line break be either.

However, just to confuse matters, be aware that a comment doesn't affect whether an element is considered "empty" or not. For example, this is still considered empty:

```
<div class="thing"><!--I'm empty, honest I am--></div>
```

> Remember to check support for your users. As we delve into CSS more and more, don't forget to visit http://caniuse.com, if you ever want to know what the current level of browser support is for a particular CSS or HTML5 feature. Alongside showing browser version support (searchable by feature), it also provides the most recent set of global usage statistics from http://gs.statcounter.com.

Let's change tack now. We've looked at how we can select items in our responsive world. But how about how we size them? We'll look at viewport-percentage lengths next.

Responsive viewport-percentage lengths (vmax, vmin, vh, and vw)

CSS Values and Units Module Level 3 (http://www.w3.org/TR/css3-values/#viewport-relative-lengths) ushered in viewport relative units. These are great for responsive web design, as each unit is a percentage length of the viewport:

- The vw unit, where each vw unit is 1% of the viewport width.
- The vh unit, where each vh unit is 1% of the viewport height.
- The vmin unit (for viewport minimum; equal to the smaller of either vw or vh).
- The vmax (viewport maximum; equal to the larger of either vw or vh).

Want a modal window that's 90% of the browser height? This is as easy as:

```
.modal {
    height: 90vh;
}
```

As useful as viewport relative units are, some browsers have curious implementations. Safari in iOS, for example, changes the viewable screen area as you scroll from the top of a page (it shrinks the address bar), but doesn't make any changes to the reported viewport height.

However, you can perhaps find more utility for these units when coupled with fonts. For example, it's now trivially easy to create text that scales in size, depending upon the viewport.

For example:

```css
.Hero-text {
  font-size: 25vw;
}
```

Now, the text will always be sized as a percentage of the viewport width.

 There is a new mathematical expression on the way to CSS called `clamp()`, which lets us specify a minimum, maximum, and variable size. For example, we might opt for a headline like this: `.headline { font-size: clamp(20px, 40vw, 80px) }`. And while our headline text might vary in size, depending upon the viewport, it would never be less than `20px` or larger than `80px`. You can read the specification for `clamp()` here: `https://www.w3.org/TR/css-values-4/#calc-notation`.

Right, we've dealt with selectors of various types, and some of the more recent length units that are particularly relevant to responsive designs. Before we move on to web typography, let's cover some important capabilities of CSS.

CSS calc

How many times have you been trying to code out a layout and thought something like, "it needs to be half the width of the parent element minus exactly 10px"? This is particularly useful with responsive web design, as we never know the size of the screen that will be viewing our web pages. Thankfully, CSS has a way to do this. It's called the `calc()` function. Here's that example in CSS:

```css
.thing {
    width: calc(50% - 10px);
}
```

Just be careful to include whitespace around your symbols. If I had written `calc(50% -10px)`, for example, missing the whitespace around the minus sign, the declaration would not have worked.

Addition, subtraction, division, and multiplication are supported, so it's possible to solve a bunch of problems that have been impossible without JavaScript in the past.

You can also use CSS custom properties in there too. If you don't know anything about CSS custom properties, you're in luck, because that's what we are going to talk about next.

CSS custom properties

CSS custom properties are often referred to as "CSS variables," although that is not necessarily their only use case.

 You can find the full specification here: `http://dev.w3.org/csswg/css-variables/`.

CSS custom properties allow us to store information in our stylesheets that can then be utilized in that stylesheet or read/written to with JavaScript.

Let's start with a simple use case; storing a `font-family` name that we can then reference more simply later in the stylesheet:

```css
:root {
  --MainFont: 'Helvetica Neue', Helvetica, Arial, sans-serif;
}
```

Here, we are using the `:root` pseudo-class to store the custom property in the document root (although you can store them inside any rule you like).

 The `:root` pseudo-class always references the top-most parent element in a document structure. In an HTML document, this would always be the HTML tag, but for an SVG document (we will look at SVG in *Chapter 8, Using SVGs for Resolution Independence*), it would reference a different element.

A custom property always begins with two dashes, then the custom name, and then, at the end of the property, just like a normal CSS property, we terminate the property with a colon.

We can reference that value elsewhere in our stylesheet with the `var()` notation, like so:

```
.Title {
    font-family: var(--MainFont);
}
```

You could obviously store as many custom properties as you need in this manner. The main benefit of this approach is that you can change the value inside the variable and every rule that makes use of the variable gets the new value without having to amend them directly.

Let me show you a very simple example of using CSS custom properties with JavaScript. You can find this in `example_06-11`. We will make a page with the poem "If," by Rudyard Kipling. At the bottom is a simple light/dark mode toggle button. All the button will do is toggle the value of two CSS custom properties: `--background` and `--foreground`.

Here is our CSS:

```
body {
    background-color: var(--background);
    color: var(--foreground);
}
```

For the curious, here is the snippet of JavaScript we are using. Essentially, it just says that if the foreground variable is `#eee` (nearly white), then make it `#333` (a dark grey); otherwise, make it `#eee`. And, if the background variable is `#333`, make it `#eee`; otherwise, make it `#333`:

```
var root = document.documentElement;
var btn = document.getElementById("colorToggle");

btn.addEventListener("click", e => {
    root.style.setProperty("--background", getComputedStyle(root).
getPropertyValue('--background') === "#333" ? "#eee" : "#333");
    root.style.setProperty("--foreground", getComputedStyle(root).
getPropertyValue('--foreground') === "#eee" ? "#333" : "#eee");
})
```

And here is a screenshot showing each state:

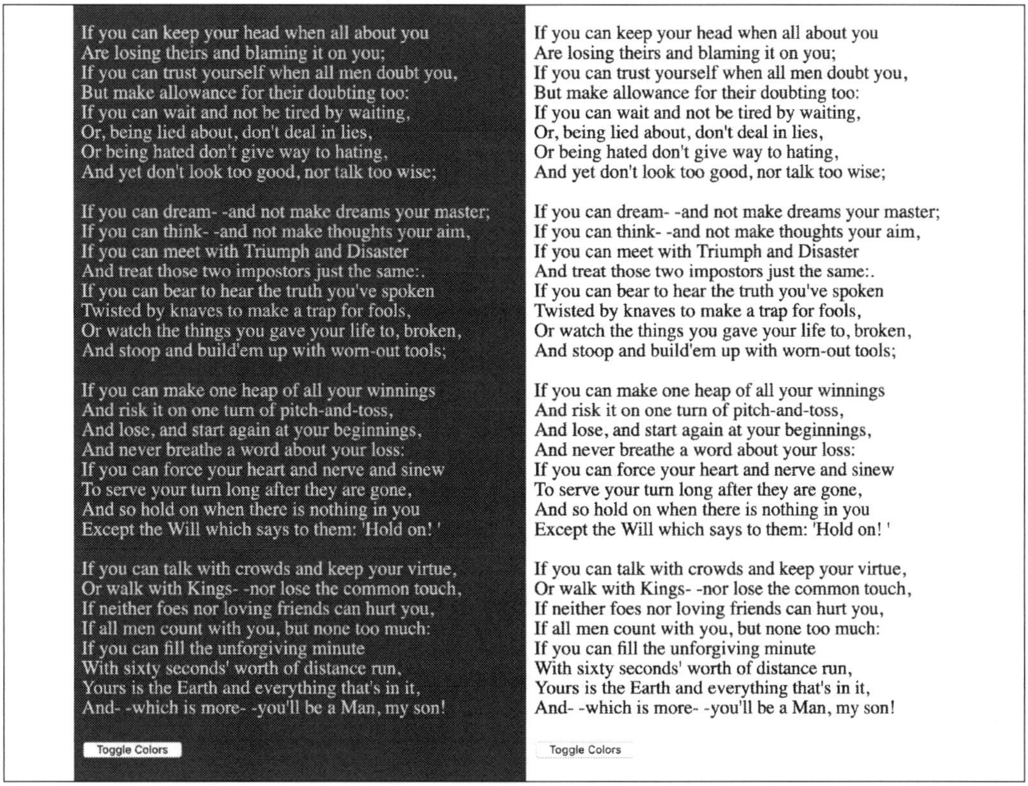

Figure 6.10: An example of each state side by side, colors easily swapped with custom properties

This example is in this chapter's code as `example_06-12`.

Custom properties also behave like other properties in terms of specificity. For example, we set our custom properties at the root level, but if they are redeclared closer to the element in question, the more specific value will override the first. Consider this CSS:

```
:root {
  --backgroundColor: red;
}


header {
  --backgroundColor: goldenrod;
}
```

The header and any elements within it that make use of the `--backgroundColor` custom property will have a "goldenrod" background color, whereas other elements will have a red background.

Setting a fallback value

There may be a situation where you want to protect against a custom property being unavailable. You can do that by providing a fallback value. The syntax is straightforward: simply provide your fallback value after the custom property name and a comma. For example, suppose I wanted to use the `--backgroundColor` custom property, but default to a dark gray color if that variable was unavailable. I could write it like this:

```
.my-Item {
    background-color: var(--backgroundColor, #555);
}
```

To be safe, it makes a lot of sense to get into the habit of supplying fallback values whenever you use custom properties.

env() environment variables

In addition to custom properties we might make for ourselves, there are occasionally properties that can be read in from the environment we are operating in. These are called "environment variables." The only solid example of these I'm currently aware of are the `safe-area-inset` properties applicable to notched mobile phones. Made famous by the iPhone X, the "safe-areas" relate to the sections at the top and bottom of the screen where areas of UI or physical buttons impinge upon the viewing area.

Environment variables are defined with the `env()` function. Values are passed into this function just like you would any other CSS function. For example, if we wanted to add padding to the top of our element equal to the height of the environments "safe area inset top," we could do this:

```
padding-top: env(safe-area-inset-top);
```

If the browser has that value available and it understands the `env()` function, it will apply the value; otherwise, it will skip over it to the next declaration.

You can read the current specification for environment variables here: `https://drafts.csswg.org/css-env-1/#env-function`.

There are a few extra peculiarities to the iPhone notched screens. For a full walkthrough of dealing with the iPhone notches, read `https://benfrain.com/css-environment-variables-iphonex/`.

I'm continually finding new use cases for CSS custom properties. The fact that they can update "on the fly" means they are useful in all manner of scenarios. The fact that they can be easily read and written to from script elevates them far beyond what was possible with the kind of variables made popular by CSS preprocessors like Sass, Less, and so on.

Custom properties, along with many of the features we have looked at and shall look at, cannot be guaranteed to work in every browser you might need to support. Thankfully, CSS has an elegant syntax for encapsulating code that pertains to the latest features. Let's look at that next.

Using @supports to fork CSS

When you're building out a responsive web design, attempting to provide a single design that works everywhere, on every device, it's a simple fact that you'll frequently encounter situations when features or techniques are not supported on certain devices. In these instances, you'll likely want to create a fork in your CSS. If the browser supports a feature, provide one chunk of code; if it doesn't, it gets different code.

This is the kind of situation that gets handled by `if/else` or `switch` statements in JavaScript. In CSS, we use the `@supports` at-rule.

Feature queries

The native solution to forking code in CSS is to use "feature queries," part of the CSS Conditional Rules Module Level 3 (`http://www.w3.org/TR/css3-conditional/`). Support was introduced in iOS and Safari 9, Firefox 22, Edge 12, and Chrome 28.

Feature queries follow a similar syntax to media queries. Consider this:

```
@supports (flashing-sausages: lincolnshire) {
  body {
    sausage-sound: sizzling;
    sausage-color: slighty-burnt;
    background-color: brown;
  }
}
```

Here, the styles will only get applied if the browser supports the `flashing-sausages` property in combination with the `lincolnshire` value. I'm quite confident that no browser is ever going to support a `flashing-sausages: lincolnshire` property/ value combination (and if they do, I want full credit), so none of the styles inside the `@supports` block will be applied.

Let's consider a more practical example. How about we use Grid when browsers support it and fall back to another layout technique when they don't? Consider this example:

```
@supports (display: grid) {
  .Item {
    display: inline-grid;
  }
}

@supports not (display: grid) {
  .Item {
    display: inline-flex;
  }
}
```

Here, we are defining one block of code for when the browser supports a feature, and another lot for when it doesn't. This pattern is fine if the browser supports `@supports` (yes, I realize that is confusing), but if it doesn't, it won't apply any of those styles.

If you want to cover off devices that don't support `@supports`, you're better off writing your default declarations first and then your `@supports`-specific one after. That way, the prior rule will be overruled if support for `@supports` exists, and the `@supports` block will be ignored if the browser doesn't support it. Our prior example could, therefore, be reworked to:

```
.Item {
  display: inline-flex;
}

@supports (display: grid) {
  .Item {
    display: inline-grid;
  }
}
```

Sorry, that explanation was tough—hopefully you got through it!

Combining conditionals

You can also combine conditionals. Let's suppose we only wanted to apply some rules if both Flexbox and `pointer: coarse` were supported (in case you missed it, we covered the `pointer` interaction media feature back in *Chapter 3, Media Queries – Supporting Differing Viewports*). Here is what that might look like:

```
@supports ((display: flex) and (pointer: coarse)) {
  .Item {
    display: inline-flex;
  }
}
```

Here, we have used the `and` keyword but we could use `or` as well as, or instead of it. For example, if we were happy to apply styles if those two prior property/value combinations were supported, or 3D transforms were supported:

```
@supports ((display: flex) and (pointer: coarse)) or
  (transform: translate3d(0, 0, 0)) {
  .Item {
    display: inline-flex;
  }
}
```

Note the extra set of parentheses that separates the `display` and `pointer` conditional from the `transform` conditional.

And that really is all there is to feature queries. As with media queries, put your "default" styles first, and then your enhancement inside a feature query `@supports` at-rule. Remember, you can combine queries and also offer differing possibilities in which the enclosed code can apply.

Web typography

Typography on the web has come on tremendously in the last few years. Where once it was necessary to include a slew of different file formats, things have pretty much settled on `.woff` and the newer `.woff2`. In addition, we have more control over the particulars of our fonts in CSS and new variable fonts are popping up on a monthly basis.

If some of that introduction was lost on you, fear not. Let's try to get through the current state of the art in web typography.

First, however, let's talk about system fonts as they represent the best performing web typography choice you can opt for.

System fonts

Each operating system has its own set of fonts that come preinstalled. However, aside from a few exceptions, there aren't many fonts you can rely upon to be installed on every device a user might view your site with.

Subsequently, we've grown accustomed to writing font "stacks," which enable us to write a font "wish list" for the browser. For example:

```
font-family: -apple-system, BlinkMacSystemFont, Roboto, Ubuntu,
'Segoe UI', 'Helvetica Neue', Arial, sans-serif;
```

The browser reads this declaration and goes left to right until it finds a font it has available and then chooses that to render the associated text.

In our example system font stack here, macOS users will get San Francisco or Helvetica (`-apple-system` tells Safari to pick San Francisco and `BlinkMacSystemFont` tells Chrome to use Helvetica), Android will get "Roboto," the popular Ubuntu Linux distribution will get "Ubuntu," Windows users will see "Segoe UI," and then we have some last ditch attempts to get something nice with "Helvetica Neue" or "Arial." If all else fails, we tell the browser to use any sans-serif font it has.

 Some font names contain whitespace, so it is necessary to surround those strings with single or double quotes. You can see in our previous example that both "Segoe UI" and "Helvetica Neue" are written this way.

For a lot of situations, using system fonts is a compelling choice. There is zero network overhead and you'll never have to worry about fonts not loading or seeing unsightly jumps on the page as one font is replaced with another.

The tradeoff is that with system fonts, you can never be entirely sure how your text is being rendered on the user's device. If specific typography is crucial to the project at hand, you'll want to look at web fonts with `@font-face`.

The @font-face CSS rule

The `@font-face` CSS rule has been around since CSS2 (but was subsequently absent in CSS 2.1). It was even supported partially by Internet Explorer 4 (no, really)! So, what's it doing here, when we're supposed to be talking about the latest CSS?

Well, as it turns out, `@font-face` was reintroduced for the CSS Fonts Module (`http://www.w3.org/TR/css3-fonts`). Due to the historic legal quagmire of using fonts on the web, it took years to gain traction as the de facto solution for web typography.

Like anything on the web that involves assets, in the beginning, there was no single file format for font delivery. The Embedded OpenType (files with an `.eot` extension) font was Internet Explorer's, and not anyone else's, preferred choice. Others favored the more common TrueType (the `.ttf` file extension), while there was also Scalable Vector Graphics (`.svg`) and then the Web Open Font Format (the `.woff` / `.woff2` extension).

Thankfully, as of 2020, you really only need to consider WOFF (Web Open Font Format), although there are two types: WOFF and WOFF2. Where a user can use WOFF2, that will always be preferable as it is simply a more efficient way of compressing the font information.

However, the good news is that adding each custom font format for every browser is easy. Let's see how!

Implementing web fonts with @font-face

There are a number of online font services for getting beautiful typefaces onto the web. Google Fonts and Adobe Fonts are probably the two most popular. They each have their own variation of the required syntax for getting their fonts onto your websites. However, as it's not always possible or preferable to use an online font provider, we will look at how to do it for ourselves.

For this exercise, I'm going to use "Inter" by Rasmus Andersson. It's the font used for the majority of the `https://rwd.education` website. Not only that, it's also what's known as a "variable" font.

Before we look at variable fonts, let's look at the kind of web fonts that you will likely spend the majority of your time dealing with. If you grab the "Inter" font from `https://rsms.me/inter/`, you will have both the standard and variable fonts at your disposal.

 If you can, download a "subset" of your font, specific to the language you intend to use. For example, if you are not going to be using Cyrillic or Greek characters, why include them? The resultant file size will be much smaller as it won't contain glyphs for languages you have no intention of using. You can often choose character sets when you are buying a font, but for an open source version, there are a growing number of services and utilities that can subset a font for you.

Having downloaded the "Inter" font, a look inside the ZIP file reveals folders of the different files available. I'm choosing the `Inter-Regular.woff2` and `Inter-Regular.woff` files for our example.

To make a web font available for use in our CSS, we use the `@font-face` at-rule. This lets us provide a name for the font that we can then reference and also tells the browser where to go and fetch this file from. Let's look at the syntax:

```css
@font-face {
    font-family: 'InterRegular';
    src: url('Inter-Regular.woff2') format('woff2'),
url('Inter-Regular.woff') format('woff');
    font-weight: normal;
    font-style: normal;
    font-display: fallback;
}
```

Inside the `@font-face` braces, we give our font the "InterRegular" name. I could have called it "FlyingBanana" had I wanted; it wouldn't affect anything other than I would then need to reference this font with that name when I wanted to use it. For example:

```css
.hero-Image {
    font-family: 'FlyingBanana', sans-serif;
}
```

So, know that you can do this, but it makes sense to use a name similar to the font you are expecting to see!

You can then see two successive `url()` and `format()` sections within our `src` property. Each pair of these separated with a comma. As we noted previously, `.woff2` is always our preference, as it is a better compressed version of the same font, so we list that first. As long as the browser can understand `.woff2` and download the file, it will do so. If, however, the browser can't find that file, or can't understand `.woff2`, it will download the `.woff` file listed afterward.

Now, although this block of code is great for fans of copy and paste, it's important to pay attention to the paths the fonts are stored in. For example, if we were to place fonts in a folder inventively called `fonts` on the same level as a `css` folder, we would need to amend our paths. So, our `@font-face` block would become:

```css
@font-face {
    font-family: 'InterRegular';
    src: url('../fonts/Inter-Regular.woff2') format('woff2'),
```

```
url('../fonts/Inter-Regular.woff') format('woff');
  font-weight: normal;
  font-style: normal;
  font-display: fallback;
}
```

Optimizing font loading with font-display

If your main font is a web font, it's a good idea to request the file up front by loading it with a link in the `head` section of your HTML with the `rel` attribute value as `preload`. For example:

```
<link
  rel="preload"
  href="fonts/inter.var.woff2"
  as="font"
  type="font/woff2"
  crossorigin
/>
```

 You can read more about this font optimization technique here: https://developers.google.com/web/fundamentals/performance/resource-prioritization.

Adding a link with `rel="preload"` added in this way triggers a request for the web font early in the critical rendering path, without having to wait for the CSSOM to be created. While this technique is recommended by Google, even if other browsers don't do the same, it is unlikely to do any harm. It's only worth doing this for the `.woff2` file. Browsers that support `.woff2` also support the `preload` value in the `rel` attribute.

We can make further optimizations with web fonts by making use of the `font-display` property.

font-display

For browsers that support it, we can also make use of the relatively new `font-display` property of CSS (older browsers ignore it):

```
font-display: fallback;
```

You can also see this property being used in the previous examples. It provides some control over how fonts should get displayed.

The `fallback` value we have provided sets an extremely short "block" period and a short "swap" period.

To understand what terms like "block" and "swap" mean in this context, we need to consider what the browser does in terms of displaying fonts. I'm talking generically here, but the concepts work for our needs.

Imagine a browser loading our web page in which we have specified a web font for our text. The browser already has the HTML and is parsing the CSS, and learns it needs to download a font in order to display the text it has as intended. Before it draws any text to screen, it hangs on, waiting for the web font so it can paint the text onto the page as needed. This delay is referred to as a "FOIT," standing for "Flash of Invisible Text."

As soon as the font arrives, the browser parses it and paints the text to the screen accordingly.

The hope is that this delay is imperceptible. Where it is not, there are two schools of thought on how best to handle things.

One option is to wait for the font to be downloaded, usually for up to a few seconds but sometimes indefinitely; Safari is the most famous proponent of this option.

The second option is to render the text with a system font initially and then replace the font with the correct font when the browser has it.

This redraw of text from system font to actual intended font is known as a "Flash of Unstyled Text," or "FOUT" for short.

All the `font-display` setting does is allow us some control over what we would like to see happen.

The possible values are:

- `auto`: Whatever the browser determines is most appropriate.
- `block`: Get a white screen for up to 3 seconds (but the delay is ultimately at the browser's discretion) and then the actual font can replace any system displayed one at any future point.
- `swap`: There is a very short blocking period (100 ms is the recommended amount) to let the web font load; otherwise, a system font shows and the web font can be swapped in whenever it is available.

- `fallback`: This option prevents a web font from replacing a system font if a set amount of time has passed (3 seconds is the recommendation). This option blocks for around 100 ms initially and allows a swap for up to 3 seconds, but after that, if the web font subsequently arrives, it doesn't get applied.

- `optional`: Here, the browser allows a very short duration for the web font to load (100 ms) but no swap period. The result of this is that the browser has the option of cancelling the font download if it hasn't arrived, or if it has, using it for subsequent page loads.

 You can read the specification on this property here: `https://www.w3.org/TR/css-fonts-4/#font-display-desc`.

There are plenty of other font-related properties and values specified in the CSS Font Module Level 4 specification, but `font-display` is currently the widest implemented and has the most direct relevance to responsive web designs and performance.

So far, we have looked at how to get font files into our project and even considered how best to deal with them from a performance point of view.

However, the most recent development in web fonts, and probably the one that has most developers excited, is "variable" fonts. What new witchery is this? I hear you cry. Let's find out.

Variable fonts

As I write this in 2020, variable fonts are just gaining decent traction. There is a W3C specification and they are supported in the latest browsers. However, as support is limited to the latest browser versions and operating systems, while we will cover variable fonts here, be aware that the reality for the next few years is that you will need to consider fallback scenarios.

A "normal" font contains the information and glyphs for one variation of a typeface; the regular version of Roboto, for example. By comparison, a variable font, in a single file would contain everything needed for every variation of Roboto. Bold, Italic, Thin, Black, Medium, and more besides!

This new devilry is not without consequence. A variable version of a font is usually considerably larger in file size terms than a "normal" version. However, it can still make sense when you are making heavy use of a single typeface.

Caveats aside, let's look at what we can do with a variable font.

font-face changes

I'm working with the "Inter" font we used before, but instead using the variable version. First, let's consider how we tell the browser we are working with a variable font in the first place. It's the `@font-face` syntax again but with a few changes:

```css
@font-face {
  font-family: 'Inter-V';
  src: url('fonts/inter.var.woff2') format('woff2-variations');
  font-weight: 100 900;
  font-style: oblique 0deg 10deg;
  font-display: fallback;
}
```

The first thing to note is the `format`. We are setting this to `woff2-variations` to tell the browser this is a font file that makes use of variations.

The next thing to keep in mind is that we are using a range for `font-weight`. The two-word value syntax we are using here is only understood by browsers that understand variable fonts. It is a way of telling the browser the range weights this font can use. While `font-weight` has a range limit of 0-999, other properties may have a different range. Others still simply accept a value of `1` or `0`.

Another thing to remember is that we have `font-style`, which is also being provided with a multiple value syntax. The oblique keyword tells the browser the next values relate to how `oblique` the font can be, and the two values after that define the range. Be aware that although the range here is positive, you can pass in negative values. We will see that in use momentarily.

Finally, note that we have used the `font-display` property here to tell the browser how we want to handle the loading and display of this font, but that is no different than non-variable fonts.

You can look at this completed example at `example_06-13`.

Using a variable font

Variable fonts use what's termed a "variation axis."

A variation axis is just a way of defining two points at either end of a scale. You can then choose any point along the scale to display your font. The scale doesn't need to be vast; in fact, it can be as simple as "on" or "off" (not much of a scale, I know).

Variation axes are subdivided into two groups: registered and custom.

Registered axis

Registered axes are the most popular ones, which the specification has deemed worthy of their own CSS property:

- **Weight**: How heavy the text appears; for example, `font-weight: 200`.
- **Width**: How narrow (condensed) or wide the text appears; for example, `font-stretch: 110%`.
- **Italic**: Whether the font is being displayed as italic or not; for example, `font-style: italic`.
- **Slant**: Don't confuse this with italic. This simply alters the angle of the text; it doesn't substitute any glyphs; for example, `font-style: oblique 4deg`.
- **Optical-size**: This is the only one of the registered axes that has required a new font property. Using `font-optical-sizing` lets you alter, yes, you guessed it, the optical sizing. But what is that? It's the practice of altering a glyph based upon the size it is displayed at to aid clarity. This means the same glyph displayed at a large size might enjoy thinner stems, for example.

The values you choose to use with these properties should fall within the capabilities of the variable font you are using. For example, there isn't much point specifying a font weight of `999` if the font you are using can only go up to `600`.

There is also a low-level property that lets you bundle up your variable font settings into a single property/value combination:

```
font-variation-settings: 'wght' 300, 'slnt' -4;
```

Here, we have set font-weight to `300` and the angle of the slant to `-4`. However, the specification offers the following cautionary advice:

> *"When possible, authors should generally use the other properties related to font variations (such as font-optical-sizing), and only use this property for special cases where its use is the only way of accessing a particular infrequently used font variation. For example, it is preferable to use font-weight: 700 rather than font-variation-settings: "wght" 700."*

I'm not really sure why this advice is given. The specification doesn't explain the rationale. Hopefully, this detail will be added when the specification is complete. You can find the current version here: `https://drafts.csswg.org/css-fonts-4/`.

 Font variation properties can be animated and transitioned, which can make for some fantastic effects!

Having covered the registered axis group, let's briefly take a look at the custom axis group.

Custom axis

Variable fonts can include their own axis. For example, the "FS Pimlico Glow VF" font has a "glow" axis. You can amend that like this:

```
font-variation-settings: 'GLOW' 500;
```

Notice how this custom axis is written in uppercase; that is, `'GLOW'`? That's how to determine the difference between a registered and custom axis in variable font settings.

If your head isn't already hurting from the seemingly endless possibilities, I also need to tell you about font features, which are sort of similar to the two different axes we just looked at. Don't worry; it will make sense shortly.

Font features

Variable fonts can also include their own "features." These features can be literally anything the font designer decides to dream up! Take a look at the choices for Inter:

Figure 6.11: On the right of the Inter settings page is the enormous possibilities for the font

All of those "features" are settings that can be turned on with CSS. You can play about with these settings for yourself here: `https://rsms.me/inter/lab/?varfont=1`.

When we want to apply these custom features, we make use of the `font-feature-settings` property. This works very similarly to the `font-variation-settings` syntax. For example, to switch on "slashed zeroes," we can do this:

```
font-feature-settings: 'zero';
```

This "slashed zeroes" option is a binary choice, so it is not necessary to write `'zero'` 1. However, if we wanted to toggle this setting off further into our styles, we could write:

```
font-feature-settings: 'zero' 0;
```

When you want to apply multiple font-feature settings, you can comma-separate them. So, if we wanted to have "Lowercase L with tail" and "Uppercase i with serif," we could write this:

```
font-feature-settings: 'cv08', 'cv05';
```

These are the options switched on in the completed `example_06-13`.

There is plenty more in the way of settings and features specified in CSS Fonts Module Level 4. We have just scratched the surface! To keep up with developments, read the specification as it happens here: `https://drafts.csswg.org/css-fonts-4/#introduction`.

Exercise

Have a look at the CSS from our example page:

```css
:root {
    --MainFont: 'Helvetica Neue', Helvetica, Arial, sans-serif;
}

@font-face {
    font-family: 'Inter-V';
    src: url('fonts/inter.var.woff2') format('woff2-variations');
    font-weight: 100 900;
    font-display: fallback;
    font-style: oblique 0deg 10deg;
}
```

```
body {
  background-color: var(--background);
  color: var(--foreground);
  transition: all 0.35s;
  font-size: 1.2em;
  font-family: 'sans-serif';
  font-family: var(--MainFont);
  font-weight: 400;
}

@supports (font-variation-settings: 'wdth' 200) {
  body {
    font-family: 'Inter-V';
    font-variation-settings: 'wght' 300, 'slnt' -4;
    font-feature-settings: 'cv08', 'cv05';
  }
}
```

How much of that can you now understand? We have a CSS custom property defined for our system font-stack, a font-face loading a variable font, complete with ranges defined for weight and slant. We have sans-serif as the default font-stack, which we then overwrite with the font-stack defined in the custom property for browsers that understand it. Finally, we feature test for variable fonts and define settings for it, also adding in some additional font features we'd like to see.

This brings us to the end of our discussion on web typography. So far in this chapter, we have looked at how CSS has given us new powers of selection and the ability to add custom typography to our designs. Now, we'll look at ways CSS allows us to work with color.

CSS color formats and alpha transparency

When we start using CSS, we typically start by defining color as a hex value. However, CSS provides more powerful ways to declare color. We are going to explore another two: RGB and HSL. In addition, these two formats enable us to use an alpha channel alongside them (RGBA and HSLA, respectively). For the remainder of this chapter, we'll take a look at how these work.

RGB color

RGB (red, green, and blue) is a coloring system that's been around for decades. It works by defining different values for the red, green, and blue components of a color. For example, a red color might be defined in CSS as a hex (hexadecimal) value, `#fe0208`:

```
.redness {
    color: #fe0208;
}
```

For a great post describing how to understand hex values more intuitively, I can recommend this blog post at Smashing Magazine: `http://www.smashingmagazine.com/2012/10/04/the-code-side-of-color/`.

However, with CSS, that color can equally be described with an RGB notation:

```
.redness {
    color: rgb(254, 2, 8);
}
```

Most image editing applications show colors as both hex and RGB values in their color picker. The Photoshop color picker has R, G, and B boxes showing the values for each channel. For example, the R value might be 254, the G value 2, and the B value 8. This is easily transferable to the CSS color property value. In the CSS, after defining the color mode (for example, RGB), the values for red, green, and blue are comma-separated in that order within parentheses (as we have done in the previous code).

HSL color

Besides RGB, CSS also allows us to declare color values as hue, saturation, and lightness (HSL).

 HSL isn't the same as HSB! Don't make the mistake of thinking that the hue, saturation, and brightness (HSB) value shown in the color picker of image editing applications such as Photoshop is the same as HSL—it isn't!

What makes HSL such a joy to use is that it's relatively simple to understand the color that will be represented based on the values given. For example, unless you're some sort of color picking ninja, I'd wager you couldn't instantly tell me what color `rgb(255, 51, 204)` is? Any takers? No, me neither.

However, show me the HSL value of `hsl(315, 100%, 60%)` and I could take a guess that it is somewhere between a magenta and a red color (it's actually a festive pink color). How do I know this? Simple: "Young Guys Can Be Messy Rascals!" This mnemonic will help you to remember the order of colors in an HSL color wheel, as you'll see shortly.

HSL works on a 360° color wheel. It looks like this:

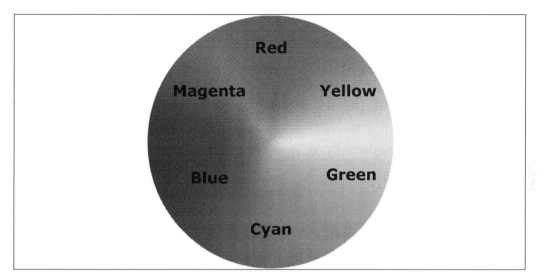

Figure 6.12: The HSL color wheel

The first figure in an HSL color definition represents hue. Looking at our wheel, we can see that yellow is at 60°, green is at 120°, cyan is at 180°, blue is at 240°, magenta is at 300°, and finally red is at 360°. So, as the aforementioned HSL color had a hue of 315, it's easy to know that it will be between magenta (at 300°) and red (at 360°).

The following two values in an HSL definition are for saturation and lightness, specified as percentages. These merely alter the base hue. For a more saturated or "colorful" appearance, use a higher percentage in the second value. The final value, controlling the lightness, can vary between 0 percent for black and 100 percent for white.

So, once you've defined a color as an HSL value, it's also easy to create variations of it, merely by altering the saturation and lightness percentages. For example, our red color can be defined in HSL values as follows:

```
.redness {
    color: hsl(359, 99%, 50%);
}
```

If we wanted to make a slightly darker color, we could use the same HSL value and merely alter the lightness (the final value) percentage value only:

```
.darker-red {
    color: hsl(359, 99%, 40%);
}
```

In conclusion, if you can remember the mnemonic "Young Guys Can Be Messy Rascals" (or any other mnemonic you care to memorize) for the HSL color wheel, you'll be able to approximately write HSL color values without resorting to a color picker, and also create variations upon it. Show that trick to the savant Ruby, Node. js, and .NET developers at the office party and earn some quick kudos!

Alpha channels

So far, you'd be forgiven for wondering why on earth we'd bother using HSL or RGB instead of our trusty hex values we've been using for years. Where HSL and RGB differ from hex is that they allow the use of an alpha transparency channel so that something beneath an element can "show through." An HSLA color declaration is similar in syntax to a standard HSL rule. However, in addition, you must declare the value as hsla (rather than merely hsl) and add an additional opacity value, given as a decimal value between 0 (completely transparent) and 1 (completely opaque). For example:

```
.redness-alpha {
    color: hsla(359, 99%, 50%, 0.5);
}
```

The RGBA syntax follows the same convention as the HSLA equivalent:

```
.redness-alpha-rgba {
    color: rgba(255, 255, 255, 0.8);
}
```

You may be wondering—why not just use opacity? As CSS allows elements to have opacity set with the opacity declaration.

When we apply opacity to an element, a value is set between zero and one in decimal increments (for example, opacity set to .1 is 10 percent). However, opacity differs from RGBA and HSLA in that setting an opacity value on an element affects the entire element, whereas setting a value with HSLA or RGBA allows particular parts of an element to have an alpha layer. For example, an element could have an HSLA value for the background but a solid color for the text within it.

What can we take from all this color talk? First, if you are given values as hex values, there's no need to convert them into anything else. Likewise, if RGB syntax makes perfect sense to you, that's a possibility and you can easily add an alpha channel with the RGBA syntax. For most of us, having some understanding of HSL is going to be very useful. I find it the most human friendly of all the ways to think about color in CSS; it's almost universally supported these days, and it also supports an alpha channel with HSLA.

Summary

In this chapter, we've learned how to select almost anything we need on the page with CSS's powerful selection capabilities. We now understand CSS's more powerful color capabilities and how we can apply colors with RGB and HSL, complete with transparent alpha layers for great aesthetic effects.

In this chapter, we've also learned how to add custom web typography to a design with the `@font-face` rule, freeing us from the shackles of the humdrum selection of web-safe fonts. We also took a dive into variable fonts and considered the possibilities they have to offer.

In among all that, we also found time to look at CSS custom properties and the `@supports` at-rule for providing feature forks in our code.

Despite all these great new features and techniques, we've only picked at the surface of what we can do with CSS.

See you in a moment for *Chapter 7, Stunning Aesthetics with CSS*. There, we will look at even more CSS with text shadows, box shadows, gradients, multiple backgrounds, and so much more!

7
Stunning Aesthetics with CSS

The aesthetically focused features of CSS are so useful in responsive web design because using CSS lets us replace images in many situations. This saves you time, makes your code more maintainable, and results in less page "weight" for the end user.

In this chapter, we will cover:

- How to create text shadows
- How to create box shadows
- How to make gradient backgrounds
- How to use multiple backgrounds
- Using CSS background gradients to make patterns
- How to implement high-resolution background images with media queries
- How to use CSS filters (and their performance implications)
- Clipping with clipping paths
- Masking elements with image masks
- Mixing the colors of elements with `mix-blend-mode`

Let's dig in.

Vendor prefixes

When implementing experimental CSS, just remember to add relevant vendor prefixes via a tool, rather than by hand. This ensures the broadest cross-browser compatibility and also negates you adding in prefixes that are no longer required. I'm mentioning Autoprefixer (`https://github.com/postcss/autoprefixer`) in most chapters as, at the time of writing, I think it's the best tool for the job.

Text shadows with CSS

Let's make a start by looking at text shadows. Text shadows are a fairly simple way to change the aesthetics of text, and therefore provide a good starting point. Support for `text-shadow` is also ubiquitous. Let's first consider the basic syntax:

```
.element {
    text-shadow: 1px 1px 1px #ccc;
}
```

Remember, the values in shorthand rules always go right and then down (or think of it as clockwise if you prefer). Therefore, the first value is the amount of shadow to the right, the second is the amount down, the third value is the amount of blur (the distance the shadow travels before fading to nothing), and the final value is the color. Shadows to the left and above can be achieved using negative values. For example:

```
.text {
    text-shadow: -4px -4px 0px #dad7d7;
}
```

The color value doesn't need to be defined as a hex value. It can just as easily be HSL(A) or RGB(A):

```
text-shadow: 4px 4px 0px hsla(140, 3%, 26%, 0.4);
```

You can also set the shadow values in any other valid CSS length units such as em, rem, ch, rem, and so on. Personally, I rarely use em or rem units for `text-shadow` values. As the length values tend to be low, using 1px or 2px generally looks good across all viewports.

Thanks to media queries, we can easily remove text shadows at different viewport sizes too. The key here is the `none` value:

```
.text {
  text-shadow: 2px 2px 0 #bfbfbf;
}
@media (min-width: 30rem) {
  .text {
    text-shadow: none;
  }
}
```

 It's worth knowing that, in CSS, where a value starts with a zero, such as `0.14s`, there is no need to write the leading zero: `.14s` is exactly the same.

Omit the blur value when it's not needed

If there is no blur to be added to a text shadow, the value can be omitted from the declaration. For example:

```
.text {
  text-shadow: -4px -4px #dad7d7;
}
```

That is perfectly valid. The browser assumes that the first two values are for the offsets if no third value is declared.

Multiple text shadows

It's possible to add multiple text shadows by comma separating two or more shadows. For example:

```
.multiple {
  text-shadow: 0px 1px #fff, 4px 4px 0px #dad7d7;
}
```

Also, as CSS is forgiving of whitespace, you can lay out the values like this if it helps with readability:

```
.text {
  font-size: calc(100vmax / 40); /* 100 of vh or vw, whichever is
larger divided by 40 */
  text-shadow:
```

```
    3px 3px #bbb, /* right and bottom */
   -3px -3px #999; /* left and top */
}
```

You can read the W3C specification for the text-shadow property here: http://www.w3.org/TR/css3-text/#text-shadow.

So, that's how you create shadows around text. What about when you want a shadow on a containing element?

Box shadows

Box shadows allow you to create a box-shaped shadow around the outside or inside of an element. Once you understand text shadows, box shadows are a piece of cake. Principally, they follow the same syntax: horizontal offset, vertical offset, blur, spread (we will get to spread in a moment), and color. Only two of the four length values are required. In the absence of the last two length values, a value of zero is assumed. Let's look at a simple example:

```
.shadow {
   box-shadow: 0px 3px 5px #444;
}
```

The default box-shadow is set on the outside of the element. Another optional keyword, inset, allows the box shadow to be applied inside the element.

Inset shadow

The box-shadow property can also be used to create an inset shadow. The syntax is identical to a normal box shadow, except that the value starts with the keyword inset:

```
.inset {
   box-shadow: inset 0 0 40px #000;
}
```

Everything functions as before, but the inset part of the declaration instructs the browser to set the effect on the inside. If you look at example_07-01, you'll see an example of each type:

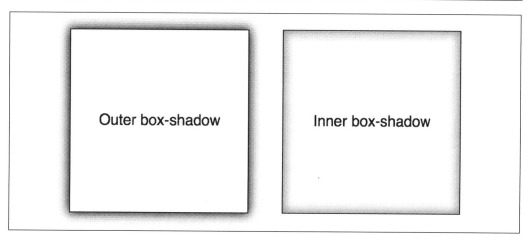

Figure 7.1: Outer shadows and inner shadows are both easily achievable

Multiple shadows

Like text shadows, you can apply multiple box shadows. Separate the box-shadow declarations with a comma. They are applied bottom to top (last to first) as they are listed. Remind yourself of the order by thinking that the declaration nearest to the top in the rule (in the code) appears nearest to the "top" of the order when displayed in the browser. As with text-shadow declarations, you may find it useful to use whitespace to visually stack the different box-shadow declarations:

```
box-shadow:
    inset 0 0 30px hsl(0, 0%, 0%),
    inset 0 0 70px hsla(0, 97%, 53%, 1);
```

 Stacking longer, multiple values, one under the other in the code, has an added benefit when using version control systems; it makes it easy to spot differences when you compare, or "diff," two versions of the same file. It can be useful to stack selectors one under the other for that same reason.

Understanding spread

I'll be honest, for literally years I didn't truly understand what the spread value of a box-shadow actually did. I don't think the name "spread" is useful. Think of it more as an offset. Let me explain.

Look at the box on the left in `example_07-02`. This has a standard box shadow applied, with no `spread`. The one on the right has a negative `spread` value applied. It's set with the fourth value. Here is the relevant code that deals with each shadow:

```
.no-spread {
    box-shadow: 0 10px 10px;
}

.spread {
    box-shadow: 0 10px 10px -10px;
}
```

Here is the effect of each (element with a `spread` value on the right):

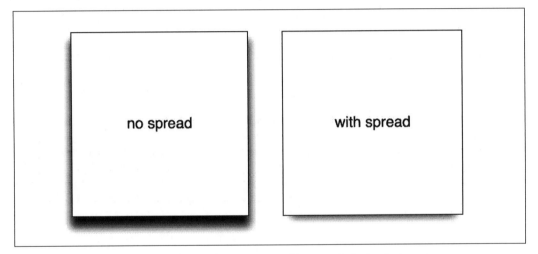

Figure 7.2: With spread, you can control how much shadow leaks out

The `spread` value lets you extend or contract the shadow in all directions by the amount specified. In this example, a negative value is pulling the shadow back in all directions. The result is that we can just see the shadow at the bottom of the right example, instead of seeing the blur "leak" out on all sides.

You can read the W3C specification for the box-shadow property here: http://www.w3.org/TR/css3-background/#the-box-shadow.

Right, so that's shadows. We will go on to deal with more shadows when we look at drop-shadow as part of CSS filters. For now, let's move on to gradients.

Background gradients

In days gone by, to achieve a background gradient on an element, it was necessary to tile a thin graphical slice of the gradient. As graphics resources go, it's quite an economical tradeoff. An image, only a pixel or two wide, isn't going to break the bandwidth bank and on a single site, it can be used on multiple elements.

However, if we need to tweak the gradient, it still requires round trips to the graphics editor. Plus, occasionally, content might "break out" of the gradient background, extending beyond the image's fixed size limitations. This problem is compounded with a responsive design, as sections of a page may increase at different viewports.

With a CSS background-image gradient, however, things are far more flexible. As part of the CSS Image Values and Replaced Content Module Level 3, CSS enables us to create linear and radial background gradients. Let's look at how we can define them.

The specification for CSS Image Values and Replaced Content Module Level 3 can be found at http://www.w3.org/TR/css3-images/.

Linear-gradient notation

The linear-gradient notation, in its simplest form, looks like this:

```
.linear-gradient {
   background: linear-gradient(red, blue);
}
```

This will create a linear gradient that starts at red (the gradient starts from the top by default) and fades to blue.

Specifying gradient direction

Now, if you want to specify a direction for the gradient, there are a couple of ways to do this. The gradient will always begin in the opposite direction to where you are sending it. However, when no direction is set, a gradient will always default to a top to bottom direction. For example:

```
.linear-gradient {
  background: linear-gradient(to top right, red, blue);
}
```

In this instance, the gradient heads to the top right. It starts red in the bottom left corner and fades to blue at the top right.

If you're more mathematically minded, you may believe it would be comparable to write the gradient like this:

```
.linear-gradient {
  background: linear-gradient(45deg, red, blue);
}
```

However, keep in mind that on a rectangular box, a gradient that heads "to top right" (always the top right of the element it's applied to) will end in a slightly different position than "45deg" (always 45 degrees from its starting point).

It's worth knowing you can also start gradients before they are visible within a box. For example:

```
.linear-gradient {
  background: linear-gradient(red -50%, blue);
}
```

This would render a gradient as if it had started before it was even visible inside the box.

We actually used a color stop in the previous example to define a place where a color should begin and end, so let's look at those more fully.

Color stops

Perhaps the handiest thing about background gradients is color stops. They provide the means to set which color is used at which point in a gradient. With color stops, you can specify something as complex as you are likely to need. Consider this example:

```
.linear-gradient {
```

```
    margin: 1rem;
    width: 400px;
    height: 200px;
    background: linear-gradient(
        #f90 0,
        #f90 2%,
        #555 2%,
        #eee 50%,
        #555 98%,
        #f90 98%,
        #f90 100%
    );
}
```

Here's how that `linear-gradient` renders:

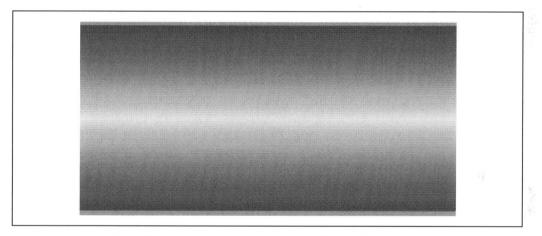

Figure 7.3: You can add as many stops as you like to a linear gradient

In this example (`example_07-03`), a direction has not been specified, so the default top to bottom direction applies.

Color stops inside a gradient are written comma separated and defined by giving first the color, and then the position of the stop. It's generally advisable not to mix units in one notation, but you can. You can have as many color stops as you like and colors can be written as a keyword, hex, RGBA, or HSLA value.

Note that there have been a number of different background gradient syntaxes over the years, so this is one area that is particularly difficult to write fallbacks for by hand.

At the risk of sounding like a broken record (kids, if you don't know what a "record" is, ask Mom or Dad), make your life easier with a tool like Autoprefixer. This lets you write the current W3C standard syntax (as detailed previously) and it will automatically create the prior versions for you.

 You can read the W3C specification for linear background gradients at `http://www.w3.org/TR/css3-images/#linear-gradients`.

Having covered linear background gradients, let's now check out radial background gradients.

Radial background gradients

It's equally simple to create a radial gradient in CSS. These typically begin from a central point and spread out smoothly in an elliptical or circular shape.

Here's the syntax for a radial background gradient (you can play with it in `example_07-04`):

```
.radial-gradient {
  margin: 1rem;
  width: 400px;
  height: 200px;
  background: radial-gradient(12rem circle at bottom, yellow,
orange, red);
}
```

Figure 7.3: We can set a gradient to start at any point. Here our "sunrise" gradient starts bottom center

Breakdown of radial gradient syntax

After specifying the property (`background:`), we begin the `radial-gradient` notation. To start with, before the first comma, we define the shape or size of the gradient and the position. We used `12rem circle` for the shape and size previously, but consider some other examples:

- `5em` would be a circle 5em in size. It's possible to omit the `circle` part if giving just a size.

- `circle` would be a circle the full size of the container (the size of a radial gradient defaults to `farthest-corner` if omitted—more on sizing keywords shortly).

- `40px 30px` would be an ellipse as if drawn inside a box 40px wide by 30px tall.

- `ellipse` would create an ellipse shape that would fit within the element.

Next, after the size and/or shape, we define the position. The default position is center, but let's look at some other possibilities and how they can be defined:

- `at top right` starts the radial gradient from the top right.

- `at right 100px top 20px` starts the gradient 100px from the right edge and 20px from the top edge.

- `at center left` starts it halfway down the left side of the element.

We end our size, shape, and position "parameters" with a comma and then define any color stops, which work in exactly the same manner as they do with linear gradients.

To simplify the notation: size, shape, and position before the first comma, then as many color stops as needed after it (with each stop separated with commas).

When it comes to sizing things such as gradients, CSS provides some keywords that are often a better choice than hardcoded values, especially with responsive designs.

Handy "extent" keywords for responsive sizing

For responsive work, you may find it advantageous to size gradients proportionally rather than using fixed pixel dimensions. That way, you know you are covered (both literally and figuratively) when the size of elements change. There are some handy sizing keywords that can be applied to gradients.

You would write them like this, in place of any size value:

```
background: radial-gradient(closest-side circle at center, #333,
blue);
```

Here is what each of them does:

- `closest-side`: The shape meets the side of the box nearest to the center (in the case of circles), or meets both the horizontal and vertical sides that are closest to the center (in the case of ellipses).

- `closest-corner`: The shape meets exactly the closest corner of the box from its center.

- `farthest-side`: The opposite of `closest-side`, in that rather than the shape meeting the nearest size, it's sized to meet the one farthest from its center (or both the furthest vertical and horizontal side in the case of an ellipse).

- `farthest-corner`: The shape expands to the farthest corner of the box from the center.

- `cover`: Identical to `farthest-corner`.

- `contain`: Identical to `closest-side`.

You can read the W3C specification for radial background gradients at http://www.w3.org/TR/css3-images/#radial-gradients.

The cheat's way to perfect CSS linear and radial gradients

If defining gradients by hand seems like hard work, there are some great online gradient generators. My favorite is http://www.colorzilla.com/gradient-editor/. It uses a graphics editor style GUI, allowing you to pick your colors, stops, gradient style (linear and radial gradients are supported), and even the color space (hex, RGB(A), HSL(A)) you'd like the final gradient in. There are also loads of preset gradients to use as starting points. Still not convinced? How about the ability to generate a CSS gradient based on the gradient values in an existing image? Thought that might swing it for you.

Repeating gradients

CSS also gives us the ability to create repeating background gradients. Let's take a look at how it's done:

```
.repeating-radial-gradient {
  background: repeating-radial-gradient(black 0px, orange 5px, red
10px);
}
```

Here's how that looks (don't look for long, it may cause nausea):

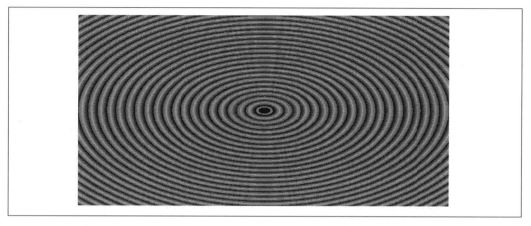

Figure 7.5: You can use repeating gradients to create all manner of visual effects

Firstly, prefix the `linear-gradient` or `radial-gradient` with `repeating-`.
It then follows the same syntax as a normal gradient. Here, I've used pixel distances between the black, orange, and red colors (0px, 5px, and 10px, respectively), but you could also choose to use percentages.

You can read the W3C information on repeating gradients at `http://www.w3.org/TR/css3-images/#repeating-gradients`.

There's one more way of using background gradients I'd like to share with you.

Background gradient patterns

Although I've often used subtle linear gradients in designs, I've found less practical use for radial gradients and repeating gradients. However, clever folks out there have harnessed the power of gradients to create background gradient patterns. Let's look at an example from CSS Ninja, Lea Verou's collection of CSS background patterns, available at `http://lea.verou.me/css3patterns/`:

```css
.carbon-fibre {
  margin: 1rem;
  width: 400px;
  height: 200px;
  background: radial-gradient(black 15%, transparent 16%) 0 0,
radial-gradient(
      black 15%,
      transparent 16%
    ) 8px 8px,
    radial-gradient(rgba(255, 255, 255, 0.1) 15%, transparent 20%) 0
1px, radial-gradient(
      rgba(255, 255, 255, 0.1) 15%,
      transparent 20%
    ) 8px 9px;
  background-color: #282828;
  background-size: 16px 16px;
}
```

Here's what that gives us in the browser, a carbon fiber background effect:

Figure 7.6: A carbon fiber effect made with pure CSS

How about that? Just a few lines of CSS and we have an easily editable, responsive, and scalable background pattern.

You might find it useful to add `background-repeat: no-repeat` at the end of the rule to better understand how it works.

As ever, thanks to media queries, different declarations can be used for different responsive scenarios. For example, although a gradient pattern might work well at smaller viewports, it might be better to go with a plain background at larger ones:

```
@media (min-width: 45rem) {
  .carbon-fibre {
    background: #333;
  }
}
```

You can view this example at `example_07-05`.

So far, we have looked at many ways of creating background images using just CSS; however, whether that is linear gradients, radial gradients, or repeating gradients, it is still just one background image. What about when you want to deal with more than one background image at the same time?

Multiple background images

Although a little out of fashion at the moment, it used to be a fairly common design requirement to build a page with a different background image at the top of the page than at the bottom. Or perhaps to use different background images for the top and bottom of a content section within a page. Back in the day, with CSS 2.1, achieving this effect typically required additional markup (one element for the header background and another for the footer background).

With CSS, you can stack as many background images as you need on an element.

Here's the syntax:

```
.bg {
  background: url('../img/1.png'), url('../img/2.png'), url('../
img/3.png');
}
```

As with the stacking order of multiple shadows, the image listed first is layered nearest to the top, or closer to the user, in the browser. You can also add a general color for the background in the same declaration if you wish, like this:

```
.bg {
    background: url('../img/1.png'), url('../img/2.png'),
      url('../img/3.png') left bottom, black;
}
```

Specify the color last and this will show up below every image specified in the preceding code snippet.

With the multiple background images, as long as your images have transparency, any partially transparent background images that sit on top of another will show through below. However, background images don't have to sit on top of one another, nor do they all have to be the same size.

Background size

To set different sizes for each image, use the background-size property. When multiple images have been used, the syntax works like this:

```
.bg {
    background-size: 100% 50%, 300px 400px, auto;
}
```

The size values (first width, then height) for each image are declared, separated by commas, in the order they are listed in the background property. As in the preceding example, you can use percentage or pixel values for each image alongside the following:

- auto: This sets the element at its native size.
- cover: This expands the image, preserving its aspect ratio, to cover the area of the element.
- contain: This expands the image to fit its longest side within the element while preserving the aspect ratio.

Having considered size, let's also think about position.

Background position

If you have different background images, at different sizes, the next thing you'll want is the ability to position them differently. Thankfully, the background-position property facilitates that.

Let's put all this background image capability together, alongside some of the responsive units we looked at in previous chapters.

Let's create a simple space scene, made with a single element and three background images, set at three different sizes, and positioned in three different ways:

```
.bg-multi {
  height: 100vh;
  width: 100vw;
  background: url('rosetta.png'), url('moon.png'), url('stars.jpg');
  background-size: 75vmax, 50vw, cover;
  background-position: top 50px right 80px, 40px 40px, top center;
  background-repeat: no-repeat;
}
```

You'll see something like this in the browser:

Figure 7.7: Multiple background images on a single element

We have the stars image at the bottom, then the moon, and finally an image of the Rosetta space probe on top. View this for yourself in `example_07-06`. Notice that if you adjust the browser window, the responsive length units work well (vmax, vh, and vw) and retain proportion, while pixel-based ones do not.

Where no `background-position` is declared, the default position of top left is applied.

Background shorthand

There is a shorthand method of combining the different background properties together.

However, my experience so far has been that it produces erratic results. Therefore, I recommend the longhand method and declare the multiple images first, then the size, and then the position.

 You can read the W3C documentation on multiple background elements here: http://www.w3.org/TR/css3-background/.

High resolution background images

Thanks to media queries, we have the ability to load in different background images, not just at different viewport sizes, but also different viewport resolutions.

For example, here is the official way of specifying a background image for a "normal" and a "high" DPI screen. You can find this in example_07-07:

```
.bg {
    background-image: url('bg.jpg');
}
@media (min-resolution: 1.5dppx) {
    .bg {
        background-image: url('bg@1_5x.jpg');
    }
}
```

The media query is written exactly as it is with width, height, or any of the other capability tests. In this example, we are defining the minimum resolution that bg@1_5x.jpg should use as 1.5dppx (device pixels per CSS pixel). We could also use dpi (dots per inch) or dpcm (dots per centimeter) units if preferable. However, despite the poorer support, I find dppx the easiest unit to think about; as 2dppx is twice the resolution, 3dppx would be three times the resolution. Thinking about that in dpi is trickier. "Standard" resolution would be 96dpi, twice that resolution would be 192dpi, and so on.

A brief note on performance: just remember that large images can potentially slow down the feel of your site and lead to a poor experience for users. While a background image won't block the rendering of the page (you'll still see the rest of the site drawn to the page while you wait for the background image), it will add to the total weight of the page, which is important if users are paying for data.

Earlier in this chapter, I told you we would look at more shadows when we got to dealing with CSS filters. That time has come.

CSS filters

There is a glaring problem with `box-shadow`. As the name implies, it is limited to the rectangular CSS box shape of the element it is applied to. Here's a screengrab of a triangle shape made with CSS with a box shadow applied:

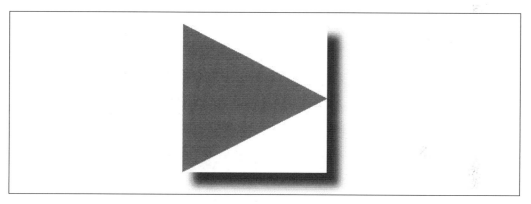

Figure 7.8: Box shadows don't always provide the effect you want

Not exactly what I was hoping for. Thankfully, we can overcome this issue with CSS filters, part of the Filter Effects Module Level 1 (`http://www.w3.org/TR/filter-effects/`).

Here is that same element with a CSS `drop-shadow` filter applied instead of a `box-shadow` (you can view the code in `example_07-08`):

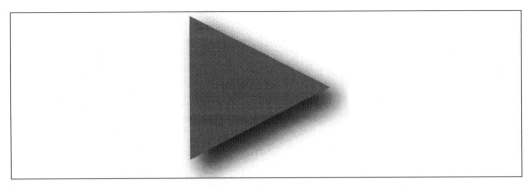

Figure 7.9: A drop-shadow filter effect can apply to more than just boxes

Here is the format for CSS filters:

```
.filter-drop-shadow {
    filter: drop-shadow(8px 8px 6px #333);
}
```

After the `filter` property, we specify the filter we want to use, which is `drop-shadow` in this example, and then pass in the arguments for the filter. `drop-shadow` follows a similar syntax to `box-shadow`, so this one is easy; x and y offset, blur, then spread radius (both optional), and finally color, also optional, although I recommend specifying a color for consistency.

CSS filters are actually based upon SVG filters, which have wider support. We'll look at the SVG-based equivalent in *Chapter 8, Using SVGs for Resolution Independence*.

Available CSS filters

There are a few filters to choose from. We will look at each. While images of most of the filters follow, those of you reading a hard copy of this book (with monochrome images) may struggle to notice the differences. If you're in that situation, remember you can still view the various filters in the browser by opening `example_07-08`. I'm going to list each out now with a suitable value specified. As you might imagine, a greater value means more of the filter applied. Where images are used, the image is shown after the relevant code:

- `filter: url('./img/filters.svg#filterRed')`: Lets you specify an SVG filter to use.

- `filter: blur(3px)`: Uses a single length value (but not as a percentage):

Figure 7.10: A blur filter applied

- `filter: brightness(2)`: With brightness, a value of 1 or 100% is normal; less than that, such as "0.5" or "50%," darkens; and more, such as "200%" or "2," lightens:

Figure 7.11: A brightness filter applied

- `filter: contrast(2)`: A value of 1 or 100% is normal; less than that, for example "0.5" or "50%," reduces contrast; and more, such as "200%" or "2," increases it:

Figure 7.12: A contrast filter applied

- `filter: drop-shadow(4px 4px 6px #333)`: We looked at `drop-shadow` in detail previously.

- `filter: grayscale(.8)`: Use a value from 0 to 1 or 0% to 100% to apply varying amounts of grayscale to the element. A value of 0 would be no grayscale, while a value of 1 would be fully grayscale:

Figure 7.13: A grayscale filter applied

- `filter: hue-rotate(25deg):` Use a value between 0 and 360 degrees to adjust the hue of the colors around the color wheel. You can use a negative value to move the "wheel" backward and a number greater than 360 just spins it around more!

Figure 7.14: A hue-rotate filter applied

- `filter: invert(75%):` Use a value from 0 to 1 or 0% to 100% to define the amount the element has its colors inverted:

Figure 7.15: An invert filter applied

- `filter: opacity(50%)`: Use a value from 0 to 1 or 0% to 100% to alter the opacity of the element. 1 or 100% is fully opaque, while 0 or 0% would be full transparency. This is similar to the `opacity` property you will already be familiar with. However, filters, as we shall see, can be combined, and this allows opacity to be combined with other filters in one go:

Figure 7.16: An opacity filter applied

- `filter: saturate(15%)`: Use a value from 0 to 1 or 0% to 100% to desaturate an image and anything above 1/100% to add extra saturation:

Figure 7.17: A saturate filter applied

- `filter: sepia(.75)`: Use a value from 0 to 1 or 0% to 100% to make the element appear with a more sepia color. 0/0% leaves the element as is, while anything above that applies greater amounts of sepia, up to a maximum of 1/100%:

Figure 7.18: A sepia filter applied

Combining CSS filters

You can also combine filters easily; simply space separate them. For example, here is how you would apply `opacity`, `blur`, and `sepia` filters at once:

```
.MultipleFilters {
    filter: opacity(10%) blur(2px) sepia(35%);
}
```

 Note: Apart from `hue-rotate`, when using filters, negative values are not allowed.

I think you'll agree, CSS filters offer some pretty powerful effects. There are also effects we can transition and transform from situation to situation. We'll look at how to do that in *Chapter 9, Transitions, Transformations, and Animations*.

However, before you go crazy with these new toys, we need to have a grown-up conversation about performance.

A warning on CSS performance

When it comes to CSS performance, I would like you to remember this one thing:

"Architecture is outside the braces, performance is inside."

– Ben Frain

Let me expand on my little maxim: as far as I can prove, worrying about whether a CSS selector (the part outside the curly braces) is fast or slow is pointless. I set out to prove this here: `http://benfrain.com/css-performance-revisited-selectors-bloat-expensive-styles/`.

However, one thing that really can grind a page to a halt, CSS-wise, is "expensive" properties (the parts inside the curly braces). When we use the term "expensive" in relation to certain styles, it simply means it costs the browser a lot of overhead. It's something the browser, or perhaps more accurately, the host hardware, finds overly taxing to do.

It's possible to make a common-sense guess about what will cause the browser extra work. It's basically anything it would have to compute before it can paint things to the screen. For example, compare a standard `div` with a flat solid background, against a semi-opaque image, on top of a background made up of multiple gradients, with rounded corners and a `drop-shadow`. The latter is more expensive; it will result in far more computational work for the browser and subsequently cause more overhead.

Therefore, when you apply effects like filters, do so judiciously and, if possible, test whether the page speed suffers on the lowest powered devices you are hoping to support. At the least, switch on development tool features such as continuous page repainting in Chrome and toggle any effects you think may cause problems. This will provide you with data (in the form of a millisecond reading of how long the current viewport is taking to paint) to make a more educated decision on which effects to apply. The lower the figure, the faster the page will perform—although be aware that browsers/platforms vary, so, as ever, test on real devices where possible.

For more on this subject, I recommend the following resource: `https://developers.google.com/web/fundamentals/performance/rendering/?hl=en:`.

Figure 7.19: Check fancy effects aren't killing your performance.

OK, grown-up talk finished with now. Let's get back to looking at the fun and powerful stuff we can do with CSS. Next on the list is clipping things.

CSS clip-path

The `clip-path` property allows you to "clip" an element with a shape. Think of clipping just like drawing a shape on a piece of paper and then cutting around it. This shape can be something simple like an ellipse, something more complicated such as a polygon, or something more complex still such as a shape defined by an inline SVG path. If you want to view each of these on a page, check out `example-07_09` in the download code.

clip-path with url

You can use the path of an inline SVG like this:

```
clip-path: url(#myPath);
```

 If the term "inline SVG" doesn't make much sense, don't worry about that for now. Come back here once you have read the next chapter on SVG.

CSS basic shapes

You can use `clip-path` with any of the CSS basic shapes. These are `inset`, `circle`, `ellipse`, and `polygon`, as described here: `https://www.w3.org/TR/css-shapes-1/#supported-basic-shapes`.

Let's take a look at how we would write each of these.

clip-path with a circle

With `clip-path: circle()`, the first argument you pass is the size, and the second, which is an optional argument, is the position of that shape. So, if you wanted to clip an element down to a circle 20% of the element's height and width:

```
clip-path: circle(20%);
```

If you wanted the same circle `clip-mask` but positioned 60% horizontally and 40% vertically:

```
.clip-circle {
    clip-path: circle(35% at 60% 40%);
}
```

Figure 7.20: A circular clip-path applied

Notice the `at` keyword in there? That's needed to communicate that the lengths after relate to positioning and not size.

It's important to know that pointer events don't occur for areas of an element that have been clipped by a clip mask! To extend our cutting a shape from a piece of paper analogy, the bits outside a clip mask are like the discarded pieces of paper that have been cut away.

clip-path with ellipse

With `clip-path: ellipse()`, the first argument is the *x* axis radius (horizontal) and the second argument is the *y* axis radius (vertical). Just like `circle()`, you specify positioning lengths after the `at` keyword:

```
.clip-ellipse {
    clip-path: ellipse(100px 50px at 60% 40%);
}
```

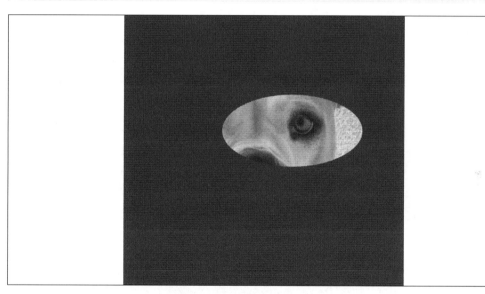

Figure 7.21: An elliptical clip-path applied

clip-path with inset

The `inset()` function for `clip-path` is a little different. You pass four lengths, and these are how much you want to inset the mask from the edges. Just like when you set `margin`, the values go clockwise: top, right, bottom, and left. Just like `margin`, you can also pass just two length values; the first will be top and bottom and the second will be left and right (the three-value syntax works the same too).

There is also an optional `round` keyword that can be used, followed by another length; that sets how much you would like each corner to be rounded by.

Here is an example with four inset values passed and four different radius values for the corners:

```
.clip-inset {
    clip-path: inset(40px 20px 40px 20px round 0 30px 15px 40px);
}
```

Figure 7.22: An inset clip-path applied

clip-path with polygon

The `polygon()` function for `clip-path` allows us to describe a simple shape with a series of comma separated *x* and *y* coordinates. This is what a triangle written with the polygon function looks like:

```
.clip-polygon {
    clip-path: polygon(50% 60px, 100% calc(100% - 40px), 0% calc(100%
    - 40px));
}
```

Figure 7.23: A clip-path applied with a polygon

Think of this as a way of describing where to start cutting (the first argument), where to go next (any subsequent arguments), and where the last point should be. The polygon then connects the final point to the first to complete the path.

Each argument is made up of an x coordinate described from the top left of the containing box (for example, 50% along), and then the y coordinate (for example, 60px from the top) in relation to the top of the containing box.

My favorite way to get started with a `clip-path` polygon is to use Bennett Feely's "Clippy" website: `https://bennettfeely.com/clippy/`.

There are a bunch of premade shapes to choose from, as well as a GUI for amending the shape. Highly recommended!

clip-path with URL (clipping source)

You can also pass the `clip-path` a "clipping-source" via a URL. The URL needs to be an SVG `clipPath` somewhere in the document.

I made a star shape as an SVG path and added an `id` of `starSymbol` to the `clipPath` element. With that in place, you can tell `clip-path` to use that path like this:

```
.clip-url {
    clip-path: url(#starSymbol);
}
```

Figure 7.24: A clip-path applied with an SVG path

You can view each of these `clip-path` examples in `example_07-09`.

Animating clip-path

As if all this clipping malarkey wasn't interesting enough, you can also animate clip-paths, as long as there remains the same number of points in the shape. For example, you can animate a triangle into a different shaped triangle, but without some tricks, you can't convert that same triangle into a star. I say "without some tricks" because you can effectively do this by hiding a few points along the lines of the polygon so your triangle has enough points to animate into a star.

Here's a grab of an extra example I added, `example_07-10`. This is just to hopefully give you an idea of what can be done by adding a few of the things we have already learned and a few things we will learn in future chapters together:

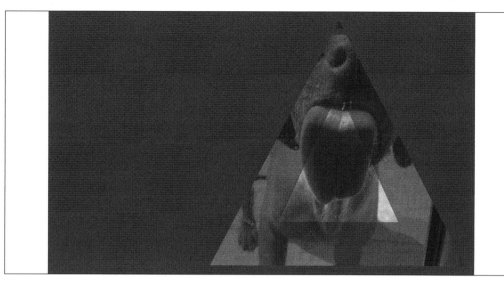

Figure 7.25: You can even animate clip-path

This shows two elements with the same background image being masked with `clip-path`. You can also tint the image with an overlay like this:

```
background: linear-gradient(hsla(0, 0%, 0%, 0.4) 0, hsla(0, 0%, 0%,
0.4) 100%),
    url('image.jpg');
```

> It's not possible to add a `background-color` above an image when using multiple background elements. However, we can create a `background-image` using a `linear-gradient` with the same HSLA color top and bottom, which creates the desired effect.

We then move the main element around the page with one set of `keyframes` animations (we will get to animations in *Chapter 9, Transitions, Transformations, and Animations*) and animate the `clip-path` with another set.

I think once you start playing about with these techniques, you're going to surprise yourself with just what you can create with relative ease!

There may be occasions when you don't just want to clip what's in an element, and you actually want to overlay it with a mask. We can do that with CSS too! Let me show you.

mask-image

You can also mask elements with images, from either an image source with transparency such as a PNG graphic, a `linear-gradient`, which we looked at earlier in this chapter, or an SVG `mask` element. You can read about all the possibilities afforded to us in the specification here: `https://www.w3.org/TR/css-masking-1/`.

In the meantime, we will just look at a fairly straightforward example so you can appreciate the kind of effect that is possible and how the syntax works to achieve it.

mask-image example

Suppose we have an image. I have one that NASA took of Mars. I'd get one I took myself but, you know, it's a bit of a jaunt.

Now, suppose we also have a PNG image that is transparent except for the word "MARS." We can use this PNG as a mask on top of our image element.

This is what we see in the browser:

Figure 7.26: A mask image applied

Here is our relevant HTML:

```
<img
  src="mars.jpg"
  alt="An image of Mars from space"
  class="mask-image-example"
/>
```

And here is our CSS:

```css
.mask-image-example {
    display: block;
    height: 1024px;
    width: 1024px;
    margin: 0 auto;
    mask-image: url('mars-text-mask.png');
}
```

The only relevant part of the mask is the `mask-image` property, which tells the browser what we want to use as a mask on this element.

Now, the cynical among you might suggest the same effect could have just been achieved in a graphics package. I'd say you were right, but then raise you this:

```css
.mask-image-example {
    display: block;
    height: 1024px;
    width: 1024px;
    margin: 0 auto;
    mask-image: url('mars-text-mask.png');
    animation: moveMask 6s infinite alternate;
}

@keyframes moveMask {
    0% {
        object-position: 0px 0px;
    }
    100% {
        object-position: 100px 100px;
    }
}
```

We will look at animations in *Chapter 9, Transitions, Transformations, and Animations,* but what we have done here is added an animation that moves the background image behind the mask so that the word "MARS" stays in position while the planet moves behind. Try doing that in Photoshop!

If we wanted to swap things around and have the mask move and the image of the planet stay put, it is as simple as swapping `object-position` in the animation for `mask-position`.

You can have a play with this example at `example_07-11`. Be aware that you might need to add vendor prefixes to the `mask-image` property as I have in the example code, and it might also be necessary to run this example from a local server. Something like BrowserSync will do the job.

There are quite a few related properties for `mask-image` that can alter the way the mask works. If you find yourself tasked with something mask-related, be sure to look through the specifications and see if there is anything in there that might aid your specific requirements.

Well, I don't know about you, but I'm almost exhausted with the visual CSS "cardio" we've just been through. Before you reach for the towel and water bottle, just let me tell you about `mix-blend-mode`.

mix-blend-mode

One final, very visual, property I want to relate before we end this chapter is `mix-blend-mode`. This property lets you decide how you want one element to "blend" with the element it sits on top of.

Here are the possible blend modes: `normal`, `multiply`, `screen`, `overlay`, `darken`, `lighten`, `color-dodge`, `color-burn`, `hard-light`, `soft-light`, `difference`, `exclusion`, `hue`, `saturation`, `color`, and `luminosity`.

Static images don't really do this property justice, so I'd encourage you to open `example_07-12` in a browser.

We're using that same image of Mars from the last example but setting it as a fixed background for the `body` element.

Then, we add some text on top that you can scroll to see `mix-blend-mode` in effect. In this example, we have used `overlay`, for no reason other than I thought it worked best. If you open the example along with your developer tools, you can cycle through the other possibilities. It's perhaps redundant to say so, but the options themselves will have different effects, depending on the foreground and background they are being applied onto.

 The specification for `mix-blend-mode` is the Compositing and Blending Level 1 specification: `https://www.w3.org/TR/compositing-1/#mix-blend-mode`.

Summary

In this chapter, we've looked at a selection of the most useful CSS features for creating lightweight aesthetics in responsive web designs. CSS's background gradients curb our reliance on images for background effects.

We considered how they can be used to create infinitely repeating background patterns. We've also learned how to use text shadows to create simple text enhancements and box shadows to add shadows to the outside and inside of elements.

We've also looked at CSS filters. They allow us to achieve even more impressive visual effects with CSS alone and can be combined for truly impressive results.

In the last part of this chapter, we looked at creating masking effects with both images and clipping paths.

We've added some considerable capabilities to our toolbelts! We will come back to CSS in *Chapter 9, Transitions, Transformations, and Animations*. But before that...

In the next chapter, we're going to turn our attention to creating and using Scalable Vector Graphics, or SVG, as they are more simply called. While it's a very mature technology, it is only in the current climate of responsive and high-performing websites that it has really come of age.

8

Using SVGs for Resolution Independence

Entire books have, are being, and will be, written about SVG (an abbreviation for Scalable Vector Graphics). SVG is an important technology for responsive web design as it provides pin-sharp and future-proof graphical assets for all screen resolutions.

Images on the web, with formats such as JPEG, GIF, or PNG, have their visual data saved as set pixels. If you save a graphic in any of those formats with a set width and height and zoom the image to twice its original size or more, their limitations can be easily exposed.

Here's a screen grab of just that; a PNG image I've zoomed into in the browser:

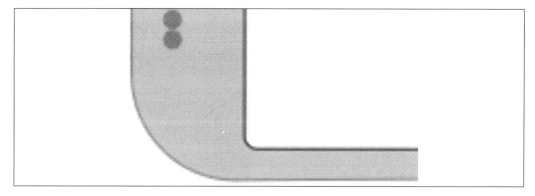

Figure 8.1: The shortcomings of raster images are easy to see on today's high-definition screens

Can you see how the image looks obviously pixelated? Here is the exact same image saved as a vector image, in SVG format, and zoomed to a similar level:

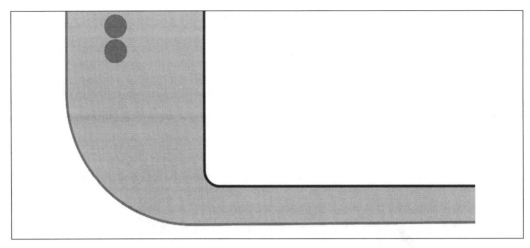

Figure 8.2: An SVG looks sharp, regardless of the display size

Hopefully, the difference is obvious.

Beyond the smallest graphical assets, where at all possible, using SVG rather than JPEG, GIF, or PNG will produce resolution-independent graphics that require far smaller file sizes compared to bitmap images.

While we will touch upon many aspects of SVG in this chapter, the focus will be on how to integrate them into your workflow, while also providing an overview of what is possible with SVG.

In this chapter, we will cover:

- SVG, a brief history, and an anatomy of a basic SVG document
- Creating SVGs with popular image editing packages and services
- Inserting SVGs into a page with `img` and `object` tags
- Inserting SVGs as background images
- Inserting SVGs directly (inline) into HTML
- Reusing SVG symbols
- Referencing external SVG symbols
- What capabilities are possible with each insertion method
- Animating SVGs with SMIL
- Styling SVGs with an external style sheet

- Styling SVGs with internal styles

- Amending and animating SVGs with CSS

- Media queries and SVGs

- Optimizing SVGs

- Using SVGs to define filters for CSS

- Manipulating SVGs with JavaScript and JavaScript libraries

- Implementation tips

- Further resources

SVG is a dense subject. Which portions of this chapter are most relevant to your needs will depend on what you actually need from SVG. Hopefully, I can offer a few shortcuts right up front.

If you simply want to replace static graphical assets on a website with SVG versions, for sharper images and/or smaller file sizes, then look at the shorter sections on using SVG as background images and within `img` tags.

If you're curious about what applications and services can help you generate and manage SVG assets, skip to the *Creating SVGs with popular image editing packages and services* section for some useful links and pointers.

If you want to understand SVG more fully, or animate and manipulate SVG, you better get yourself comfy and get a double size of your favorite beverage as this may take a while.

To begin our journey of understanding, step back with me into 2001.

A brief history of SVG

The first release of SVG was in 2001. That was not a typo. SVG has been "a thing" since 2001. While it gained traction along the way, it's only since the advent of high-resolution devices that SVGs have received widespread interest and adoption. Here is the introduction to SVGs from the 1.1 specification (`http://www.w3.org/TR/SVG11/intro.html`):

> *"SVG is a language for describing two-dimensional graphics in XML [XML10]. SVG allows for three types of graphic objects: vector graphic shapes (for example, paths consisting of straight lines and curves), images, and text."*

As the name implies, Scalable Vector Graphics allow two-dimensional images to be described in code as vector points. This makes them a great candidate for icons, line drawings, and charts.

As vectors describe relative points, they can scale to any size, without loss of fidelity. Furthermore, in terms of data, as SVG are described as vector points, it tends to make them tiny, compared to a comparably sized JPEG, GIF, or PNG file.

Browser support for SVG is now also very good. Android 2.3 and above, and Internet Explorer 9 and above support them: `http://caniuse.com/#search=svg`.

An image that is also a readable web document

Ordinarily, if you view the code of an image file in a text editor, the resultant text is completely unintelligible.

Where SVG graphics differ is that they are actually described in a markup style language. SVG is written in **Extensible Markup Language** (**XML**), a close relative of HTML. Although you may not realize it, XML is everywhere on the internet. Do you use an RSS reader? That's XML right there. XML is the language that wraps up the content of an RSS feed and makes it consumable to a variety of tools and services.

So, not only can machines read and understand SVG graphics, but we can too.

Let me give you an example. Take a look at this star graphic:

Figure 8.3: A basic SVG

This is an SVG graphic, called `Star.svg`, inside `example_08-01`. You can either open this example in the browser where it will appear as the star, or you can open it in a text editor, and you can see the code that generates it. Consider this:

```
<?xml version="1.0" encoding="UTF-8" standalone="no"?>
<svg
  width="198px"
  height="188px"
  viewBox="0 0 198 188"
```

```
    version="1.1"
    xmlns="http://www.w3.org/2000/svg"
    xmlns:xlink="http://www.w3.org/1999/xlink"
    xmlns:sketch="http://www.bohemiancoding.com/sketch/ns"
>
    <!-- Generator: Sketch 3.2.2 (9983) - http://www.bohemiancoding.
com/sketch -->
    <title>Star 1</title>
    <desc>Created with Sketch.</desc>
    <defs></defs>
    <g
        id="Page-1"
        stroke="none"
        stroke-width="1"
        fill="none"
        fill-rule="evenodd"
        sketch:type="MSPage"
    >
    <polygon
        id="Star-1"
        stroke="#979797"
        stroke-width="3"
        fill="#F8E81C"
        sketch:type="MSShapeGroup"
        points="99 154 40.2214748 184.901699 51.4471742 119.45085
3.89434837 73.0983006 69.6107374 63.5491503 99 4 128.389263
63.5491503 194.105652 73.0983006 146.552826 119.45085 157.778525
184.901699 "
    ></polygon>
    </g>
</svg>
```

That is the entirety of the code needed to generate that star as an SVG graphic.

Now, ordinarily, if you've never looked at the code of an SVG graphic before, you may be wondering why you would ever want to. If all you want is vector graphics displayed on the web, you certainly don't need to. Just find a graphics application that will save your vector artwork as an SVG and you're done.

We will list a few of those packages in the coming pages. However, although it's certainly common and possible to only work with SVG graphics from within a graphics editing application, understanding exactly how an SVG fits together and how you can tweak it to your exact will can become very useful if you need to start manipulating and animating an SVG.

So, let's take a closer look at that SVG markup and get an appreciation of what exactly is going on in there. I'd like to draw your attention to a few key things.

The root SVG element

The root SVG element here has attributes for `width`, `height`, and `viewBox`:

```
<svg width="198px" height="188px" viewBox="0 0 198 188"
```

Each of these plays an important role in how an SVG is displayed.

Hopefully, at this point, you understand the term "viewport." It's been used in most chapters of this book to describe the area of a device through which content is viewed. For example, a mobile device might have a 320px by 480px viewport. A desktop computer might have a 1,920px by 1,080px viewport.

The `width` and `height` attributes of the SVG effectively create a viewport. Through this defined viewport, we can peek in to see the shapes defined inside the SVG. Just like a web page, the contents of the SVG may be bigger than the viewport, but that doesn't mean the rest isn't there; it's merely hidden from our current view.

The `viewBox`, on the other hand, defines the coordinate system in which all the shapes of the SVG are governed. You can think of the `viewBox` values `0 0 198 188` as describing the top left and bottom right area of a rectangle. The first two values, known technically as `min-x` and `min-y`, describe the top left corner, while the second two, known technically as width and height, describe the bottom right corner. Having the `viewBox` attribute allows you to do things like zoom an image in or out. For example, if you halve the `width` and `height` in the `viewBox` attribute like this:

```
<svg width="198px" height="188px" viewBox="0 0 99 94"
```

The shape will "zoom" to fill the size of the SVG width and height.

 To really understand `viewBox` and the SVG coordinate system and the opportunities it presents, I recommend this post by Sara Soueidan: `http://sarasoueidan.com/blog/svg-coordinate-systems/` and this post by Jakob Jenkov: `http://tutorials.jenkov.com/svg/svg-viewport-view-box.html`.

namespace

This SVG has an additional namespace defined for the Sketch graphics program that generated it (xmlns is short for XML namespace):

```
xmlns:sketch="http://www.bohemiancoding.com/sketch/ns"
```

These namespace references tend to only be used by the program that generated the SVG, so they are often not needed when the SVG is bound for the web. Optimization processes for reducing the size of SVGs will often strip them out.

The title and desc tags

There are title and desc tags that make an SVG document highly accessible:

```
<title>Star 1</title>
    <desc>Created with Sketch.</desc>
```

These tags can be used to describe the contents of the graphics when they cannot be seen. However, when SVG graphics are used for background graphics, these tags can be stripped to further reduce the file size.

The defs tag

There is an empty defs tag in our example code:

```
<defs></defs>
```

Despite being empty in our example, this is an important element. It is used to store definitions of all manner of reusable content such as gradients, symbols, paths, and more.

The g element

The g element is used to group other elements together. For example, if you were drawing an SVG of a car, you might group the shapes that make up an entire wheel inside a g tag:

```
<g id="Page-1" stroke="none" stroke-width="1" fill="none" fill-
rule="evenodd" sketch:type="MSPage">
```

In our g tag, we can see the earlier namespace of Sketch being reused here. It will help that graphics application open this graphic again, but it serves no further purpose should this image be bound elsewhere.

SVG shapes

The innermost node in this example is a polygon:

```
<polygon id="Star-1" stroke="#979797" stroke-width="3" fill="#F8E81C"
sketch:type="MSShapeGroup" points="99 154 40.2214748 184.901699
51.4471742 119.45085 3.89434837 73.0983006 69.6107374 63.5491503 99
4 128.389263 63.5491503 194.105652 73.0983006 146.552826 119.45085
157.778525 184.901699 "></polygon>
```

SVGs have a number of readymade shapes available (`path`, `rect`, `circle`, `ellipse`, `line`, `polyline`, and `polygon`).

SVG paths

SVG paths differ from the other shapes of SVG as they are composed of any number of connected points (giving you the freedom to create any shape you like).

So, that's the guts of an SVG file, and hopefully now you have a high-level understanding of what's going on. While some will relish the opportunity to handwrite or edit SVG files in code, a great many more would rather generate SVGs with a graphics package. Let's consider some of the more popular choices.

Creating SVGs with popular image editing packages and services

While SVGs can be opened, edited, and written in a text editor, there are plenty of applications offering a **graphical user interface** (GUI) that make authoring complex SVG graphics easier if you come from a graphics editing background. Perhaps the most obvious choice is Adobe's Illustrator (PC/Mac). However, it is expensive for casual users, so my own preference is either Bohemian Coding's Sketch (Mac only: `http://bohemiancoding.com/sketch/`), which still isn't cheap at $99, or Figma, which is cross-platform and uses a subscription-based model that is currently free for the starter plan. Check out Figma at `https://www.figma.com/`.

If you use Windows/Linux and/or are looking for cheap options, consider the free and open source Inkscape (`https://inkscape.org/en/`). It's by no means the prettiest tool to work with, but it is very capable (if you want any proof, view the Inkscape gallery: `https://inkscape.org/en/community/gallery/`).

Finally, there are a few online editors. Google has svg-edit (`https://svg-edit.github.io/svgedit/editor/svg-editor.html`). There is also DRAW SVG (`http://www.drawsvg.org/`) and Method Draw, an arguably better-looking fork of svg-edit (`http://editor.method.ac/`).

Saving time with SVG icon services

The aforementioned applications all give you the capability to create SVG graphics from scratch. However, if it's icons you're after, you can probably save a lot of time (and for me, get better results) by downloading SVG versions of icons from an online icon service.

My personal favorite is `https://icomoon.io`, although `http://fontastic.me` is also great. To quickly illustrate the benefits of an online icon service, loading the `https://icomoon.io` application gives you a searchable library of icons (some free, some paid):

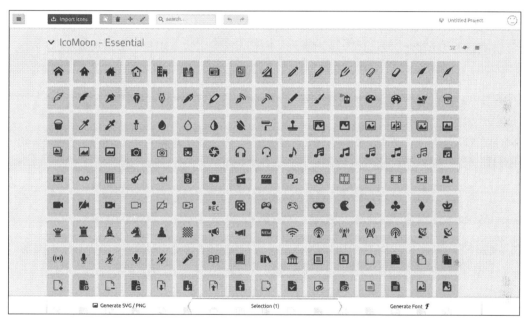

Figure 8.4: Online services can make it simple to get started incorporating SVGs

You select the ones you want and then click download. The resultant file contains the icons as SVGs, PNGs, and also SVG symbols for placement in the `defs` element (remember that the `defs` element is a container element for referenced elements).

To see for yourself, open `example_08-02`. You can see the resultant downloaded files after I'd chosen five icons from `https://icomoon.io`.

Inserting SVGs into your web pages

There are a number of things that you can do (browser-dependent) with SVG images that you can't do with normal image formats (JPEG, GIF, and PNG). The range of what's possible is largely dependent upon the way that the SVG is inserted into the page.

So, before we get to what we can actually do with SVGs, we'll consider the various ways we can actually get them on the page in the first place.

Using an img tag

The most straightforward way to use an SVG graphic is exactly how you would insert any image into an HTML document. We just use a good ol' `img` tag:

```
<img src="mySconeVector.svg" alt="Amazing line art of a scone" />
```

This makes the SVG behave more or less like any other image. There isn't much else to say about that.

With an object tag

The `object` tag is the container recommended by the W3C for holding non-HTML content in a web page (the specification for `object` is here: `http://www.w3.org/TR/html5/embedded-content-0.html#the-object-element`). We can make use of it to insert an SVG into our page like this:

```
<object data="img/svgfile.svg" type="image/svg+xml">
<span class="fallback-info">Your browser doesn't support SVG</span>
</object>
```

Either a `data` or `type` attribute is required, although I would always recommend adding both. The `data` attribute is where you link out to the SVG asset in the same manner you would link to any other asset. The `type` attribute describes the MIME type relevant for the content. In this instance, `image/svg+xml` is the MIME (internet media type) type to indicate that the data is SVG. You can also add a `width` and `height` attribute too if you want to constrain the size of the SVG with this container.

An SVG inserted into the page via an `object` tag is also accessible with JavaScript, so that's one reason to insert them this way. However, an additional bonus of using the `object` tag is that it provides a simple mechanism for when a browser doesn't understand the data type.

For example, if that prior object element was viewed in Internet Explorer 8 (which has no support for SVG), it would simply see the message "Your browser doesn't support SVG." You can use this space to provide a fallback image in an `img` tag. However, be warned that from my cursory testing, the browser will always download the fallback image, regardless of whether it actually needs it. Therefore, if you want your site to load in the shortest possible time (you do, trust me), this might not actually be the best choice.

An alternative approach to providing a fallback would be to add a `background-image` via the CSS. For example, in our previous example, our fallback `span` has a `class` of `.fallback-info`. We could make use of this in CSS to link to a suitable `background-image`. That way, the background image will only be downloaded if required.

Inserting an SVG as a background image

SVGs can be used as a background image in CSS, much the same way as any other image format (PNG, JPG, or GIF). There's nothing special about the way you reference them:

```
.item {
  background-image: url('image.svg');
}
```

If you find yourself in the unlikely situation of needing to support browsers that don't support SVG (Android 2 and Internet Explorer 8, for example) you can use CSS feature queries, which we looked at in *Chapter 6, CSS Selectors, Typography, Color Modes, and More*:

```
.item {
  background-image: url('image.png');
}

@supports (fill: black) {
  .item {
    background-image: url('image.svg');
  }
}
```

The `@supports` rule works here because `fill` is an SVG property, so if the browser understands that, it will take the lower rule over the first.

If your needs for SVG are primarily static background images, perhaps for icons and the like, I highly recommend implementing SVGs as background images. That's because there are a number of tools that will automatically create image sprites or style sheet assets (which means including the SVGs as data URIs), fallback PNG assets, and requisite style sheets from any individual SVGs you create. Using SVGs this way is very well supported; the images themselves cache well (so performance-wise, they work very well), and it's simple to implement.

A brief aside on data URIs

After reading the previous section, you might wonder what on earth is a **data uniform resource identifier (URI)**. In relation to CSS, it's a means of including what would ordinarily be an external asset, such as an image, within the CSS file itself. Therefore, where we might do this to link to an external image file:

```
.external {
  background-image: url('Star.svg');
}
```

We could simply include the image inside our style sheet with a data URI, like this:

```
.data-uri {
  background-image: url(data:image/svg+xml,%3C%3Fxml%20
version%3D%221.0%22%20encoding%3D%22UTF-8%22%20standalone%3D%22
no%22%3F%3E%0A%3Csvg%20width%3D%22198px%22%20height%3D%22188px-
%22%20viewBox%3D%220%200%20198%20188%22%20version%3D%221.1%22%20
xmlns%3D%22http%3A%2F%2Fwww.w3.org%2F2000%2Fsvg%22%20xmlns
%3Axlink%3D%22http%3A%2F%2Fwww.w3.org%2F1999%2Fxlink%22%20
xmlns%3Asketch%3D%22http%3A%2F%2Fwww.bohemiancoding.
com%2Fsketch%2Fns%22%3E%0A%20%20%20%20%3C%21--%20Generator%3A%20
Sketch%203.2.2%20%289983%29%20-%20http%3A%2F%2Fwww.bohemiancoding.
com%2Fsketch%20--%3E%0A%20%20%20%20%3Ctitle%3EStar%20
1%3C%2Ftitle%3E%0A%20%20%20%20%3Cdesc%3ECreated%20with%20
Sketch.%3C%2Fdesc%3E%0A%20%20%20%20%3Cdefs%3E%3C%2Fdefs%3E%0A%20
%20%20%20%3Cg%20id%3D%22Page-1%22%20stroke%3D%22none%22%20stroke-
width%3D%221%22%20fill%3D%22none%22%20fill-rule%3D%22evenodd%22%20
sketch%3Atype%3D%22MSPage%22%3E%0A%20%20%20%20%20%20%20%20
%3Cpolygon%20id%3D%22Star-1%22%20stroke%3D%22%23979797%22%20stroke-
width%3D%223%22%20fill%3D%22%23F8E81C%22%20sketch%3Atype%3D%22MSS
hapeGroup%22%20points%3D%2299%20154%2040.2214748%20184.901699%20
51.4471742%20119.45085%203.89434837%2073.0983006%2069.6107374%20
63.5491503%2099%204%20128.389263%2063.5491503%20194.105652%20
73.0983006%20146.552826%20119.45085%20157.778525%20184.901699%20
%22%3E%3C%2Fpolygon%3E%0A%20%20%20%20%3C%2Fg%3E%0A%3C%2Fsvg%3E);
}
```

It's not pretty, but it provides us with a way to negate a separate request over the network. There are different encoding methods for data URIs and plenty of tools available to create data URIs from your assets.

If you're encoding SVGs in this manner, I would suggest avoiding the Base64 method as it doesn't compress as well as text for SVG content.

Generating image sprites

My personal recommendation, tool-wise, for generating image sprites or data URI assets, is iconizr (`http://iconizr.com`). It gives you complete control over how you would like your resultant SVG and fallback PNG assets. You can have the SVGs and fallback PNG files output as data URIs or image sprites, and it even includes the requisite JavaScript snippet for loading the correct asset if you opt for data URIs. This is highly recommended.

Also, if you are wondering whether to choose data URIs or image sprites for your projects, I did further research on the pros and cons of data URIs or image sprites that you may be interested in, should you be facing the same choice: `http://benfrain.com/image-sprites-data-uris-icon-fonts-v-svgs/`.

While I'm a big fan of SVGs as background images, if you want to animate them dynamically, or inject values into them via JavaScript, then it will be best to opt for inserting SVG data "inline" into the HTML.

Inserting an SVG inline

As SVG is merely an XML document, you can insert it directly into the HTML. For example:

```
<div>
    <h3>Inserted 'inline':</h3>
    <span class="inlineSVG">
        <svg id="svgInline" width="198" height="188" viewBox="0 0
198 188" xmlns="http://www.w3.org/2000/svg" xmlns:xlink="http://www.
w3.org/1999/xlink">
        <title>Star 1</title>
            <g class="star_Wrapper" fill="none" fill-rule="evenodd">
                <path id="star_Path" stroke="#979797" stroke-
width="3" fill="#F8E81C" d="M99 154l-58.78 30.902 11.227-65.45L3.894
73.097l65.717-9.55L99 4l29.39 59.55 65.716 9.548-47.553 46.353
11.226 65.452z" />
            </g>
```

```
        </svg>
    </span>
</div>
```

There is no special wrapping element needed; you literally just insert the SVG markup inside the HTML markup. It's also worth noting that if you remove any `width` and `height` attributes on the `svg` element, the SVG will scale fluidly to fit the containing element.

Inserting SVG as markup into your documents is probably the most versatile option in terms of accessing the broadest range of SVG features.

Let's consider some of those features that inserting SVGs inline allows next.

Reusing graphical objects from symbols

Earlier in this chapter, I mentioned that I had picked and downloaded some icons from IcoMoon (`http://icomoon.io`). They were icons depicting touch gestures: swipe, pinch, drag, and more. Suppose, in a website you are building, you need to make use of them multiple times. Remember I mentioned that there was a version of those icons as SVG symbol definitions? That's what we will make use of now.

In `example_08-09`, we insert the various symbol definitions inside the `defs` element of an SVG in the page. You'll notice that, on the `svg` element, an inline style is used, `display:none`, and the `height` and `width` attributes have both been set to `0` (those styles could be set in CSS if you prefer). This is so that this SVG takes up no space. We are only using this SVG to house symbols of the graphical objects we want to use elsewhere. So, our markup starts like this:

```
<body>
    <svg display="none" width="0" height="0" version="1.1"
xmlns="http://www.w3.org/2000/svg" xmlns:xlink="http://www.
w3.org/1999/xlink">
    <defs>
    <symbol id="icon-drag-left-right" viewBox="0 0 1344 1024">
        <title>drag-left-right</title>
        <path class="path1" d="M256 192v-160l-224 224 224
224v-160h256v-128z"></path>
```

Notice the `symbol` element inside the `defs` element? This is the element to use when we want to define a shape for later reuse.

You can create symbols for use inside the defs tag by taking an existing SVG, changing the svg tag to symbol, removing the namespace attribute, and then nesting it inside the defs tag.

After the SVG has defined all necessary symbols for our work, we have all our "normal" HTML markup. Then, when we want to make use of one of those symbols, we can do this:

```
<svg class="icon-drag-left-right">
    <use xlink:href="#icon-drag-left-right"></use>
</svg>
```

That will display the drag left and right icon:

Figure 8.5: With SVGs inserted inline, it's possible to reuse graphics

The magic here is the use element. As you might have guessed from the name, it's used to make use of existing graphical objects that have already been defined elsewhere. The mechanism for choosing what to reference is the xlink attribute, which, in this case, is referencing the symbol ID of the "drag left and right" icon (#icon-drag-left-right) we have inline at the beginning of the markup.

When you reuse a symbol, unless you explicitly set a size (either with attributes on the element itself or with CSS), `use` will be set to a width and height of 100%. So, to resize our icon, we could do this:

```
.icon-drag-left-right {
  width: 2.5rem;
  height: 2.5rem;
}
```

The `use` element can be used to reuse all sorts of SVG content: gradients, shapes, symbols, and more.

Inline SVGs allow different colors in different contexts

With inline SVGs, you can also do useful things like change colors based on context, and that's great when you need multiple versions of the same icon in different colors:

```
.icon-drag-left-right {
  fill: #f90;
}


.different-context .icon-drag-left-right {
  fill: #ddd;
}
```

Making dual-tone icons that inherit the color of their parent

With inline SVGs, you can also have some fun and create two-tone effects from a single color icon (as long as the SVG is made up of more than one path) with the use of `currentColor`, the oldest CSS variable. To do this, inside the SVG symbol, set the `fill` of the path you want to be one color as `currentColor`. Then, use the `color` value in your CSS to color the element. For the paths in the SVG symbol without the fill, set them as `currentColor`; they will receive the `fill` value. To exemplify this:

```
.icon-drag-left-right {
  width: 2.5rem;
  height: 2.5rem;
  fill: #f90;
  color: #ccc; /* this gets applied to the path that has it's fill
  attribute set to currentColor in the symbol */
}
```

Here's that same symbol reused three times, each with different colors and sizes:

Figure 8.6: Making dual-color SVGs by inheriting colors

Remember, you can dig around the code in `example_08-09`. It's also worth noting that the `color` doesn't have to be set on that element itself—it can be on any parent element; `currentColor` will inherit a value from up the DOM tree to the nearest parent with a `color` value set.

Recoloring SVGs with CSS custom properties

Nowadays, I find the most effective way to recolor the same SVG or symbol is by using CSS custom properties. Let me show you an example. This example can be found at `example_08-11`.

I have made a pentagon shape using two paths. Each path has a `fill` and a `stroke` value. Here is the SVG:

```
<svg class="shape" width="268" height="254" xmlns="http://www.
w3.org/2000/svg">
  <g fill="none" fill-rule="evenodd" stroke-width="10">
    <path d="M134 6.18L6.73 98.647l48.613 149.615h157.314L261.27
98.647 134 6.18z" stroke="var(--stroke1)" fill="var(--fill1)"/>
    <path d="M134 36.18l-98.738 71.738 37.714 116.074h122.048l37.714-
116.074L134 36.18z" stroke="var(--stroke2)" fill="var(--fill2)"/>
  </g>
</svg>
```

Notice how for each `path` element, both the `stroke` and `fill` values have been set to a CSS custom property. With those values in place, I can then set any colors I want for that SVG with CSS, JavaScript, or a combination of the two!

In our example, I have set default colors and hover colors, like this:

```
.shape {
  display: block;
  --stroke1: #ddd;
  --fill1: #444;
```

```
    --stroke2: #f90;
    --fill2: #663d00;
}


.shape:hover {
    --stroke1: #333;
    --fill1: #444;
    --stroke2: #fff;
    --fill2: #ffc266;
}
```

Sadly, grayscale images fail us a little here, but this is the default coloring. I made the example document background dark just to make it clearer:

Figure 8.7: CSS custom properties make recoloring SVGs simple

Then, to prove how easy it is to amend further still, if you open the example, you will see a button that uses a tiny bit of JavaScript to toggle a class on the page, adding or removing the .amended class. This allows us to have two further sets of colors for this shape:

```
.amended .shape {
    --stroke1: #080b2b;
    --fill1: #141a67;
    --fill2: #192183;
    --stroke2: #2d3ad7;
}


.amended .shape:hover {
```

```
    --stroke1: #092b08;
    --fill1: #125610;
    --fill2: #2dd728;
    --stroke2: #1b8118;
}
```

This results in four blue colors ordinarily and four green colors when hovered over:

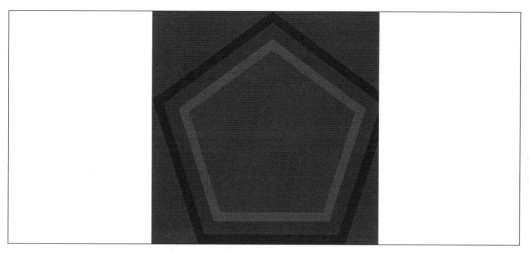

Figure 8.8: CSS custom properties create near limitless possibilities

As you can see, there are a lot of positives to placing SVGs inside the markup. The only downside is that it's necessary to include the same SVG data on every page where you want to use the icons. Sadly, this is bad for performance, as the assets (the SVG data) aren't going to be cached easily. However, there is another option (if you are happy to add a script to support Internet Explorer).

Reusing graphical objects from external sources

Rather than paste in an enormous set of SVG symbols in each page, while still using the use element, it's possible to link out to external SVG files and grab the portion of the document you want to use. Take a look at example_08-10 and the same three icons as we had in example_08-09, which are put on the page in this manner:

```
<svg class="icon-drag-left-right">
  <use xlink:href="defs.svg#icon-drag-left-right"></use>
</svg>
```

Be aware that some of these examples might require to run them on a server. Two simple solutions. Either use something like BrowserSync to create a simple local server or paste the code into a service like Codepen.io

The important part to understand is `href`. We are linking to an external SVG file (the `defs.svg` part) and then specifying the ID of the symbol within that file we want to use (the `#icon-drag-left-right` part). The benefits of this approach are that the asset is cached by the browser (just like any other external image would/could be) and it saves littering our markup with an SVG full of symbol definitions. The downside is that, unlike when `defs` are placed inline, any dynamic changes made to `defs.svg` (for example, if a path was being manipulated by JavaScript) won't be updated in the `use` tags.

Sadly, Internet Explorer does not allow referencing symbols from external assets. However, there's a polyfill script for IE 9-11, called *SVG For Everybody*, that allows us to use this technique regardless. Head over to `https://github.com/jonathantneal/svg4everybody` for more information.

When using that piece of JavaScript, you can happily reference external assets and the polyfill will insert the SVG data directly into the body of the document for Internet Explorer.

What you can do with each SVG insertion method (inline, object, background-image, and img)

As mentioned previously, SVGs differ from other graphical assets. They can behave differently, depending upon the way they are inserted into a page. As we have seen, there are four main ways in which to place SVG onto the page:

- Inside an `img` tag
- Inside an `object` tag
- As a background-image
- Inline

And depending upon the insertion method, certain capabilities will or will not be available to you. To understand what should be possible with each insertion method, it might be simpler to consider this table:

Feature	img	object	inline	bg image
SMIL	Y	Y	Y	Y
External CSS	N	*1	Y	N
Internal CSS	Y	Y	Y	Y
Access via JS	N	Y	Y	N
Cacheable	Y	Y	*2	Y
MQ in SVG	Y	Y	*3	Y
Use possible	N	Y	Y	N

Figure 8.9: Depending upon the insertion method, differing capabilities are possible

Now, there are caveats to consider, marked within numbers:

1. When using an SVG inside an object, you can use an external style sheet to style the SVG, but you have to link to that style sheet from within the SVG.

2. You can use SVGs in an external asset (which is cacheable), but it doesn't work by default in Internet Explorer.

3. A media query inside the styles section of an "inlined" SVG works on the size of the document it lives in (not the size of the SVG itself).

Be aware that browser implementations of SVG also vary. Therefore, just because those things should be possible (as indicated previously) doesn't mean they will be in every browser, or that they will behave consistently!

Browser schisms

The results in the preceding table are based upon the test page in `example_08-03`.

The behavior of the test page is comparable in the latest versions of Firefox, Chrome, and Safari. However, Internet Explorer sometimes does things a little differently.

For example, in all the SVG-capable versions of Internet Explorer (at this point, that's 9, 10, and 11), as we have already seen, it is not possible to reference external SVG sources. Furthermore, Internet Explorer applies the styles from the external style sheet onto the SVGs, regardless of how they have been inserted (all the other browsers only apply styles from external style sheets if the SVGs have been inserted via an object or inline).

Internet Explorer also doesn't allow any animation of SVG via CSS; animation of SVG in Internet Explorer has to be done via JavaScript. I'll say that one again for the folks at the back in the cheap seats: you cannot animate SVGs in Internet Explorer by any means other than JavaScript.

Obviously, Internet Explorer is a diminishing concern, but it's worth knowing about these issues if you need to support it.

Extra SVG capabilities and oddities

Let's put aside the foibles of browsers for a moment and consider what some of these features in the table actually allow, and why you may or may not want to make use of them.

SVGs will always render as sharp as the viewing device will allow and regardless of the manner of insertion. For most practical situations, resolution independence is usually reason enough to use SVG. It's then just a question of choosing whichever insertion method suits your workflow and the task at hand.

However, there are other capabilities and oddities that are worth knowing about, such as SMIL animation, different ways to link to external style sheets, marking internal styles with Character Data delimiters, amending an SVG with JavaScript, and making use of media queries within an SVG. Let's cover those next.

SMIL animation

SMIL animations (`http://www.w3.org/TR/smil-animation/`) are a way to define animations for an SVG within the SVG document itself. SMIL (pronounced "smile," in case you were wondering) stands for Synchronized Multimedia Integration Language and was developed as a method of defining animations inside an XML document (remember, SVG is XML-based).

Here's an example of how to define a SMIL-based animation:

```
<g class="star_Wrapper" fill="none" fill-rule="evenodd">
  <animate
    xlink:href="#star_Path"
    attributeName="fill"
    attributeType="XML"
    begin="0s"
    dur="2s"
    fill="freeze"
    from="#F8E81C"
```

```
        to="#14805e"
    />

    <path
      id="star_Path"
      stroke="#979797"
      stroke-width="3"
      fill="#F8E81C"
      d="M99 1541-58.78 30.902 11.227-65.45L3.894 73.097l65.717-
  9.55L99 4l29.39 59.55 65.716 9.548-47.553 46.353 11.226 65.452z"
    />
  </g>
```

I've grabbed a section of the earlier SVG we looked at. The `g` is a grouping element in SVG, and this one includes both a star shape (the `path` element with `id="star_Path"`) and the SMIL animation within the `animate` element. That simple animation tweens the fill color of the star from yellow to green in 2 seconds.

"Tweening"

In case you didn't already know (I didn't), "tweening" as a term is simply a shortening of "inbetweening" as it merely indicates all the in-between stages from one animation point to another.

What's more, it does that whether the SVG is put on the page in an `img`, `object`, background-image, or inline (no, honestly, open up `example_08-03` in any recent browser other than Internet Explorer to see).

Wow! Great, right? Well, kind of. Despite being a standard for some time, SMIL remains on shaky ground. In the last edition of this book, released in August 2015, it looked like the Chrome browser was going to deprecate SMIL in Chrome.

It's also important to know that SMIL has no support in Internet Explorer. None. Nada. Zip. Zilch. I could go on with other words that amount to very little, but I trust you understand there's no support for SMIL in Internet Explorer.

However, since Microsoft now has the Edge browser, which in turn is based on Chromium (the same code Chrome runs on), SMIL is now in the most modern Microsoft browser. Plus, like a phoenix from the flames, Chrome provided a "stay of execution" of their intention to deprecate SMIL: `https://groups.google.com/a/chromium.org/d/msg/blink-dev/5o0yiO440LM/YGEJBsjUAwAJ`.

So, while theoretically, SMIL is good to use for some use cases, I tend to quarantine it mentally in a "use as a last resort" technique.

However, if you still have a need to use SMIL, Sara Soueidan wrote an excellent, in-depth article about SMIL animations here: `http://css-tricks.com/guide-svg-animations-smil/`.

Thankfully, there are plenty of other ways we can animate SVGs, which we will come to shortly. So, if you have to support Internet Explorer, hang on in there.

Styling an SVG with an external style sheet

It's possible to style an SVG with CSS. This can be CSS enclosed in the SVG itself, or in the CSS style sheets you would write all your "normal" CSS in.

Now, if you refer back to our features table from earlier in this chapter, you can see that styling SVG with external CSS isn't possible when the SVG is included via an `img` tag or as a background-image (apart from Internet Explorer). It's only possible when SVGs are inserted via an `object` tag or inline.

There are two syntaxes for linking to an external style sheet from an SVG. The most straightforward way is like this (you would typically add this in the `defs` section):

```
<link href="styles.css" type="text/css" rel="stylesheet"/>
```

It's akin to the way we used to link to style sheets prior to HTML5 (for example, note the `type` attribute is no longer necessary in HTML5). However, despite this working in many browsers, it isn't the way the specifications define how external style sheets should be linked in SVG (`http://www.w3.org/TR/SVG/styling.html#ReferencingExternalStyleSheets`). Here is the correct/official way, actually defined for XML back in 1999 (`http://www.w3.org/1999/06/REC-xml-stylesheet-19990629/`):

```
<?xml-stylesheet href="styles.css" type="text/css"?>
```

You need to add this above the opening SVG element in your file. For example:

```
<?xml-stylesheet href="styles.css" type="text/css"?>
<svg
  width="198"
  height="188"
  viewBox="0 0 198 188"
  xmlns="http://www.w3.org/2000/svg"
  xmlns:xlink="http://www.w3.org/1999/xlink"
></svg>
```

Interestingly, the latter syntax is the only one that works in Internet Explorer. So, when you need to link out to a style sheet from your SVG, I'd recommend using this second syntax for wider support. You don't have to use an external style sheet; you can use inline styles directly in the SVG itself if you would rather.

Styling an SVG with internal styles

You can place styles for an SVG within the SVG itself. They should be placed within the `defs` element. As SVG is XML-based, it's safest to include the **Character Data marker (CDATA)**. The Character Data marker simply tells the browser that the information within the Character Data delimited section could possibly be interpreted as XML markup but should not be. The syntax is like this:

```
<defs>
  <style type="text/css">
    <![CDATA[
       #star_Path {
          stroke: red;
       }
    ]]>
  </style>
</defs>
```

SVG properties and values within CSS

Notice the `stroke` property in the prior code block? This isn't a CSS property; it's an SVG property. There are quite a few specific SVG properties you can use in styles (regardless of whether they are declared inline or via an external style sheet). For example, with an SVG, as you have seen in an earlier example, you don't specify a `background-color`; instead, you specify a `fill`. You don't specify a `border`; you specify a `stroke-width`.

 For the full list of SVG-specific properties, take a look at the specification here: `http://www.w3.org/TR/SVG/styling.html`.

With either inline or external CSS, it's possible to do all the "normal" CSS things you would expect; change an element's appearance, animate and transform elements, and so on.

Animating an SVG with CSS

Let's consider a quick example of adding a CSS animation inside an SVG (remember, these styles could just as easily be in an external style sheet too). Let's take the star example we have looked at throughout this chapter and make it spin. You can look at the finished example in `example_08-07`:

```
<div class="wrapper">
  <svg
    width="198"
    height="188"
    viewBox="0 0 220 200"
    xmlns="http://www.w3.org/2000/svg"
    xmlns:xlink="http://www.w3.org/1999/xlink"
  >
    <title>Star 1</title>
    <defs>
      <style type="text/css">
        <![CDATA[
        @keyframes spin {
            0% {
                transform: rotate(0deg);
            }
            100% {
                transform: rotate(360deg);
            }
        }
        .star_Wrapper {
            animation: spin 2s 1s;
            transform-origin: 50% 50%;
        }
        .wrapper {
            padding: 2rem;
            margin: 2rem;
        }
        ]]>
      </style>
      <g id="shape">
        <path fill="#14805e" d="M50 50h50v50H50z" />
        <circle fill="#ebebeb" cx="50" cy="50" r="50" />
      </g>
    </defs>
```

```
    <g class="star_Wrapper" fill="none" fill-rule="evenodd">
      <path
        id="star_Path"
        stroke="#333"
        stroke-width="3"
        fill="#F8E81C"
        d="M99 1541-58.78 30.902 11.227-65.45L3.894 73.097165.717-
  9.55L99 4129.39 59.55 65.716 9.548-47.553 46.353 11.226 65.453z"
      />
    </g>
  </svg>
</div>
```

If you load that example in the browser, after a 1 second delay, the star will spin a full circle over the course of 2 seconds.

 Notice how a `transform-origin` of 50% 50% has been set on the SVG? This is because, unlike CSS, the default `transform-origin` of an SVG is not 50% 50% (center in both axis); it's actually 0 0 (top left). Without that property set, the star would rotate around the top left point.

You can get quite far animating SVGs with CSS animations alone (well, assuming you don't need to worry about Internet Explorer). However, when you want to add interactivity, support Internet Explorer, or synchronize several events, it's generally best to lean on JavaScript. And the good news is that there are great libraries that make animating SVGs really easy. Let's look at an example of that now.

Animating SVG with JavaScript

With an SVG inserted into the page via an `object` tag or inline, it's possible to manipulate the SVG directly or indirectly with JavaScript. By indirectly, I mean it's possible with JavaScript to change a class on or above the SVG that would cause a CSS animation to start. For example:

```
svg {
  /* no animation */
}


.added-with-js svg {
  /* animation */
}
```

However, it's also possible to animate an SVG via JavaScript directly.

If you're animating just one or two things independently, it's probable things would be lighter, code wise, by writing the JavaScript by hand. However, if you need to animate lots of elements or synchronize the animation of elements as if on a timeline, JavaScript libraries can really help. Ultimately, you will need to judge whether the weight of including the library in your page can be justified for the goal you are trying to achieve.

My recommendation for animating SVGs via JavaScript is the GreenSock Animation Platform (`http://greensock.com`), Velocity.js (`http://julian.com/research/velocity/`), or Snap.svg (`http://snapsvg.io/`). For the next example, we'll cover a very simple example using GreenSock.

A simple example of animating an SVG with GreenSock

Suppose we want to make an interface dial that animates when we click a button from zero to whatever value we input. We want not only the stroke of the dial to animate in both length and color, but also the number from zero to the value we input. You can view the completed implementation in `example_08-08`.

So, if we entered a value of 75 and clicked **Animate!!**, the dial would fill around to look like this:

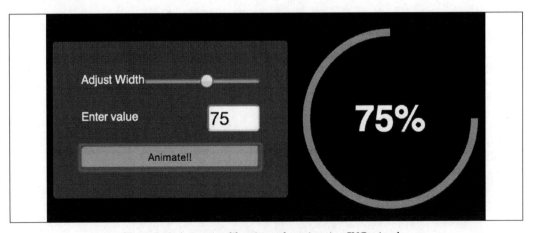

Figure 8.10: Animation libraries make animating SVGs simpler

Instead of listing out the entire JavaScript file (which is heavily commented, so it should make some sense to read in isolation), for brevity's sake, we'll just consider the key points.

The basic idea is that we have made a circle as an SVG `<path>` (rather than a `<circle>` element). As it's a path, it means we can animate the path as if it were being drawn using the `stroke-dashoffset` technique. There's more info on this technique in the boxed out section that follows, but briefly, we use JavaScript to measure the length of the path and then use the `stroke-dasharray` attribute to specify the length of the rendered part of the line and the length of the gap.

Then, we use `stroke-dashoffset` to change where that `dasharray` starts. This means you can effectively start the stroke "off" the path and animate it in. This gives the illusion that the path is being drawn.

If the value to animate `dasharray` was a static, known value, this effect would be relatively simple to achieve with a CSS animation and a little trial and error (more on CSS animations in the next chapter). However, besides a dynamic value, at the same time as we are "drawing" the line, we want to fade in the stroke color from one value to another and visually count up to the input value in the text node. This is an animation equivalent of patting our heads, rubbing our tummy, and counting backward from 10,000. GreenSock makes those things easy (the animation part; it won't rub your tummy or pat your head, although it can count back from 10,000, should you need it to).

Here are the lines of JavaScript needed to make GreenSock do all three:

```
// Animate the drawing of the line and color change
TweenLite.to(circlePath, 1.5, {
  'stroke-dashoffset': '-' + amount,
  stroke: strokeEndColour,
});
// Set a counter to zero and animate to the input value
var counter = {var: 0};
TweenLite.to(counter, 1.5, {
  var: inputValue,
  onUpdate: function() {
    text.textContent = Math.ceil(counter.var) + '%';
  },
  ease: Circ.easeOut,
});
```

In essence, with the `TweenLite.to()` function, you pass in the thing you want to animate, the time over which the animation should occur, and then the values you want to change (and what you want them to change to).

The GreenSock site has excellent documentation and support forums, so if you find yourself needing to synchronize a number of animations at once, be sure to clear a day from your diary and familiarize yourself with GreenSock.

 In case you haven't come across the SVG "line drawing" technique before, it was popularized by Polygon magazine when Vox Media animated a couple of line drawings of the Xbox One and PlayStation 4 games consoles. You can read the original post here: `http://product.voxmedia.com/2013/11/25/5426880/polygon-feature-design-svg-animations-for-fun-and-profit`.

There's also an excellent and more thorough explanation of the technique by Jake Archibald here: `http://jakearchibald.com/2013/animated-line-drawing-svg/`.

Optimizing SVGs

As conscientious developers, we want to ensure that assets are as small as possible. The easiest way to do this with SVGs is to make use of automation tools that can optimize various particulars of SVG documents. Besides obvious economies such as removing elements (for example, stripping the title and description elements), it's also possible to perform a raft of micro-optimizations that, when added up, make for far leaner SVG assets. Presently, for this task, I would recommend SVGO (`https://github.com/svg/svgo`).

If you have never used SVGO before, I would recommend starting with SVGOMG (`https://jakearchibald.github.io/svgomg/`). It's a browser-based version of SVGO that enables you to toggle the various optimization plugins and get instant feedback on the file savings. Remember our example star SVG markup from the beginning of this chapter? By default, that simple SVG is 489 bytes in size. By passing that through SVGO, it's possible to get the size down to just 218 bytes, and that's leaving the `viewBox` in. That's a saving of 55.42%. If you're using a raft of SVG images, these savings can really add up. Here's what the optimized SVG markup looks like:

```
<svg
  width="198"
  height="188"
  viewBox="0 0 198 188"
  xmlns="http://www.w3.org/2000/svg"
>
  <path
    stroke="#979797"
    stroke-width="3"
    fill="#F8E81C"
    d="M99 1541-58.78 30.902 11.227-65.45L3.894 73.097l65.717-
```

```
9.55L99 4129.39 59.55 65.716 9.548-47.553 46.353 11.226 65.454z"
  />
</svg>
```

Before you spend too long with SVGO, be aware that, such is the popularity of SVGO, plenty of other SVG tools also make use of it. For example, the aforementioned iconizr (`http://iconizr.com`) tool runs your SVG files through SVGO by default anyway, before creating your assets, so ensure you aren't unnecessarily double optimizing.

Using SVGs as filters

In *Chapter 7, Stunning Aesthetics with CSS3*, we looked at the CSS filter effects. CSS filters aren't supported in older browsers like Internet Explorer 10 or 11. That can be frustrating if you have a project that requires filters and you want/need to support those browsers.

Luckily, with help from SVG, we can create filters that work in Internet Explorer 10 and 11 too, but as ever, it's perhaps not as straightforward as you might imagine. For example, in `example_08-05`, we have a page with the following markup inside the body:

```
<img class="HRH" src="queen@2x-1024x747.png" />
```

It's an image of the Queen of England. Ordinarily, it looks like this:

Figure 8.11: An image with no SVG filter applied

Now, also in that example folder, is an SVG with a filter defined in the `defs` elements. The SVG markup looks like this:

```
<svg xmlns="http://www.w3.org/2000/svg" version="1.1">
  <defs>
    <filter id="myfilter" x="0" y="0">
      <feColorMatrix
        in="SourceGraphic"
        type="hueRotate"
        values="90"
        result="A"
      />
      <feGaussianBlur in="A" stdDeviation="6" />
    </filter>
  </defs>
</svg>
```

Within the filter, we are first defining a hue rotation of 90 (using `feColorMatrix`, and then passing that effect, via the `result` attribute, to the next filter (`feGaussianBlur`) with a blur value of 6. Be aware that I've been deliberately heavy handed here. This doesn't produce a nice aesthetic, but it should leave you in no doubt that the effect has worked!

Now, rather than add that SVG markup to the HTML, we can leave it where it is and reference it using the same CSS filter syntax we saw in the previous chapter.

```
.HRH {
  filter: url('filter.svg#myfilter');
}
```

In most evergreen browsers (Chrome, Safari, and Firefox), this is the effect:

Figure 8.12: An image with an SVG filter applied

Sadly, this method doesn't work in IE 10 or 11. However, there is another way to achieve our goal, and that's using SVG's own image tag to include the image within the SVG. Inside example_08-06, we have the following markup:

```
<svg
  height="747px"
  width="1024px"
  viewBox="0 0 1024 747"
  xmlns="http://www.w3.org/2000/svg"
  version="1.1"
>
  <defs>
    <filter id="myfilter" x="0" y="0">
      <feColorMatrix
        in="SourceGraphic"
        type="hueRotate"
        values="90"
        result="A"
      />
      <feGaussianBlur in="A" stdDeviation="6" />
    </filter>
  </defs>
  <image
    x="0"
    y="0"
```

```
        height="747px"
        width="1024px"
        xmlns:xlink="http://www.w3.org/1999/xlink"
        xlink:href="queen@2x-1024x747.png"
        filter="url(#myfilter)"
    ></image>
</svg>
```

The SVG markup here is very similar to the external `filter.svg` filter we used in the previous example but the `height`, `width`, and `viewBox` attributes have been added. In addition, the image we want to apply the filter to is the only content in the SVG outside of the `defs` element. To link to the filter, we are using the `filter` attribute and passing the ID of the filter we want to use (in this case, from within the `defs` element).

Although this approach is a little more involved, it means you can get the many and varied filter effects that SVG affords, even in versions 10 and 11 of Internet Explorer.

A note on media queries inside SVGs

All browsers that understand SVG should respect the CSS media queries defined inside. However, when it comes to media queries inside SVGs, there are a few things to remember.

For example, suppose you insert a media query inside an SVG, like this:

```
<style type="text/css"><![CDATA[
    #star_Path {
        stroke: red;
    }
    @media (min-width: 800px) {
        #star_Path {
            stroke: violet;
        }
    }
]]></style>
```

And that SVG is displayed on the page at a width of 200px, while the viewport is 1,200px wide.

We might expect the stroke of the star to be violet when the screen is 800px and above. After all, that's what we have our media query set to. However, when the SVG is placed on the page via an `img` tag, as a background image, or inside an `object` tag, it has no knowledge of the outer HTML document. Hence, in this situation, `min-width` means the minimum width of the SVG itself. So, unless the SVG itself displayed on the page at a width of 800px or more, the stroke wouldn't be violet.

Conversely, when you insert an SVG inline, it merges (in a manner of speaking), with the outer HTML document. The `min-width` media query here is looking to the viewport (as is the HTML) to decide when the media query matches.

To solve this particular problem and make the same media query behave consistently, we could amend our media query to this:

```
@media (min-device-width: 800px) {
  #star_Path {
    stroke: violet;
  }
}
```

That way, regardless of the SVG size or how it is embedded, it is looking to the device width (effectively the viewport).

SVG implementation tips

We're almost at the end of this chapter now and there is still so much we could talk about regarding SVG. Therefore, at this point, I'll just list a few unrelated considerations. They aren't necessarily worthy of protracted explanations, but I'll list them here in note form in case they save you from hours of searching Stack Overflow:

- If you have no need to animate your SVGs, opt for an image sprite of your assets or a data URI style sheet. It's far easier to provide fallback assets and they almost always perform better from a performance perspective.

- Automate as many steps in the asset creation process as possible; this reduces human error and produces predictable results faster.

- To insert static SVGs in a project, pick a single delivery mechanism and stick to it (image sprite, data URI, or inline). It can become a burden to produce some assets one way and some another and maintain the various implementations.

- There is no easy "one size fits all" choice with SVG animation. For occasional and simple animations, use CSS. For complex interactive or timeline style animations that will also work in Internet Explorer, lean on a proven library such as GreenSock, Velocity.js, or Snap.svg.

Summary

This has been a dense chapter. We have covered a lot of the essential information needed to start making sense of, and implementing, SVGs in a responsive project. We have considered the different graphics applications and online solutions available to create SVG assets, then the various insertion methods possible and the capabilities each allows, along with the various browser peculiarities to be aware of.

We've also considered how to link to external style sheets and reuse SVG symbols from within the same page and when referenced externally. We even looked at how we can make filters with SVG that can be referenced and used in CSS for wider support than CSS filters.

Finally, we considered how to make use of JavaScript libraries to aid animating SVGs, as well as how to optimize SVGs with the aid of the SVGO tool.

In the next chapter, we'll be looking at CSS transitions, transforms, and animations. It's also worth reading that chapter in relation to SVG, as many of the syntaxes and techniques can be used and applied in SVG documents too.

Further resources

As I mentioned at the start of this chapter, I have neither the space, nor the knowledge, to impart all there is to know about SVG. Therefore, I'd like to make you aware of the following excellent resources, which provide additional depth and range on the subject:

- *SVG Essentials, 2nd Edition* by J. David Eisenberg and Amelia Bellamy-Royds: `http://shop.oreilly.com/product/0636920032335.do`

- *A Guide to SVG Animations (SMIL)* by Sara Soueidan: `http://css-tricks.com/guide-svg-animations-smil/`

- *Media Queries inside SVGs Test* by Jeremie Patonnier: `http://jeremie.patonnier.net/experiences/svg/media-queries/test.html`

- *An SVG Primer for Today's Browsers*: `http://www.w3.org/Graphics/SVG/IG/resources/svgprimer.html`

- *Understanding SVG Coordinate Systems and Transformations (Part 1)* by Sara Soueidan: `http://sarasoueidan.com/blog/svg-coordinate-systems/`

- *Hands On: SVG Filter Effects*: `https://testdrive-archive.azurewebsites.net/Graphics/hands-on-css3/hands-on_svg-filter-effects.htm`

- The full set of SVG tutorials by Jakob Jenkov: `http://tutorials.jenkov.com/svg/index.html`

9
Transitions, Transformations, and Animations

Historically, whenever elements needed to be moved or animated on screen, it was essential to call upon JavaScript. Nowadays, CSS can handle the majority of motion requirements using CSS transitions and CSS transforms, or CSS animations.

To clearly understand what transitions, transforms, and animations do, I will offer this, perhaps overly simplistic, summary:

- A CSS transition is used to define how one visual state should move (transition) to another, differing visual state.

- A CSS transform is used to take an existing element and transform it into something or someplace else without affecting any other elements on the page. For example, "make this twice as big" and "move this 100px to the right" are plain text descriptions of tasks we can achieve with CSS transforms. However, the transform doesn't control HOW the element makes that change; that is the job of the transition.

- A CSS animation is typically used to make a series of changes to an element at various key points over time.

If those differences seem a little vague at this point, hopefully, by the end of this chapter, they won't.

In this chapter, we'll cover:

- What CSS transitions are, and how to use them
- Writing CSS transitions and understanding the shorthand syntax
- CSS transition timing functions (`ease`, `cubic-bezier`, and so on)
- What CSS transforms are, and how to use them
- Understanding different 2D transforms (`scale`, `rotate`, `skew`, `translate`)
- Understanding 3D transforms
- How to animate with CSS using keyframes

Let's get started with an introduction to CSS transitions.

What CSS transitions are and how we can use them

Transitions are the simplest way to create some visual "effect" between one state and another with CSS. Let's consider a simple example: an element that transitions from one state to another when hovered over.

When styling hyperlinks in CSS, it's common practice to create a `hover` state; an obvious way to make users aware that the item they are hovering over can be interacted with. Hover states are of little relevance to the growing number of touch screen devices but for mouse users, they're a great and simple interaction between website and user. They're also handy for illustrating transitions, so that's what we will start with.

Traditionally, using only CSS, `hover` states are an on/off affair. There is one set of properties and values on an element as the default, and when a pointer is hovered over that element, the properties and values are instantly changed. However, CSS transitions, as the name implies, allow us to transition between one or more properties and values to other properties and values.

A couple of important things to know up front. Firstly, you can't transition from `display: none;`. When something is set to `display: none;` it isn't actually "painted" on the screen, so it has no existing state you can transition from.

 Although you can't transition from `display: none`, it is possible to run an animation on an element at the same time its display property is changed. So, you could, for example, fade an element in from 0% opacity with an animation while changing its `display` property from `display: none`. We'll cover animations later in this chapter.

In order to create the effect of something fading in, you would have to transition opacity or position values. Secondly, not all properties can be transitioned. To ensure you're not attempting the impossible, here is the list of transitionable (I know, it's not even a word) properties: `https://developer.mozilla.org/en-US/docs/Web/CSS/CSS_animated_properties`.

 Older versions of the specifications used to include a list of animatable properties. You can still view this older version of the specification at `https://www.w3.org/TR/2017/WD-css-transitions-1-20171130/#animatable-properties` but it's likely to be incomplete.

If you open up `example_09-01`, you'll see a few links in a `nav`. Here's the relevant markup:

```
<nav>
  <a href="#">link1</a>
  <a href="#">link2</a>
  <a href="#">link3</a>
  <a href="#">link4</a>
  <a href="#">link5</a>
</nav>
```

And here's the relevant CSS:

```
a {
  font-family: sans-serif;
  color: #fff;
  text-indent: 1rem;
  background-color: #ccc;
  display: inline-flex;
  flex: 1 1 20%;
  align-self: stretch;
  align-items: center;
  text-decoration: none;
  transition: box-shadow 1s;
}

a + a {
  border-left: 1px solid #aaa;
}
```

```
a:hover {
    box-shadow: inset 0 -3px 0 #cc3232;
}
```

And here are the two states, first the default:

Figure 9.1: Two links, in their default state

And then here's the `hover` state:

Figure 9.2: When hovered, we underline the link

Ordinarily, hovering over the link snaps from the first state (no red line) to the second (red line); it's an on/off affair. However, this line:

```
transition: box-shadow 1s;
```

adds a transition to the `box-shadow` from the existing state to the `hover` state over 1 second.

 You'll notice in the CSS of the preceding example we're using the adjacent sibling selector +. You'll remember this selector from *Chapter 6, CSS Selectors, Typography, Color Modes, and More.* This means if an element (an anchor tag in our example) directly follows another element (another anchor tag), then apply the enclosed styles. It's useful here as we don't want a left border on the first element.

The `transition` property is applied on the "from" state, not the "to" state of a selector. In our case, we add the `transition` property and values on the element in its default state, not the `hover` state. You could add a `transition` property to the `hover` state too, but this would apply when you transition away from the `hover` state and back to default. This implementation is so that multiple different states such as `:active`, `:focus`, `:hover`, and more can also have different styles set and enjoy the same transition to them.

The properties of a transition

A transition can be declared using up to four properties:

- `transition-property`: The name of the CSS property to be transitioned (such as `background-color`, `text-shadow`, or `all` to transition every possible property).

- `transition-duration`: The length of time over which the transition should occur (defined in seconds, for example, `.3s`, `2s`, or `1.5s`).

- `transition-timing-function`: How the transition changes speed during the duration (for example, `ease`, `linear`, `ease-in`, `ease-out`, or `cubic-bezier`).

- `transition-delay`: An optional value to determine a delay before the transition commences. Alternatively, a negative value can be used to commence a transition immediately but part way through its transition "journey." It's defined in seconds, for example, `.3s`, `1s`, or `2.5s`.

 For any duration defined in seconds with s in CSS, you can also define in milliseconds, if you prefer. For example, instead of `0.5s` for half a second, you could write `500ms`. It's purely a preference thing but for predictability, I would advise you choose one or the other and stick to it throughout a project.

Used separately, the various transition properties can be used to create a transition like this:

```css
.style {
  /*...(more styles)...*/
  transition-property: all;
  transition-duration: 1s;
  transition-timing-function: ease;
  transition-delay: 0s;
}
```

The transition shorthand property

We can roll these individual declarations into a single, shorthand version:

```css
transition: all 1s ease 0s;
```

One important point to note when writing the shorthand version is that the first time-related value provided is always parsed to be the `transition-duration`. The second time-related value is parsed to be the `transition-delay`. The shorthand version is the one I favor, as I generally only need to define the duration of the transition and the properties that should be transitioned.

Furthermore, the shorthand syntax is much easier to write as you can get away with only providing the property you want to transition and the duration it should transition over. To exemplify, suppose I wanted the `background-color` to transition over 2 seconds:

```
transition: background-color 2s;
```

If no timing function is provided, the default timing function of `ease` is applied.

I would also advise only defining the property or properties you actually need to transition. It's really handy to just set `all`, but if you only need to transition `opacity`, then only define `opacity` as the transition property. Otherwise, you're making the browser work harder than necessary. In most cases, this isn't a big deal, but if you're hoping to have the best performing site possible, even on lower powered devices, then every little helps.

Transitioning different properties over different periods of time

Where a rule has multiple properties declared, you don't have to transition all of them in the same way. Consider this rule:

```
.style {
  /* ...(more styles)... */
  transition-property: border, color, text-shadow;
  transition-duration: 2s, 3s, 8s;
}
```

Here, we have specified with `transition-property` that we'd like to transition the `border`, `color`, and `text-shadow`. Then, with the `transition-duration` declaration, we are stating that the `border` should transition over 2 seconds, the `color` over 3 seconds, and the `text-shadow` over 8 seconds. The comma-separated durations match the comma-separated order of the transition properties.

You can also perform the same job with the shorthand syntax, and again this is my preferred way to do it:

```
.style {
    transition: border 2s, color 3s, text-shadow 8s;
}
```

I think it is far easier to reason about each property and its timing when they are written next to each other.

So far, we have dealt with transitioning different properties over different durations. However, there is also a fairly limitless number of timing functions that change how an element property changes over a duration.

Understanding timing functions

When you declare a `transition`, the properties, durations, and delays are relatively simple to understand. However, understanding what each timing function does can be a little trickier. Just what do `ease`, `linear`, `ease-in`, `ease-out`, `ease-in-out`, and `cubic-bezier` actually do? Each of them is actually a predefined `cubic-bezier` curve, essentially the same as an easing function. Or, more simplistically, a mathematical description of how the transition should look. It's generally easier to visualize these curves, so I recommend you head over to http://cubic-bezier.com/ or http://easings.net.

Both these sites let you compare timing functions and see the difference each one makes. Here is a screenshot of `http://easings.net` — on the website you can hover over each line for a demonstration of the easing function:

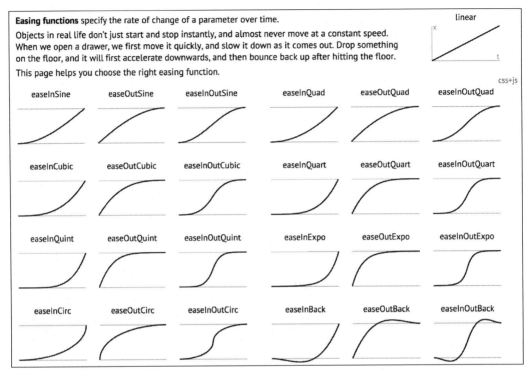

Figure 9.3: Easings.net provides a handy visualization of a number of different timing functions

However, even if you can write your own `cubic-bezier` curves blindfolded, the likelihood is, for most practical situations, it makes little difference. The reason for this is that like any enhancement, it's necessary to employ transition effects subtly. For "real-world" implementations, transitions that occur over too great a period of time tend to make a site feel slow. For example, navigation links that take 5 seconds to transition are going to frustrate rather than wow your users. The perception of speed is incredibly important for our users, and you and I must concentrate on making websites and applications feel as fast as possible.

Therefore, unless there is a compelling reason to do so, using the default transition (`ease`) over a short interval is often best; a maximum of 1 second is my own preference.

Fun transitions for responsive websites

Did you ever have one of those occasions growing up when one parent was out for the day and the other parent said something to the effect of, "OK, while your mom/dad is out, we're going to put sugar all over your breakfast cereal, but you have to promise not to tell them when they come back." I'm certainly guilty of that with my little ankle biters. So, here's the thing. While no one is looking, let's have a bit of fun. I don't recommend this for production, but try adding this to your responsive project:

```
* {
    transition: all 1s;
}
```

Here, we are using the CSS universal selector * to select everything and then setting a transition on all properties for 1 second (1s). As we have omitted to specify the timing function, ease will be used by default and there will be no delay as, again, a default of 0 is assumed if an alternative value is not added. The effect? Well, try resizing your browser window and most things (links, hover states, and the like) behave as you would expect. However, because everything transitions, it also includes any rules within media queries, so as the browser window is resized, elements sort of flow from one state to the next. Is it essential? Absolutely not! Is it fun to watch and play around with? Certainly! Now, remove that rule before your mom sees it!

Right, hopefully, we have transitions licked. Now, we can have some fun because we are going to learn how to effortlessly move elements around the screen with transforms. There are 2D and 3D variants; we will start with 2D and if that gets a bit flat (see what I did there? No? I'll see myself out) then we will move on to 3D.

CSS 2D transforms

Despite sounding similar to CSS transitions, CSS transforms are entirely different. As we already established, transitions deal with the transition from one state to another. Transforms, on the other hand, are a means of defining what the state should actually be.

My own (admittedly childish) way of remembering the difference is like this: Imagine a Transformer robot like Optimus Prime. When he has changed into a truck, he has transformed. However, the period between robot and truck is a transition (he's transitioning from one state to another). Obviously, if you have no idea who or what Optimus Prime even is, feel free to mentally discard the last few sentences. Hopefully, all will become clear when we get to the examples in a moment.

There are two groups of CSS transforms available: 2D and 3D. 2D variants are probably a little more straightforward, so let's look at those first. The CSS 2D Transforms Module allows us to use the following transforms:

- `scale`: Scale an element (larger or smaller)
- `translate`: Move an element on the screen (up, down, left, and right)
- `rotate`: Rotate the element by a specified amount (defined in degrees or turns)
- `skew`: Skew an element with its X and Y coordinates
- `matrix`: Allows you to move and shape transformations in multiple ways

An essential concept to understand is that transforms occur outside of the document flow. More simply, any element that is transformed will not affect the position of any other element that is not a child of it. This is quite different to adding a transition to an element when you change the margin, height, or other transitionable/animatable property.

Open `example_09-09` and you will see two sentences; the first has `margin-left: 10px` applied to the bold word "item" on hover, while the second sentence has `transform: translateX(10px)` applied to the same word on hover. Both have a transition of 1 second applied.

With nothing hovered over, they look like this:

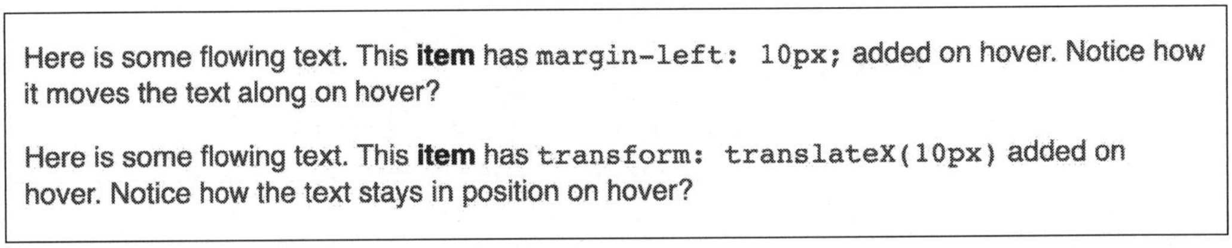

Here is some flowing text. This **item** has `margin-left: 10px;` added on hover. Notice how it moves the text along on hover?

Here is some flowing text. This **item** has `transform: translateX(10px)` added on hover. Notice how the text stays in position on hover?

Figure 9.4: Two paragraphs in their default state

Hover over "item" in the first paragraph and the following happens; notice the text after that word has been shunted along?

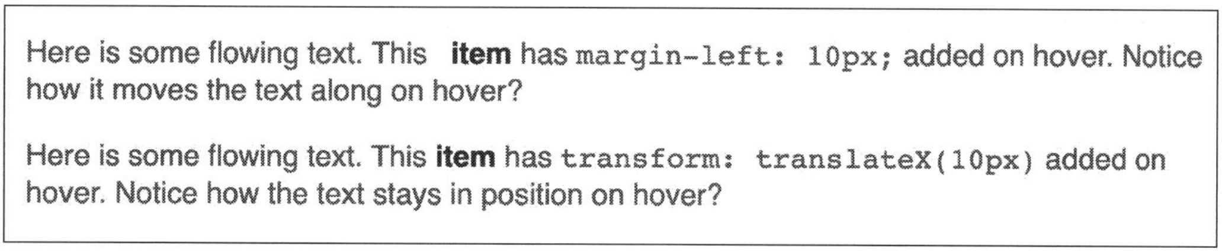

Here is some flowing text. This item has margin-left: 10px; added on hover. Notice how it moves the text along on hover?
Here is some flowing text. This item has transform: translateX(10px) added on hover. Notice how the text stays in position on hover?

Figure 9.5: When the first paragraph is hovered over, "item" gets a margin applied, moving all the text after it too

Now, hover over "item" in the second paragraph and notice how just that word moves? The words around it are unaffected.

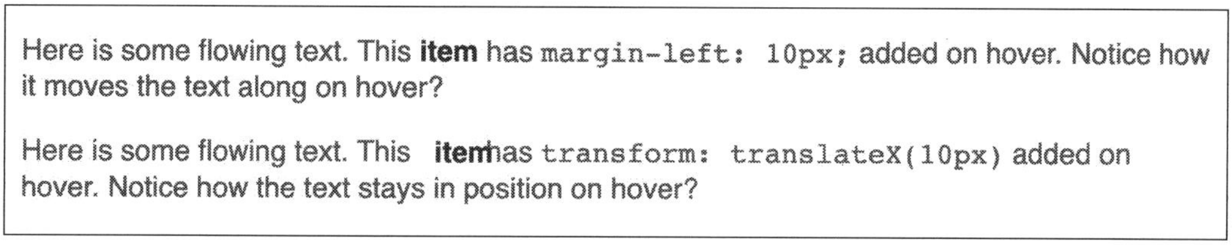

Here is some flowing text. This item has margin-left: 10px; added on hover. Notice how it moves the text along on hover?
Here is some flowing text. This itemhas transform: translateX(10px) added on hover. Notice how the text stays in position on hover?

Figure 9.6: In the second paragraph, "item" is transformed, moving to the right without affecting anything else

So, transforms, either 2D or 3D, do not affect document flow.

Let's try out the various 2D transitions. You can test each of these out by opening `example_09-02` in the browser. There's a transition applied to all of the transforms so that you get a better idea of what's happening.

Scale

Here's the syntax for `scale`:

```
.scale:hover {
  transform: scale(1.4);
}
```

Hovering over the "scale" link in our example produces this effect:

scale(1.4)
ranslate(-20px, -20px)
rotate(30deg)

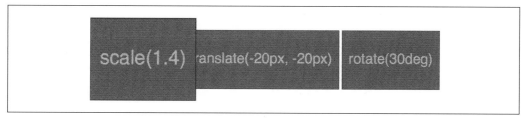

Figure 9.7: You can scale elements up or down in size

We've told the browser that when this element is hovered over, we want the element to scale to 1.4 times its original value.

Besides the values we've already used to enlarge elements, by using values below 1, we can shrink elements; the following will shrink the element to half its size:

```
transform: scale(0.5);
```

Translate

Here's the syntax for `translate`:

```
.translate:hover {
  transform: translate(-20px, -20px);
}
```

Here's the effect that rule has in our example:

Figure 9.8: Translate lets you move an element anywhere in the *x* or *y* axis

The `translate` property tells the browser to move an element by an amount, defined by a length (for example, vw, px, %, and so on). The first value is the *x* axis and the second value is the *y* axis. Positive values given within parentheses move the element right or down; negative values move it left or up. If you only pass one value, then it is applied to the *x* axis.

If you want to specify just one axis to translate an element, you can also use `translateX(-20px)`, which, in this instance, would move the element left 20px, or you could use `translateY(-20px)`, which, in this case, would move the element 20px up.

Using translate to center absolutely positioned elements

`translate` provides a really useful way to center absolutely positioned elements within a relatively positioned container. You can view this example at `example_09-03`.

Consider this markup:

```
<div class="outer">
  <div class="inner"></div>
</div>
```

And then this CSS:

```
.outer {
  position: relative;
  height: 400px;
  background-color: #f90;
}

.inner {
  position: absolute;
  height: 200px;
  width: 200px;
  margin-top: -100px;
  margin-left: -100px;
  top: 50%;
  left: 50%;
}
```

You've perhaps done something similar to this yourself. When the dimensions of the absolutely positioned element are known (200px × 200px in this case), we can use negative margins to "pull" the item back to the center. However, what happens when you want to include content and have no way of knowing how tall it will be?

For example, let's add some random content to the inner box:

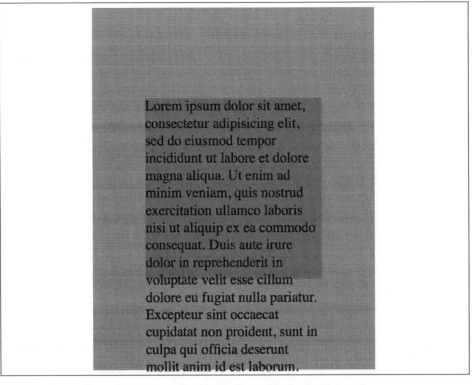

Figure 9.9: Text overflowing our box can be fixed with transform

Yes, that problem! Right, let's use `transform` to sort this mess out:

```
.inner {
  position: absolute;
  width: 200px;
  background-color: #999;
  top: 50%;
  left: 50%;
  transform: translate(-50%, -50%);
}
```

And here is the result:

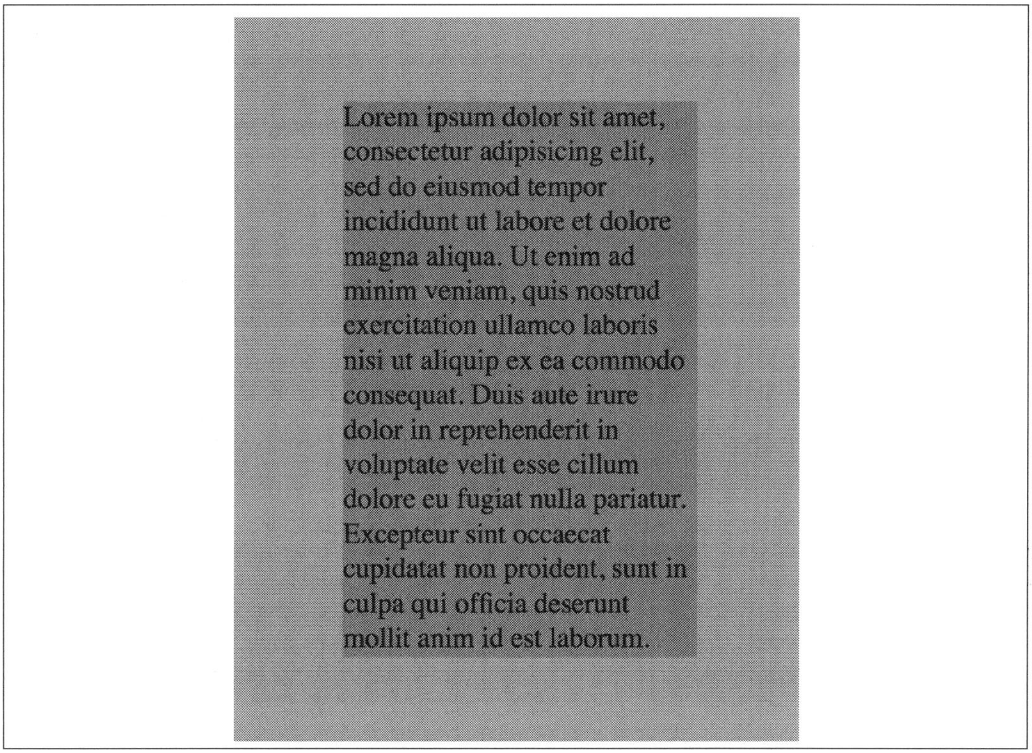

Figure 9.10: With a smart application of transform, overflow issues are avoided

Here, `top` and `left` are positioning the inner box inside its container so that the top left corner of the inner box starts at a point 50% along and 50% down the outer box. Then, `transform` is working on the inner element and positioning it negatively in those axes by half (-50%) of its own width and height. Nice!

Rotate

The `rotate` transform allows you to rotate an element. Here's the syntax:

```
.rotate:hover {
  transform: rotate(30deg);
}
```

In the browser, here's what happens:

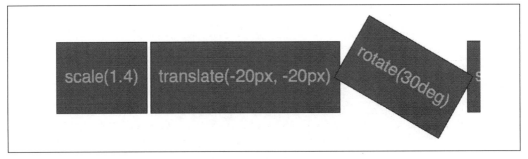

Figure 9.11: Rotating elements is straightforward with a transform

The value in parentheses should always be an angle. The angle can be expressed in degrees, gradians, radians, or turns. Personally, I default to using degrees (for example, 90deg), but all units are equally valid. While positive angle values always apply clockwise, using negative values will rotate the element counter-clockwise.

Pass an angle greater than a full revolution and the element will keep turning until it has turned around to the required degree. Therefore, you can also go crazy and make elements spin by specifying a value like the following:

```
transform: rotate(3600deg);
```

This will rotate the element 10 times in a complete circle. Practical uses for this particular value are few and far between but you know, if you ever find yourself designing websites for a windmill company, it may come in handy.

Skew

If you've spent any time working in Photoshop, you'll have a good idea what skew will do. It allows an element to be skewed on either or both of its axes. Here's the code for our example:

```
.skew:hover {
  transform: skew(40deg, 12deg);
}
```

Setting this on the hover state produces the following effect on hover:

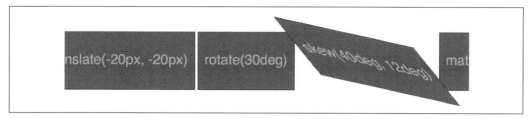

Figure 9.12: Just like it sounds, a skew can produce some dramatic effects

The first value is the `skew` applied to the *x* axis (in our example, `40deg`), while the second (`12deg`) is for the *y* axis. Omitting the second value means any value will merely be applied to the *x* axis (horizontal). For example:

```
transform: skew(10deg);
```

Just like with `translate`, you can apply skews to just one axis with `skewX()` and `skewY()`.

Matrix

Did somebody mention a completely overrated film? No? What's that? You want to know about the CSS `matrix`, not the film? Oh, okay.

The `matrix` transform syntax looks rather impenetrable. Here's our example code:

```
.matrix:hover {
    transform: matrix(1.178, -0.256, 1.122, 1.333, -41.533, -1.989);
}
```

It essentially allows you to combine a number of other transforms (`scale`, `rotate`, `skew`, and so on) into a single declaration. The preceding declaration results in the following effect in the browser:

Figure 9.13: Not for the faint-hearted, the matrix value

If you find yourself doing work with animations in JavaScript without the help of an animation library, you'll probably need to become a little more acquainted with `matrix`. It's the syntax all the other transforms get computed into behind the scenes, so if you're grabbing the current state of an animation with JavaScript, it will be the `matrix` value you will need to inspect and understand.

Now, I like a challenge (unless, you know, it's sitting through the Twilight films), but I think the majority of us would agree that syntax is a bit testing. The specification doesn't exactly clear matters up: `https://www.w3.org/TR/css-transforms-1/#mathematical-description`.

However, the truth is I can count on the fingers of one hand how many times I've needed to write or understand a CSS transform described as a `matrix`, so it likely isn't something to concern yourself with.

If you do find yourself needing to create one, I'd suggest heading over to `http://www.useragentman.com/matrix/`.

The Matrix Construction Set website allows you to drag and drop the element exactly where you want it and includes good ol' copy and paste code for your CSS file.

Transform-origin property

Notice how, with CSS, the default transform origin – the point at which the browser uses as the center for the transform – is in the middle: 50% along the x axis and 50% along the y axis of the element. This differs from SVG, which defaults to the top left (or 0 0).

Using the `transform-origin` property, we can amend the point from which transforms originate.

Consider our earlier `matrix` transform. The default `transform-origin` is `50% 50%` (the center of the element). The Firefox developer tools show how the transform is applied:

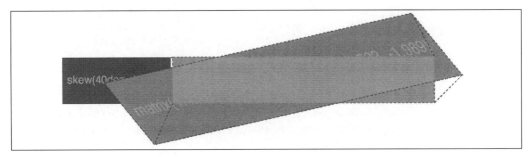

Figure 9.14: Default transform-origin applied

Now, if we adjust the `transform-origin` like this:

```
.matrix:hover {
  transform: matrix(1.678, -0.256, 1.522, 2.333, -51.533, -1.989);
  transform-origin: 270px 20px;
}
```

Then you can see the effect this has:

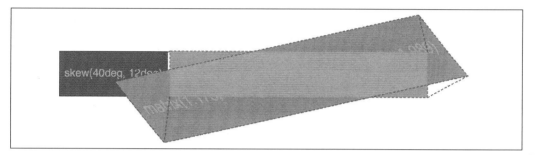

Figure 9.15: You can amend the origin of transforms as needed

The first value is the horizontal offset and the second value is the vertical offset. You can use keywords. For example, `left` is equal to 0% horizontal, `right` is equal to 100% horizontal, `top` is equal to 0% vertical, and `bottom` is equal to 100% vertical. Alternatively, you can use a length, using any of the CSS length units.

If you use a percentage for the `transform-origin` values, then the horizontal/vertical offset is relative to the height/width of the elements bounding box.

If you use a length, then the values are measured from the top left corner of the element's bounding box.

The specification for CSS Transforms Module Level 1 can be found here: `https://www.w3.org/TR/css-transforms-1`.

For more on the benefits of moving elements with transform, read this old but great post by Paul Irish, `http://www.paulirish.com/2012/why-moving-elements-with-translate-is-better-than-posabs-topleft/`, which provides some good data.

And, for a fantastic overview of how browsers actually deal with transitions and animations, and why transforms can be so effective, I highly recommend the following blog post: `http://blogs.adobe.com/webplatform/2014/03/18/css-animations-and-transitions-performance/`.

So far, we have dealt with transforming in two dimensions, the *x* and *y* axis. However, CSS can also handle elements in 3D space. Let's look at what extra fun we can have with 3D transforms.

CSS 3D transformations

As you've probably already realized, a 3D transform allows us to manipulate an element in an imaginary 3D space. Let's look at our first example. All we have in our example are two elements that each flip in 3D when hovered over. I've used `hover` here to invoke the flip as it's simple for the sake of illustration. However, the flipping action could just as easily be initiated with any other state change — a class change (via JavaScript) or when an element has received focus, for example.

The only difference between these two elements is that one flips horizontally and the other vertically. You can view them in a browser by opening `example_09-04`. Images fail to fully convey this technique, but the idea is that the element flips from the green "face" to the red "face," giving the illusion of doing so through 3D space with the aid of perspective. Here's a grab partway through the transition from green to red, which hopefully conveys some of the effect:

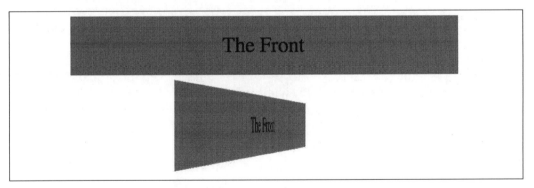

Figure 9.16: Halfway through a 3D transform

 It's also worth knowing that while positioning an element absolutely with top/left/bottom/right values can only be calculated to whole pixels, a transform can interpolate at subpixel positions.

Here's the markup for the flipping element:

```
<div class="flipper">
  <span class="flipper-object flipper-vertical">
    <span class="panel front">The Front</span>
```

```
      <span class="panel back">The Back</span>
    </span>
  </div>
```

The only difference with the horizontal one, markup wise, is the `flipper-vertical` class is replaced with `flipper-horizontal`.

As the majority of the styles relate to aesthetics, we'll merely look at the essential ingredients in our styles to make the flipping effect possible. Refer to the full style sheet in the example for the aesthetic styles.

When dealing with 3D transforms, the first essential ingredient required is to define some kind of 3D space.

For our example, we need to set some perspective for `.flipper-object`, whether horizontal or vertical, to flip within. For that, we use the `perspective` property. This takes a length value, attempting to simulate the distance from the viewer's screen to the edge of the elements' 3D space. We set this on the outer-most element to provide the 3D context for our nested elements to move within.

The value you assign to `perspective` is arguably counter-intuitive — if you set a low number like 20px for the perspective value, the 3D space of the element will extend right out to only 20px from your screen; the result being a more pronounced 3D effect.

Setting a high number, on the other hand, will mean the edge of that imaginary 3D space will be further away, and therefore produce a less pronounced 3D effect. I recommend opening the example in the browser and playing with the perspective in the developer tools to get a feel for it:

```
.flipper {
  perspective: 400px;
  position: relative;
}
```

We use `position: relative` on the outer `flipper` element to provide a positioning context for `flipper-object` to be absolutely positioned within:

```
.flipper-object {
  position: absolute;
  width: 100%;
  height: 100%;
  transition: transform 1s;
  transform-style: preserve-3d;
}
```

Besides positioning `.flipper-object` absolutely, we set the `height` and `width` to `100%` so that it fills the same space as the outer container. We have also set a transition for the transform. If you remember from earlier in this chapter, when we dealt with transitions, you will know that by just setting the time for transition, the default timing function will be used.

The key thing here, 3D wise, is `transform-style: preserve-3d`. This declaration tells the browser that when we transform this element, we want any child elements to preserve any 3D effect.

If we didn't set `preserve-3d` on `.flipper-object`, we would never get to see the back (the red part) of the flipping element.

 You can read the specification for this property here: `http://www.w3.org/TR/2009/WD-css3-3d-transforms-20090320/#transform-style-property`.

Each "panel" in our flipping element needs positioning at the top of its container, but we also want to make sure that, if rotated, we don't see the "rear" of it (otherwise we would never see the green panel as it sits "behind" the red one). To do that, we use the `backface-visibility` property. We set this to `hidden` so that the back face of the element is, you guessed it, hidden:

```
.panel {
  top: 0;
  position: absolute;
  backface-visibility: hidden;
}
```

Next, we want to make our back panel flipped by default (so that when we flip the whole thing, it will actually be in the correct position). To do that, we apply a `rotate` transform. Hopefully, having covered these in the previous section, you'll understand what they are doing here:

```
.flipper-vertical .back {
  transform: rotateX(180deg);
}


.flipper-horizontal .back {
  transform: rotateY(180deg);
}
```

Now that everything is in place, all we want to do is flip the entire inner element when the outer one is hovered over:

```
.flipper:hover .flipper-vertical {
  transform: rotateX(180deg);
}


.flipper:hover .flipper-horizontal {
  transform: rotateY(180deg);
}
```

As you can imagine, there are a bazillion (by the way, bazillion is definitely not a real amount, I just checked) ways you can use these techniques. If you're wondering what a fancy navigation effect, or off-canvas menu, might look like with a spot of perspective, I highly recommend paying Codrops a visit: `http://tympanus.net/Development/PerspectivePageViewNavigation/index.html`.

 You can read the W3C specification for the CSS Transforms Module Level 1 at `https://www.w3.org/TR/css-transforms-1/`.

It turns out there is a very handy property when working with transforms that can do all your *x*, *y*, and *z* movement in one go. Let's take a look at that next.

The translate3d property

I've found great utility in the `translate3d` function. With this single function, it is possible to move an element in the *x* (left/right), *y* (up/down), and *z* (forward/backward) axes.

Let's amend our previous example and make use of the `translate3d()` function. You can view this example at `example_09-06`.

Besides setting the elements into the page a little more with padding, the only changes from our previous example can be seen here:

```
.flipper:hover .flipper-vertical {
  transform: rotateX(180deg) translate3d(0, 0, -120px);
  animation: pulse 1s 1s infinite alternate both;
}


.flipper:hover .flipper-horizontal {
```

```
    transform: rotateY(180deg) translate3d(0, 0, 120px);
    animation: pulse 1s 1s infinite alternate both;
}
```

We're still applying a transform, but this time, in addition to our rotate, we have also made use of `translate3d()`. The syntax for the comma-separated "arguments" you can pass into `translate3d` are *x* axis movement, *y* axis movement, and *z* axis movement.

In our two examples, I'm not moving the element in the *x* or *y* axis (left to right, and up and down); instead, I'm moving toward or further away from you as you look at it.

If you look at the top example, you will see it flip behind the bottom button and end 120px closer to the screen (minus values effectively pull it back toward you):

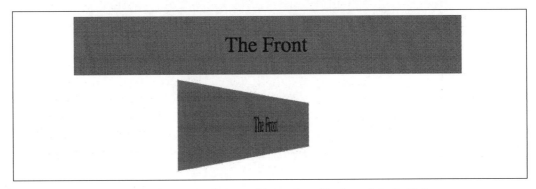

Figure 9.17: Elements can be moved forwards and backwards in the Z plane

On the other hand, the bottom button flips around horizontally and ends with the button 120px further away from you:

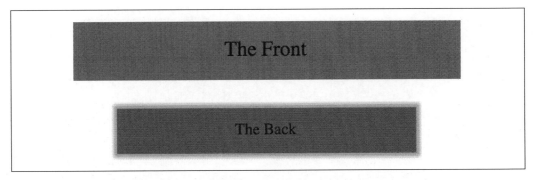

Figure 9.18: Here, the element ends "further away"

Although `translate3d()` is very well supported, it's now part of the CSS Transforms Module Level 2 specification. You can read that here: `https://drafts.csswg.org/css-transforms-2/#three-d-transform-functions`.

A progressive enhancement example using translate3d

An area I have found great utility with `translate3d` is in sliding panels on and off the screen, particularly "off-canvas" navigation patterns. If you open `example_09-07`, you'll see I have created a basic, progressively enhanced, off-canvas pattern.

Whenever you create interaction with JavaScript and modern CSS features like transforms, it makes sense to consider things from the lowest possible device you want to support. What about the two people that don't have JavaScript (yes, those guys), or if there is a problem with the JavaScript loading or executing? What if somebody's device doesn't support `translate3d()`? Don't worry. It's possible, with a little effort, to ensure a working interface for every eventuality.

When building these kinds of interface patterns, I find it most useful to start with the lowest set of features and enhance from there. First, establish what someone sees if they don't have JavaScript available. After all, it's no use parking a menu off-screen when JavaScript isn't available, if the method for displaying the menu relies upon JavaScript. Instead, in this case, we are relying upon markup to place the navigation area in the normal document flow. Worst case, whatever the viewport width, they can merely scroll down the page and click a link:

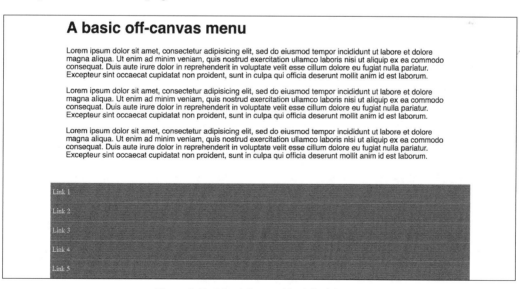

Figure 9.19: A basic but usable default layout

If JavaScript is available, for smaller screens, we "pull" the menu off to the left. When the menu button is clicked, we add a class onto the `body` tag (with JavaScript) and use this class as a hook to move the navigation back into view with CSS:

Figure 9.20: With a click, we slide over our menu

For larger viewports, we hide the menu button and merely position the navigation to the left and move the main content over to accommodate this:

Figure 9.21: Where screen size allows, we can show the menu by default

So, that's the no-JavaScript eventuality handled. Now, what about the situation where a device can't handle `translate3d`?

First, for browsers that only support 2D `translate` transforms (very old Android phones, for example), we can use a simple `translateX`. Here is the relevant part of the code:

```
@supports (transform: translateX(-200px)) {
  .js .navigation-menu {
    left: auto;
    transform: translateX(-200px);
  }
  /*when transforms are supported and the menu button is clicked,
reset the nav to default position*/
  .js .OffCanvas-Active .navigation-menu {
    transform: translateX(0);
  }
}
```

For browsers that support `translate3d`, we use `translate3d` instead. This will provide the best visual performance, where supported, as it's a process typically offloaded to the graphics processor, which excels at such tasks:

```
@supports (transform: translate3d(-200px, 0, 0)) {
  /*where transform3d is supported reset left and pull off screen
with a translate3d instead*/
  .js .navigation-menu {
    left: auto;
    transform: translate3d(-200px, 0, 0);
  }
  /*when transform3d is supported and the menu button is clicked,
reset the nav to default position*/
  .js .OffCanvas-Active .navigation-menu {
    transform: translate3d(0, 0, 0);
  }
}
```

If you open the example in the browser, you can simulate the different eventualities with the developer tools by changing the `js` class on the `html` element to `no-js` to see how it would look without JavaScript. Also, you can change the CSS `@supports` rules related to `translate3d()` in the CSS to something no browser supports, such as `@supports (scones: delicious)`.

This is a simplified example, but hopefully it's apparent that embracing a progressive enhancement approach ensures the widest possible audience will get a workable experience from your design. Remember, your users don't need visual parity, but they might appreciate functional parity.

Animating with CSS

If you've worked with applications like Final Cut Pro or After Effects, you'll have an instant advantage when working with CSS animations. CSS employs animation keyframing conventions found in timeline-based applications.

If you have never worked with keyframes or even come across the term, here is all you need to know. When you are devising an animation, you will choose key moments where things need to be in a certain position. Imagine a bouncing ball. At first, it is in the air, which would be one "keyframe," and then it is on the floor, another keyframe. When you specify keyframes, the animation knows how to fill in the blanks between them and create the animation.

There are two components to a CSS animation; first, writing a set of keyframes inside an `@keyframes` "at-rule" declaration and then employing that keyframe animation with the `animation` property and associated values. Let's take a look.

In a previous example, we made a simple flip effect on elements that combined transforms and transitions. Let's bring together all the techniques we have learned in this chapter and add an animation to the previous example. In the following example, `example_09-05`, let's add a pulsing animation effect around our element once it has flipped.

Firstly, we will create a keyframes at-rule:

```
@keyframes pulse {
  100% {
    text-shadow: 0 0 5px #bbb;
    box-shadow: 0 0 3px 4px #bbb;
  }
}
```

As you can see, after writing `@keyframes` to define a new keyframes at-rule, we name this particular animation (`pulse`, in this instance). The `@keyframes` at-rule describes what you want to happen for each cycle of your animation loop.

It's generally best to use a name that represents what the animation does, not where you intend to use the animation, as a single `@keyframes` rule can be used as many times as you need throughout a project.

We have used a single "keyframe selector" here: 100%. However, you can set as many keyframe selectors (defined as percentage points) as you like within a @ keyframes at-rule. Think of these as points along a timeline. For example, at 10%, make the background blue, at 30%, make the background purple, at 60%, make the element semi-opaque. On and on as you need.

There is also the keyword from, which is equivalent to 0% and to, which is equivalent to 100%. You can use the keywords like this:

```
@keyframes pulse {
  to {
    text-shadow: 0 0 5px #bbb;
    box-shadow: 0 0 3px 4px #bbb;
  }
}
```

However, WebKit browsers (iOS, Safari) don't always play happily with from and to values (preferring 0% and 100%), so I'd recommend sticking with percentage keyframe selectors.

You'll notice here that we haven't bothered to define a starting point. That's because the starting point is the state each of those properties is already at. Here's the part of the specification that explains that (http://www.w3.org/TR/css3-animations/#keyframes):

"If a 0% or from keyframe is not specified, then the user agent constructs a 0% keyframe using the computed values of the properties being animated. If a 100% or to keyframe is not specified, then the user agent constructs a 100% keyframe using the computed values of the properties being animated."

In this @keyframes at-rule, we've added a text-shadow and box-shadow at 100%. We can then expect the keyframes, when applied to an element, to animate the text shadow and box shadow to the defined amount. But how long does the animation last? How do we make it repeat, reverse, and more? This is how we actually apply a keyframes animation to an element:

```
.flipper:hover .flipper-horizontal {
  transform: rotateY(180deg);
  animation: pulse 1s 1s infinite alternate both;
}
```

The `animation` property here is a shorthand for several animation-related properties. In this example, we are declaring (in order):

1. The name of the keyframes declaration to use (`pulse`);

2. The `animation-duration` (1 second);

3. The `animation-delay` before the animation begins (1 second, to allow time for our button to first flip);

4. The number of times the animation will run (infinitely);

5. The direction of the animation (`alternate`, so it animates first one way and then back the other); and

6. That we want the `animation-fill-mode` to retain the values that are defined in the keyframes, whether going forward or backward (both).

The shorthand property can actually accept all seven animation properties. In addition to those used in the preceding example, it's also possible to specify `animation-play-state`. This can be set to `running` or `paused` to effectively play and pause an animation. Of course, you don't need to use the shorthand property; sometimes, it can make more sense (and help when you revisit the code in the future) to set each property separately. The following are the individual properties and example values. Where appropriate, alternate values have been listed with a comment:

```css
.animation-properties {
  animation-name: warning;
  animation-duration: 1.5s;
  animation-timing-function: ease-in-out;
  animation-iteration-count: infinite;
  animation-play-state: running; /* could also be 'paused' */
  animation-delay: 0s;
  animation-fill-mode: none; /* could also be 'forwards', 'backwards'
or 'both' */
  animation-direction: normal; /* could also be set to 'reverse',
'alternate' or 'alternate-reverse' */
}
```

You can read the full definition for each of these animation properties in the CSS Animations Level 1 specification at `https://www.w3.org/TR/css-animations-1/`.

> You can run multiple animations on an element with the shorthand property by comma separating them. For example: `animation: animOne 1s alternate both, animTwo 0.3s forwards`.

As mentioned previously, it's simple to reuse a declared `keyframes` on other elements and with completely different settings:

```
.flipper:hover .flipper-vertical {
  transform: rotateX(180deg);
  animation: pulse 2s 1s cubic-bezier(0.68, -0.55, 0.265, 1.55) 5
alternate both;
}
```

Here, the pulse animation would run over 2 seconds and uses an `ease-in-out-back` timing function (defined as a `cubic-bezier` curve). It runs five times in both directions. This declaration has been applied to the vertically flipping element in the example file.

The animation-fill-mode property

The `animation-fill-mode` is worthy of a special mention. Consider an animation that starts with a yellow background and animates to a red background over 3 seconds. You can view this in `example_09-08`.

We apply the animation like this:

```
.background-change {
  animation: fillBg 3s;
  height: 200px;
  width: 400px;
  border: 1px solid #ccc;
}

@keyframes fillBg {
  0% {
    background-color: yellow;
  }
  100% {
    background-color: red;
  }
}
```

However, once the animation completes, the background of the `div` will return to nothing. That's because, by default, when an animation ends, the element goes back to exactly how it was before the animation ran. In order to override this behavior, we have the `animation-fill-mode` property. In this instance, we could apply this:

```
animation-fill-mode: forwards;
```

This makes the item retain any values that have been applied by the animation end. In our case, the div would retain the red background color that the animation ended on. More on the `animation-fill-mode` property here: `https://www.w3.org/TR/css-animations-1/#animation-fill-mode`.

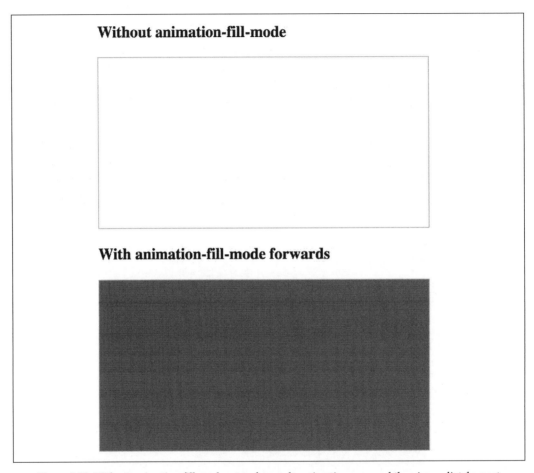

Figure 9.22: Without animation-fill-mode set to forwards, animations run and then immediately reset

Exercises and training

At this point, you might find it useful to find a site using transitions, transforms, and animations and try playing with the settings in the developer tools. Inspect any moving elements and then tweak the relevant values and properties. Can you send elements in the opposite direction? Can you make transitions take longer or shorter? Are there any 2D transforms you can amend to use the `transform3d()` function?

You can make a start on `https://rwd.education` — I won't mind!

Summary

It would be entirely possible to fill multiple books covering the possibilities of CSS transforms, transitions, and animations. Hopefully, by dipping your toe in the water with this chapter, you've been able to pick up the basics and run with them.

In this chapter, we've learned what CSS transitions are and how to write them. We got a handle on timing functions like `ease` and `linear`, and then used them to create simple but fun effects. We then learned all about 2D transforms like `scale` and `skew`, and then how to use them in tandem with transitions. We also looked briefly at 3D transformations before learning all about the power and relative simplicity of CSS animations. You'd better believe our CSS muscles are growing!

However, if there's one area of site design that I always avoid where possible, it's making forms. I don't know why; I've just always found making them a tedious and largely frustrating task. Imagine my joy when I learned that HTML5 and CSS can make the whole form building, styling, and even validating (yes, validating!) process easier than ever before. I was quite joyous. As joyous as you can be about building web forms, that is. In the next chapter, I'd like to share this knowledge with you.

10
Conquer Forms with HTML5 and CSS

Before HTML5, adding things like date pickers, placeholder text, and range sliders into forms has always needed JavaScript. Similarly, there has been no easy way to help users input the kind of data we expect them to into certain input fields, for example, whether we want users to input telephone numbers, email addresses, or URLs.

The good news is that HTML5 largely solves these common problems.

We have two main aims in this chapter. Firstly, to understand HTML5 form features and secondly, to understand how we can lay out forms more simply for multiple devices with the latest CSS features. In this chapter, we will learn how to:

- Easily add placeholder text into relevant form input fields
- Disable auto-completion of form fields where necessary
- Set certain fields to be required before submission
- Specify different input types such as email, telephone number, and URL
- Create number range sliders for easy value selection
- Place date and color pickers into a form
- Use a regular expression to define an allowed form value
- Style forms using Flexbox
- Change caret color

HTML5 forms

I think the easiest way to get to grips with HTML5 forms is to work our way through an example form. Just like in daytime TV cooking shows, I have one I made earlier! A minor introduction is needed. Two facts: firstly, I love films. Secondly, I'm very opinionated on what is a good film and what is not.

Every year, when the Oscar nominations are announced, I can't help feeling the wrong films have got "the nod" from the Academy. Therefore, we will start with an HTML5 form that enables fellow cinephiles to vent their frustrations at the continual travesties of the Oscar nominations.

It's made up of a few `fieldset` elements, within which we are including a raft of the HTML5 form input types and attributes. Besides standard form input fields and text areas, we have a number spinner, a range slider, and placeholder text for many of the fields.

Here's how it looks with no styles applied in Chrome:

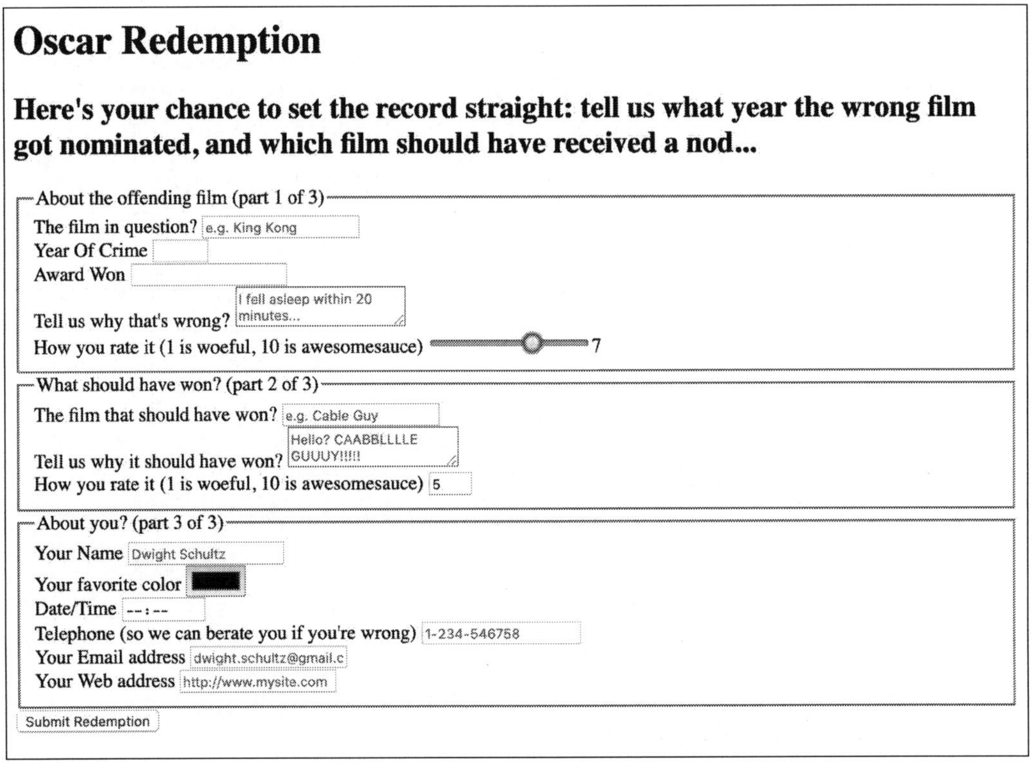

Figure 10.1: A basic form with no styling

If we "focus" on the first field and start inputting text, the placeholder text is removed. If we blur focus without entering anything (by clicking outside of the input box again), the placeholder text reappears. If we submit the form (without entering anything), the following happens:

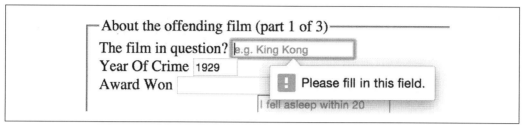

Figure 10.2: A standard browser warning from a required field

The great news is that all these user interface elements, including the aforementioned slider, placeholder text, spinner, and the input validation, are all being handled natively by the browser via HTML5, and no JavaScript. Now, the form validation isn't entirely cross-browser compatible, but we will get to that shortly. First of all, let's get a handle on all the new capabilities of HTML5 that relate to forms and make all this possible. Once we understand all the mechanics, we can get to work styling it up.

Understanding the component parts of HTML5 forms

There's a lot going on in our HTML5 powered form, so let's break it down. The three sections of the form are each wrapped in a fieldset, which semantically groups the related sets of form fields, and a legend, which provides the textual explanation of what that fieldset is:

```
<fieldset>
  <legend>About the offending film (part 1 of 3)</legend>
  <div>
    <label for="film">The film in question?</label>
    <input
      id="film"
      name="film"
      type="text"
      placeholder="e.g. King Kong"
      required
      aria-required="true"
```

```
            />
        </div>
    </fieldset>
```

You can see from the previous code snippet that each `input` element of the form is also wrapped in a `div` with a `label` associated with each `input` (we could have wrapped the `input` with the `label` element if we wanted to too). So far, so normal. However, within this first `input`, we've just stumbled upon our first HTML5 form feature. After the common attributes of `id`, `name`, and `type`, we have `placeholder`.

The placeholder attribute

As the name suggests, the `placeholder` attribute offers a means of providing a hint or some placeholder data to indicate the kind of input we are expecting. An obvious example would be the word "Search" in a search box.

Needing placeholder text within form fields is such a common requirement that the folks creating HTML5 decided it should be a standard feature of HTML. To add placeholder text for an `input`, simply add the `placeholder` attribute. Its value will be displayed in the input until the field gains focus. When it loses focus, if a value has not been entered, it will redisplay the placeholder text.

In our example, the `placeholder` attribute is filled in like this:

```
placeholder="e.g. King Kong"
```

Styling the placeholder text

You can style the `placeholder` attribute with the `:placeholder-shown` pseudo selector:

 You should be aware that this selector has been through a number of iterations, so ensure you have a prefixer tool set up to provide the fallback selectors for older implementations in browsers.

```
input:placeholder-shown {
    color: #333;
}
```

You can also change the text size of the placeholder text; it doesn't need to be the same as the values. As ever, be mindful of accessibility. You don't want to be using a text size below 10px.

When it comes to color accessibility, ensure you use appropriate contrast. If you don't already have a tool to check acceptable contrast levels, I'd recommend bookmarking `https://webaim.org/resources/contrastchecker/`.

Styling the input caret with the caret-color property

Caret, in our context here, refers to the insertion point in an input area. You might think of that typically blinking vertical line as a "cursor," but it is purposely named differently in CSS to make the distinction from other cursors, such as the one produced by mouse input.

By the way, it's generally pronounced like your favorite orange vegetable, "carrot," but depending upon your accent, you might need to alter your pronunciation to "carrit;" such as we have to in the UK, which is fine, as long as the Queen doesn't hear you!

The `caret-color` property is a fairly recent addition to CSS. It allows us to change the color of the input insertion point cursor; the caret.

Suppose we wanted an orange input insert point; we could style it like this:

```
.my-Input {
  caret-color: #f90;
}
```

Sadly, apart from color, we don't get any real control over how the caret appears. We can't change the shape, thickness, or blink rate and style, for example. Hopefully, by the next edition of this book, all that will be possible!

> In case you weren't aware, there is an attribute called `contenteditable` that can make the contents of an everyday element, such as a `div` or `span` editable. You can also make use of `:caret-color` in those situations too.

The required attribute

`required` is a Boolean attribute, with "Boolean" meaning it has only two possibilities. In this case, you either include it or not.

When it is present, like this:

```
<input type="text" value="" placeholder="hal@2001.com" required />
```

It means that adding a value to this input will be required before the form can be submitted.

If the form submission is attempted without the input containing a requisite value, a warning message is displayed. The message itself differs both in content and styling depending upon the browser and the input type used.

We've already seen what the `required` field browser message looks like in Chrome. The following screenshot shows the same message in Firefox:

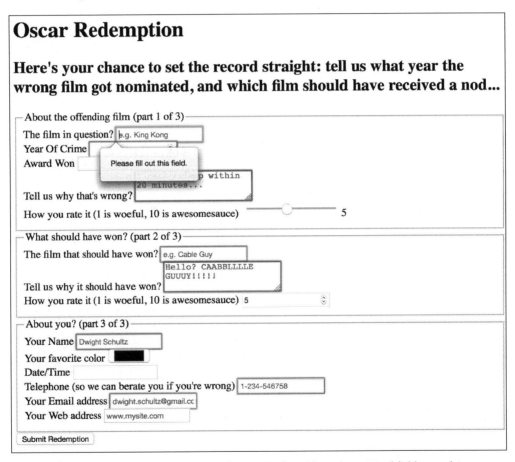

Figure 10.3: Errors when submitting a form in Firefox without the required fields complete

The `required` value can be used alongside many input types to ensure a value is entered. Notable exceptions are the `range`, `color`, `button`, and `hidden` input types as they almost always have a default value.

The autofocus attribute

The HTML5 `autofocus` attribute allows a form to have a field focused, ready for user input, as soon as the page loads. The following code is an example of an input field wrapped in a `div` with the `autofocus` attribute added at the end:

```
<div>
  <label for="search">Search the site...</label>
  <input
    id="search"
    name="search"
    type="search"
    placeholder="Wyatt Earp"
    autofocus
  />
</div>
```

Tread carefully with `autofocus`; it's easy to make a worse experience for users.

For example, it's important that you only add one `autofocus` per page. If multiple fields have `autofocus` added, in Safari, the last field with `autofocus` added is focused on page load. However, Firefox and Chrome do the opposite, with the first autofocused field focused.

It's also worth considering that some users use the space bar to quickly skip down the content of a web page once it's loaded. On a page where a form has an autofocused input field, it prevents this capability; instead, it adds a space to the focused input field. It's easy to see how that could be a source of frustration for users.

In addition, users of assistive technology will be instantly transported to a location on the page they have no control of—not exactly the best user experience!

If using the `autofocus` attribute, be certain it's only used once in a form and be sure you understand the implications.

The autocomplete attribute

By default, most browsers aid user input by autocompleting the value of form fields where possible.

While the user can turn this preference on and off within the browser, we can now also indicate to the browser when we don't want a form or field to allow autocompletion with the `autocomplete` attribute. This is useful not just for sensitive data (bank account numbers, for example) but also if you want to ensure users pay attention and enter something by hand.

For example, for many forms I complete, if a telephone number is required, I enter a "spoof" telephone number. I know I'm not the only one that does that (doesn't everyone?), but I can ensure that users don't enter an autocompleted spoof number by setting the value of the `autocomplete` attribute to `off` on the relevant input field. The following is a code example of a field with the `autocomplete` attribute set to `off`:

```
<div>
   <label for="tel">Telephone (so we can berate you if you're
wrong)</label>
   <input
     id="tel"
     name="tel"
     type="tel"
     placeholder="1-234-546758"
     autocomplete="off"
     required
   />
</div>
```

It's not possible to stop autocomplete on entire fieldsets in one go, but you can stop autocomplete on entire forms. Just add the `autocomplete` attribute to the `form` element itself. Here's an example:

```
<form id="redemption" method="post" autocomplete="off">
  <!-- content -->
</form>
```

The list attribute and the associated datalist element

This `list` attribute and the associated `datalist` element allow a number of selections to be presented to a user once they start entering a value in the field. The following is a code example of the `list` attribute in use with an associated `datalist`, all wrapped in a `div`:

```
<div>
  <label for="awardWon">Award Won</label>
  <input id="awardWon" name="awardWon" type="text" list="awards" />
  <datalist id="awards">
    <select>
      <option value="Best Picture"></option>
      <option value="Best Director"></option>
      <option value="Best Adapted Screenplay"></option>
      <option value="Best Original Screenplay"></option>
    </select>
  </datalist>
</div>
```

`datalist` contains the list of possible values for the `input`. To connect the `datalist` to the `input`, you have to set the value of the `list` attribute on the `input` to the `id` of the `datalist`.

In our example, we have added an `id` of `awards` to the `datalist` element and then set the value of the `list` attribute on the `input` to that.

Although wrapping the options with a `<select>` element isn't strictly necessary, it helps when applying scripts to add comparable functionality for browsers that haven't implemented the feature.

With our `list` and `datalist` wired up, the input field still appears initially to be just a normal text input field. However, when typing in the input, a selection box appears below it with matching results from the `datalist`. In the following screenshot, we can see the `list` in action (Firefox).

In this instance, as "B" is present in all options within the `datalist`, all the values are shown for the user to select from:

Figure 10.4: The datalist element showing the matching possible choices

However, when typing "D" instead, only the matching suggestions appear, as shown in the following screenshot:

Figure 10.5: The datalist narrows based upon input

`list` and `datalist` don't prevent a user entering different text in the input box, but they do provide another great way of adding common functionality and user enhancement through HTML5 markup alone.

Support for `list` and `datalist` was pretty sketchy in the past. Where it isn't supported, the `input` will just behave like a standard input. If you have to support older browsers and need to be sure what they will see, be sure to check the support at `http://caniuse.com/#search=datalist`.

You can read the specification for `datalist` here: `http://www.w3.org/TR/html5/forms.html#the-datalist-element`.

When we started this chapter, I mentioned that there are ways of hinting to the user and, depending on the device, aiding the user in entering the appropriate data for the input at hand. We can do that with HTML5 input types. Let me show you how.

HTML5 input types

HTML5 adds a number of extra `input` types. These have been a great addition because when they are supported, they offer great additional functionality and, when not supported, they still behave like a standard text type input. Let's take a look at them.

The email input type

You can set an `input` to the type of `email` like this:

```
type="email"
```

Supporting browsers will expect a user input that matches the syntax of an email address. In the following code example, `type="email"` is used alongside `required` and `placeholder`:

```
<div>
  <label for="email">Your Email address</label>
  <input
    type="email"
    id="email"
    name="email"
    placeholder="dwight.schultz@gmail.com"
    required
  />
</div>
```

When used in conjunction with `required`, trying to input a non-conforming value will generate a warning message:

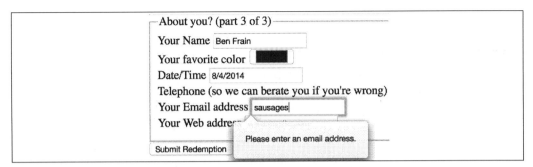

Figure 10.6: An error shows when incorrect data is entered

Perhaps most usefully, most touchscreen devices (Android, iPhone, and so on) change the software keyboard presented to the user based upon this input type. The following screenshot shows how the software keyboard on an iPad is shown when focusing an input with `type="email"`. Notice the "@" symbol has been added for easy email address completion:

Figure 10.7: Software keyboards will often adapt to the input type

The number input type

You can set an input field to expect a number like this:

```
type="number"
```

With the type of input set to `number`, browsers also sometimes add pieces of UI called "spinner" controls. These are tiny pieces of user interface that allow users to easily click up or down to alter the value input.

The following is a code example:

```
<div>
  <label for="yearOfCrime">Year Of Crime</label>
  <input
    id="yearOfCrime"
    name="yearOfCrime"
    type="number"
    min="1929"
    max="2015"
    required
  />
</div>
```

The following screenshot shows how it looks in Chrome, complete with "spinners:"

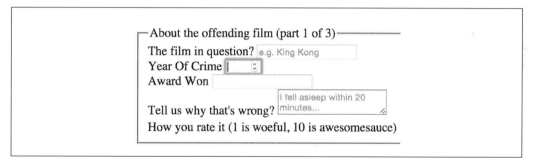

Figure 10.8: On desktop browsers, "spinners" are shown for number inputs

And here is how `type="number"` makes the software keyboard appear on an iPad. Notice how all the numerical keys display by default:

Figure 10.9: Software keyboards default to showing numbers for number inputs

What happens if you don't enter a number that varies between browser implementations? For example, Firefox does nothing until the form is submitted, at which point it displays a warning. Safari, on the other hand, simply does nothing, and merely lets the form be submitted.

Using min and max to create number ranges

You'll notice in the previous code example that we set a minimum and maximum allowed range:

```
type="number" min="1929" max="2015"
```

Numbers outside of this range (should) get special treatment.

However, you probably won't be surprised to learn that browser implementation of `min` and `max` ranges is varied. For example, Chrome and Firefox display a warning, while Safari does nothing.

Changing the step increments

You can alter the step increments (granularity) for the spinner controls of various input types with the use of the `step` attribute. For example, to step 10 units at a time:

```
<input type="number" step="10" />
```

The url input type

You can set an input field to expect a URL like this:

```
type="url"
```

As you might expect, the `url` input type is for URL values. Similar to the `tel` and `email` input types, it behaves almost identically to a standard text input. However, some browsers add specific information to the warning message provided when submitted with incorrect values. The following is a code example including the `placeholder` attribute:

```
<div>
  <label for="web">Your Web address</label>
  <input id="web" name="web" type="url" placeholder="http://www.
mysite.com" />
</div>
```

The following screenshot shows what happens when an incorrectly entered URL field is submitted in Chrome:

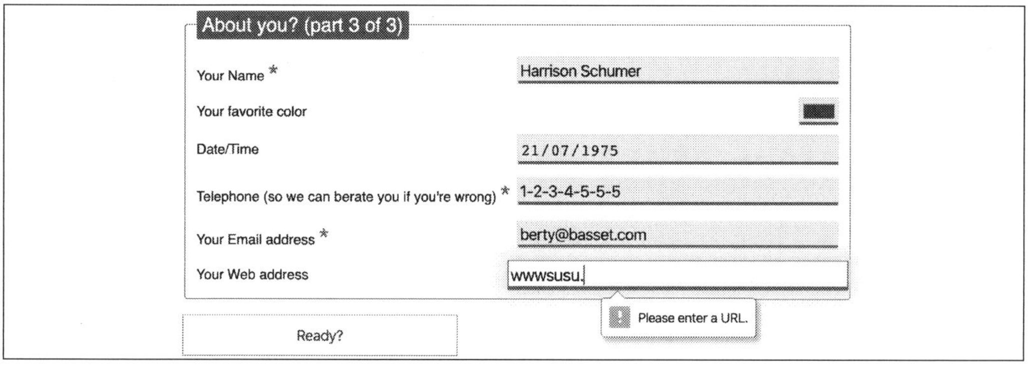

Figure 10.10: Chrome will show a warning when the input doesn't match the type

Like `type="email"`, touchscreen devices often amend the software keyboard based upon this input type. The following screenshot shows how the software keyboard of an iPad is changed with an input type set to `url`:

Figure 10.11: Software keyboard adapting for url input

Notice the ".com" key? Because we've used a `url` input type, the software keyboard provides a key for easy top-level domain completion.

On iOS, if you're not going to a .com site, you can press and hold that button for a few other popular top-level domains.

The tel input type

You can set an input field to expect a telephone number type of value, like this:

```
type="tel"
```

Here's a more complete example:

```
<div>
  <label for="tel">Telephone (so we can berate you if you're
wrong)</label>
  <input
    id="tel"
    name="tel"
    type="tel"
    placeholder="1-234-546758"
    autocomplete="off"
    required
  />
</div>
```

Browsers do little validation on the `tel` input type. When an incorrect value is input, they fail to provide a suitable warning message.

However, better news is that, like the `email` and `url` input types, touchscreen devices often thoughtfully accommodate this kind of input with an amended software keyboard for easy completion; here's the `tel` input type when accessed with an iPad (running iOS 13.3):

Figure 10.12: Software keyboard adapting to telephone input

Notice the lack of alphabet characters in the keyboard area? This makes it much faster for users to enter a value in the correct format.

 If the default blue color of telephone numbers in iOS Safari annoys you when you use a `tel` input, you can amend it with the following selector: `a[href^=tel] { color: inherit; }`. That will set them to the color of the parent element.

The search input type

You can set an input as a search type like this:

```
type="search"
```

The `search` input type works like a standard text input. Here's an example:

```
<div>
```

```
    <label for="search">Search the site...</label>
    <input id="search" name="search" type="search" placeholder="Wyatt
Earp">
</div>
```

As with many of the prior input types, software keyboards (such as those found on mobile devices) often provide a more tailored keyboard.

The pattern input attribute

You can set an input to expect a certain pattern input like this:

```
pattern=""
```

Note that this isn't an input type. However, it is a means of communicating to the browser that we expect input of a certain pattern.

The `pattern` attribute allows you to specify, via a regular expression, the syntax of data that should be allowed in a given input field.

Learn about regular expressions

If you've never encountered regular expressions before, I'd suggest starting here: `http://en.wikipedia.org/wiki/Regular_expressions`. Regular expressions are used across many programming languages as a means of matching strings. While the format is intimidating at first, they are incredibly powerful and flexible. For example, you could build a regular expression to match a password format or select a certain style CSS class naming pattern. To help build up your own regex pattern and get a visual understanding of how they work, I'd recommend starting with a browser-based tool like `http://www.regexr.com/`.

The following code is an example:

```
<div>
  <label for="name">Your Name (first and last)</label>
  <input
    id="name"
    name="name"
    pattern="^([\D]{2,30}\s+)+([a-zA-Z]{2,30})$"
    placeholder="Dwight Schultz"
    required
  />
</div>
```

Such is my commitment to this book, I searched the Internet for an entire 458 seconds to find a regular expression that would match a basic first and last name syntax (Western languages only, sorry). This is by no means bulletproof but should ensure that the value entered is not a number (sorry, "R2D2," you will have to register your film complaints elsewhere) and is made of at least two space separated values between 2 and 30 characters long.

By entering the regular expression value within the `pattern` attribute, it makes supporting browsers expect a matching input syntax. Then, when used in conjunction with the required attribute, incorrect entries get the following treatment in supporting browsers. In this instance, I tried submitting the form without providing a last name:

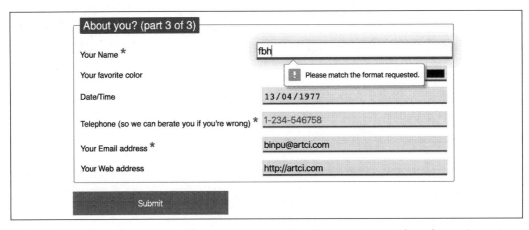

Figure 10.13: The pattern type provides a vaguer warning but allows you to create bespoke requirements

The color type input

Want to set an input field to receive a hexadecimal color value?

```
input type="color"
```

The `color` input type invokes the host operating system's color picker, allowing users to select a color value in a hexadecimal value. The following code is an example:

```
<div>
  <label for="color">Your favorite color</label>
  <input id="color" name="color" type="color" />
</div>
```

I'll be honest, it's not a type I've yet to need in practice, but it's not hard to imagine scenarios where it would be very handy.

Date and time

If you've ever bought tickets to an event online, chances are that you have used a date picker of one sort or another. The thinking behind the new `date` and `time` input types is so that the browser can provide a consistent piece of user interface for that situation.

Sadly, as I write this in 2020, it's hard to recommend using the native date and time input types as support is completely absent from iOS and Safari on Mac. It's not a completely useless situation, as with all the HTML5 input types without support the input will behave like a normal input box. However, if you have any users on those browsers (and the overwhelming likelihood is you do), chances are you're going to need a JavaScript solution to provide any kind of consistent experience.

Regardless, in the hope that support gets added to those browsers soon, let's consider the core capabilities of the `date` and `time` input types.

The date input type

The following code is an example:

```
<input id="date" type="date" name="date" />
```

And here is the UI that generates in a supporting browser:

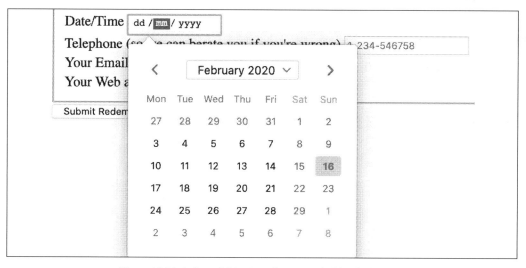

Figure 10.14: A date picking interface provided by the browser

There are a variety of different date and time input types available. What follows is a brief overview of the others.

The month input type

The following code is an example:

```
<input id="month" type="month" name="month" />
```

The interface allows the user to select a single month and sets the value of the input to a year and month; for example, "2012-06." Here is a grab of the user interface that iOS displays:

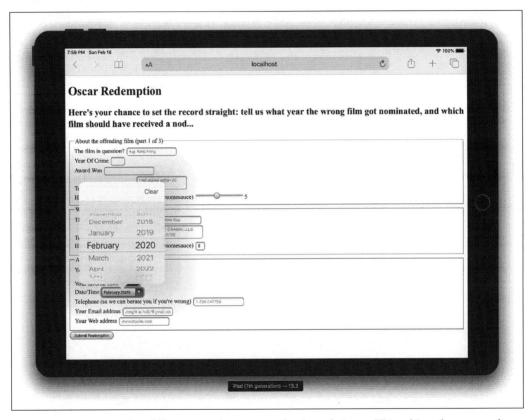

Figure 10.15: Remember, different operating systems often have their own UI to achieve the same goal

The week input type

The following code is an example:

```
<input id="week" type="week" name="week" />
```

When the `week` input type is used, the picker allows the user to select a single week within a year and provides the input in "2012-W47" format.

The following screenshot shows how it looks in Chrome and Microsoft Edge, which are both the same code under the hood, and currently the only browsers that support it:

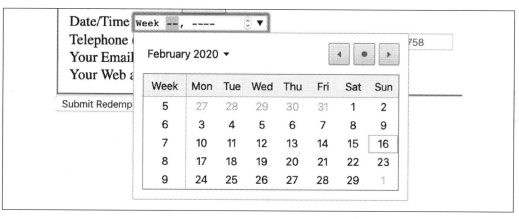

Figure 10.16: The week input type gets its own data picker style in supporting browsers

The time input type

The following code is an example:

```
<input id="time" type="time" name="time" />
```

The `time` input type allows a value in the 24-hour format; for example, "23:50."

It displays like a standard input in supporting browsers but with additional spinner controls, and it only allows relevant time values.

Touch devices show their own UI. Here's how it looks on iOS:

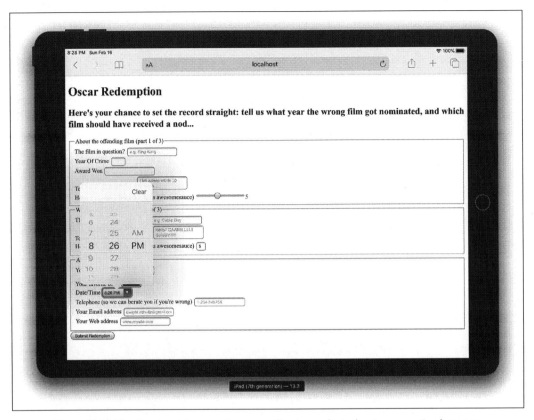

Figure 10.17: The time input type produces specific pieces of interface in supporting browsers

The range input type

The range input type creates a slider interface element. Here's an example:

```
<input type="range" min="1" max="10" value="5" />
```

And the following screenshot shows how it looks in Firefox:

Figure 10.18: A range slider doesn't show numerical values by default

The default range is from 0 to 100. However, by specifying a `min` and `max` value, in our example, we have limited it to between 1 and 10.

One big problem I've encountered with the `range` input type is that the current value is never displayed to the user. Although the range slider is only intended for vague number selections, I've often wanted to display the value as it changes. Currently, there is no way to do this using HTML5. However, if you absolutely must display the current value of the slider, it can be achieved easily with some simple JavaScript. Amend the previous example to the following code:

```
<input
  id="howYouRateIt"
  name="howYouRateIt"
  type="range"
  min="1"
  max="10"
  value="5"
  onchange="showValue(this.value)"
/>
<span id="range">5</span>
```

We've added two things, an `onchange` attribute and also a `span` element with the `id` of range. Now, we'll add the following tiny piece of JavaScript:

```
<script>
  function showValue(newValue)
  {
    document.getElementById("range").innerHTML=newValue;
  }
</script>
```

All this does is get the current value of the range slider and display it in the element with an `id` of range (our span tag). You can then use whatever CSS you deem appropriate to change the appearance of the value. We will do that ourselves in a moment once we start styling our form.

There are a few other form-related features that are new in HTML5. You can read the full specification here: `http://www.w3.org/TR/html5/forms.html`.

How to work around non-supporting browsers

Depending on the kind of form you are building and the kind of browser support you need, you might find `https://github.com/Modernizr/Modernizr/wiki/HTML5-Cross-Browser-Polyfills#web-forms` useful. It's a list of JavaScript libraries that can be used to add support to browsers for many of the features we have just looked at.

Styling HTML5 forms with CSS

We have our HTML5 powered form built now, but we need to make it a little more visually appealing across different viewport sizes. By applying some of the techniques we've learned throughout the previous chapters, I think we can improve the aesthetics of our form considerably.

You can view the styled form at `example_10-02`, and remember, if you don't already have the example code, you can grab it at `http://rwd.education`.

In this example, I've also included two versions of the style sheet: `styles.css` is the version that includes vendor prefixes (added with Autoprefixer) and `styles-unprefixed.css` is the CSS as originally written. The latter is probably easier to look at if you want to see how anything is being applied.

Here's how the form looks in a small viewport with our basic styling applied:

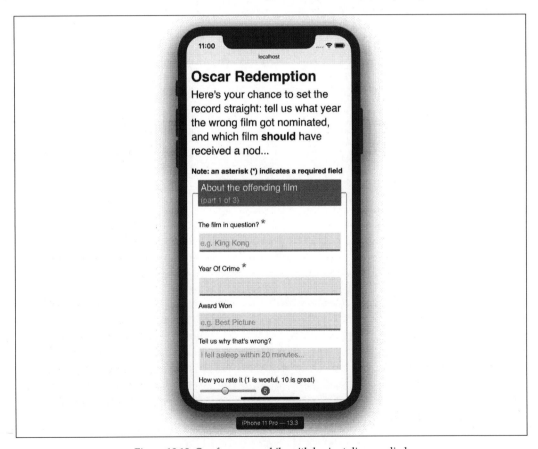

Figure 10.19: Our form on mobile with basic styling applied

And here it is with a larger viewport:

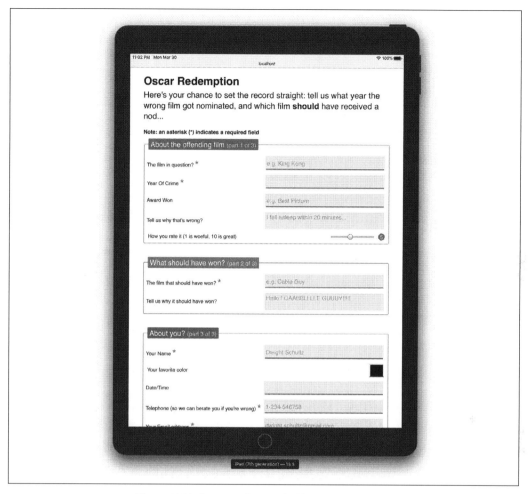

Figure 10.20: Our same form styled for wider viewports

If you look at the CSS, you'll see many of the techniques we've looked at throughout previous chapters applied. For example, Flexbox (*Chapter 4*) is used to create uniform spacing and flexibility for elements. Transforms and transitions (*Chapter 9*) are used so that the focused input fields grow and the ready/submit button flips vertically when it gains focus. Box shadows and gradients (*Chapter 7*) are used to emphasize different areas of the form. Media queries (*Chapter 3*) are used to switch the Flexbox direction for different viewport sizes, and more recent CSS selectors (*Chapter 6*) are used for selector negation.

We won't go over those techniques in detail here again. Instead, we will focus on a couple of peculiarities. Firstly, how to visually indicate required fields (and for bonus points, indicate a value has been entered) and secondly, how to create a "fill" effect when a field gets user focus.

Indicating required fields

We can indicate required input fields to a user using CSS alone. For example:

```
input:required {
  /* styles */
}
```

With that selector, we could add a border or outline to the required fields or add a `background-image` inside the field. Basically, the sky's the limit! We could also use a specific selector to target an input field that is required, but only when it gains focus. For example:

```
input:focus:required {
  /* styles */
}
```

However, that would apply styles to the `input` itself. What if we want to amend styles on the associated `label` element? I've decided I'd like to indicate required fields with a little asterisk symbol to the side of the label. But this presents a problem. Generally, CSS only lets us affect a change on elements if they are children of an element, the element itself, or a general or adjacent sibling of an element that receives "state" (when I say state, I'm talking about `hover`, `focus`, `active`, `checked`, and so on). In the following examples, I'm using `hover`, but that would obviously be problematic for touch-based devices:

```
.item:hover .item-child {
}
```

With the preceding selector, styles are applied to `item-child` when the item is hovered over:

```
.item:hover ~ .item-general-sibling {
}
```

With this selector, when the item is hovered over, styles are applied to `item-general-sibling` if it is at the same DOM level as `item` and follows it:

```
.item:hover + .item-adjacent-sibling {
}
```

Here, when the item is hovered over, styles are applied to `item-adjacent-sibling` if it is the adjacent sibling element of `item` (straight after it in the DOM).

So, back to our issue. If we have a form with labels and fields like this, with the `label` above the `input` (to give us the requisite basic layout), it leaves us a little stuck:

```
<div class="form-Input_Wrapper">
  <label for="film">The film in question?</label>
  <input
    id="film"
    name="film"
    type="text"
    placeholder="e.g. King Kong"
    required
  />
</div>
```

In this situation, using just CSS, there is no way to change the style of the `label` based upon whether the `input` is required or not (as it comes after the `label` in the markup). We could switch the order of those two elements in the markup, but then we would end up with the label underneath the input.

However, have you remembered that both Flexbox and Grid give us the ability to visually reverse the order of elements (read all about them in *Chapter 4* and *Chapter 5* if you haven't done so already) with ease?

That allows us to use this markup:

```
<div class="form-Input_Wrapper">
  <input
    id="film"
    name="film"
    type="text"
    placeholder="e.g. King Kong"
    required
  />
  <label for="film">The film in question?</label>
</div>
```

And then simply apply `flex-direction: row-reverse` or `flex-direction: column-reverse` to the parent. These declarations reverse the visual order of their child elements, allowing the desired aesthetic of the label above (smaller viewports) or to the left (larger viewports) of the input.

Now, we can get on with actually providing some indication of required fields and when they have received input.

Thanks to our revised markup, the adjacent sibling selector now makes this possible:

```
input:required + label:after {
}
```

This selector essentially says that for every label that follows an input with a required attribute, apply the enclosed rules. Here is the CSS for that section:

```
input:required + label:after {
    content: '*';
    font-size: 2.1em;
    position: relative;
    top: 6px;
    display: inline-flex;
    margin-left: 0.2ch;
    transition: color 1s;
}

input:required:invalid + label:after {
    color: red;
}

input:required:valid + label:after {
    color: green;
}
```

Then, if you focus on a required input and enter a relevant value, the asterisk changes color to green. It's a subtle but helpful touch.

Creating a background fill effect

Back in *Chapter 7, Stunning Aesthetics with CSS*, we learned how to generate linear and radial gradients as background images. Sadly, it isn't possible to transition between two background images (which makes sense as the browser effectively rasterizes the declaration into an image). However, we can transition between values of associated properties like `background-position` and `background-size`. We'll use this capability to create a fill effect when an `input` or `textarea` receives focus.

Here are the properties and values added to the `input`:

```
input:not([type='range']),
textarea {
  min-height: 40px;
  padding: 2px;
  font-size: 17px;
  border: 1px solid #ebebeb;
  outline: none;
  transition: transform 0.4s, box-shadow 0.4s, background-position
0.2s;
  background: radial-gradient(400px circle, #fff 99%, transparent
99%), #f1f1f1;
  background-position: -400px 90px, 0 0;
  background-repeat: no-repeat, no-repeat;
  border-radius: 0;
  position: relative;
}

input:not([type='range']):focus,
textarea:focus {
  background-position: 0 0, 0 0;
}
```

In the first rule, a solid white radial gradient is being generated but positioned out of view. The background color that sits behind (the hex value after `radial-gradient`) is not offset and so provides a default color. When `input` gains focus, `background-position` on `radial-gradient` is set back to the default and because we have a `transition` on `background-image` set, we get a nice transition between the two. The visual result of this is the appearance of the input being "filled" with a different color when it gains focus.

Summary

In this chapter, we learned how to use a host of new HTML5 form attributes. They have enabled us to make forms more usable, and therefore the data they capture more relevant.

We've also made use of some techniques we have learned throughout this book to restyle our form and make its layout respond to the constraints of the device on which it is used.

We're nearing the end of our responsive HTML5 and CSS journey. While we have covered an enormous amount in our time together, I'm conscious I'll never manage to impart all the information for every eventuality you'll encounter. Therefore, in the last chapter of this book, I'd like to take a higher-level look at approaching responsive web design and try to relate some solid best practices for getting your next/first responsive project off on the right footing.

11

Bonus Techniques and Parting Advice

In my favorite stories and films, there's usually a scene where a mentor passes on valuable advice and some magical items to the hero. You know those items will prove useful; you just don't know when or how.

Well, I'd like to assume the role of mentor in this final chapter—besides, my hair has waned, and I don't have the looks for the hero role. I would like you, my fine apprentice, to spare me just a few more moments of your time while I offer up some final words of advice before you set forth on your responsive quest.

This chapter will be half philosophical musings and guidance, and half a grab bag of unrelated tips and techniques. I hope, at some point in your responsive adventures, these tips will prove useful.

Here's the grab bag of tips we'll cover:

- Breaking up long URLs
- Truncating text
- Creating horizontal scrolling panels
- Using CSS Scroll Snap
- Smooth scrolling with CSS scroll-behavior
- Communicating CSS breakpoints to JavaScript

And here are our suggestions for guidance:

- Get designs in the browser
- Test on real devices
- Embrace progressive enhancement
- Define a browser support matrix
- Avoid CSS frameworks in production
- Using the simplest solution possible
- Hiding, showing, and loading content at different viewports
- Validators and linting tools
- Performance
- The next big things

Right, now pay attention, 007...

In my day-to-day work, I've found that I use some CSS features constantly and others hardly ever. I thought it might be useful to share those I've used most often, especially those that pop up time and again with responsive projects.

These are in no particular order. None are more important than any other. Just dip in if and when you need them.

Breaking up long URLs

How many times have you had to add a big URL into a tiny space and then, well, despaired? Take a look at `example_11-04`. The problem can also be seen in the following screenshot; notice that the URL is breaking out of its allocated space:

Figure 11.1: Long URLs can present a problem

It's easy to fix this issue with a simple CSS declaration, which, as chance would have it, also works in older versions of Internet Explorer as far back as 5.5! Just add:

```
word-wrap: break-word;
```

to the containing element, which gives the following effect:

Figure 11.2: Using break-word, we can tame long URLs

Hey presto, the long URL now wraps perfectly!

Truncating text

Sometimes, you have a situation where, if space is limited, you would rather have text truncated rather than wrapped. We've been trained to spot this with the ellipsis symbol "...".

This is straightforward in CSS, even if a little long-winded.

Consider this markup (you can view this example in `example_11-03`):

```
<p class="truncate">
  OK, listen up, I've figured out the key eternal happiness. All you
need to do is eat lots of scones.
</p>
```

However, we actually want to truncate the text to be 520px wide, so it looks like this:

> OK, listen up, I've figured out the key eternal happiness. All you need to do is ...

Figure 11.3: Truncation is handy when keeping vertical height constant is of paramount importance

Here is the CSS to make that happen:

```
.truncate {
  width: 520px;
  overflow: hidden;
```

```
    text-overflow: ellipsis;
    white-space: nowrap;
}
```

Each one of those properties is needed to make the truncation occur.

 You can read the specification for the `text-overflow` property here: `https://drafts.csswg.org/css-overflow-3/#text-overflow`.

Whenever the width of the content exceeds the `width` defined, it will be truncated. The `width` can just as happily be set as a percentage, such as 100% if it's inside a flexible container.

We set `overflow: hidden` to ensure that anything that overruns the box is hidden.

When the content does overrun, `text-overflow: ellipsis` creates the ellipsis symbol in the correct place to indicate the overrunning content. This could be set to `clip` if preferred. In that instance, the content just gets clipped where it overflows, possibly mid-character.

The `white-space: nowrap` property/value pair is needed to ensure that the content doesn't wrap inside the surrounding element, which is what it would do by default.

 There still isn't a solid, cross browser way to do multiline truncation, although there is a specification: `https://drafts.csswg.org/css-overflow-3/#propdef--webkit-line-clamp`. Right now, you can use `-webkit-line-clamp`. However, I wouldn't advise that as it is only supported for compatibility reasons and is likely to be superseded as soon as a "real" version is widely implemented.

Creating horizontal scrolling panels

When I say horizontal scrolling panel, hopefully, you know the kind of thing I mean. Horizontal scrolling panels are common on the iOS App and Google Play Store for showing panels of related content (movies, albums, and more). Where there is enough horizontal space, all of the items are viewable. However, when space is limited (think mobile devices), the panel is scrollable from side to side.

I've created a scrolling panel of the top 10 grossing films of 2014. You'll remember this scenario from *Chapter 6*, and that there is no significance to the year; I just picked one!

It looks like this on an iPhone running iOS 13.3:

Figure 11.4: A horizontal scrolling panel

The markup pattern looks like this; note that I'm just showing the first item in the list for brevity:

```
<nav class="Scroll_Wrapper">
  <figure class="Item">
    <img src="f1.jpg" alt="Movie poster of Guardians of the Galaxy"
/>
    <figcaption class="Caption">Guardians of the Galaxy</figcaption>
  </figure>
</nav>
```

You can find the full code in `example_11_02`.

Ordinarily, if you add more and more items in a container, it will wrap onto the next line. The key to this technique is the `white-space` property, which has actually been around since CSS 2.1 (`http://www.w3.org/TR/CSS2/text.html#white-space-prop`). Additionally, we used it a moment ago for text truncation too. By setting it to `nowrap`, we can prevent the content from wrapping.

To get the scrolling working, we just need a wrapper that is narrower than the sum of its contents and set it to overflow automatically in the *x* axis. That way, it won't scroll if there is enough space, but it will if there isn't.

At its simplest, we need this CSS:

```css
.Scroll_Wrapper {
  width: 100%;
  white-space: nowrap;
  overflow-x: auto;
  overflow-y: hidden;
}


.Item {
  display: inline-flex;
}
```

We're using `inline-flex` here for the child items of the wrapping element, but it could just as easily be `inline`, `inline-block`, or `inline-table`.

To make things a little more aesthetically pleasing, let's hide the scroll bar where we can.

Unfortunately, to do this, we need to apply a few different declarations to cover the different browser implementations. There is one for the very old Internet Explorer, one for Chrome, Safari, and Microsoft Edge, and one standardized in a new draft specification, which is the implementation that Firefox has. Now the updated `.Scroll_Wrapper` rule looks like this:

```css
.Scroll_Wrapper {
  width: 100%;
  white-space: nowrap;
  overflow-x: auto;
  overflow-y: hidden;
  /*Remove the scrollbars in supporting versions of older IE*/
  -ms-overflow-style: none;
```

```
    /* Hide scrollbar in Firefox */
    scrollbar-width: none;
}


/*Stops the scrollbar appearing in Safari, Chrome and MS Edge
browsers*/
.Scroll_Wrapper::-webkit-scrollbar {
    display: none;
}
```

 The draft standard for the CSS Scrollbars Module Level 1 can be found at `https://drafts.csswg.org/css-scrollbars-1/`.

The rest of the code is simply aesthetic niceties and doesn't directly relate to the scrolling. However, it is a pattern we can remake with Grid.

Horizontal scrolling panels with Grid

While playing with Grid I realized it's possible to make a horizontal scrolling panel just as easily with CSS Grid. Let's suppose we want to take advantage of Grid. We can leave our existing pattern as it is and progressively enhance for Grid:

```
@supports (display: grid) {
    .Scroll_Wrapper {
        display: grid;
        grid-auto-flow: column;
        max-width: min-content;
        grid-template-rows: auto;
    }
}
```

In this instance, we are making the wrapping element a grid and letting it flow automatically into as many columns as needed. It is key to set `max-width: min-content`, otherwise, the columns would grow when more space was available, which, in this instance, isn't what we want.

Right, as we've come this far, we may as well "stick a cherry on top" by adding CSS Scroll Snap into the mix!

CSS Scroll Snap

CSS Scroll Snap snaps the scrolling of content to predefined points in the container. Again, it is a user interface pattern that is commonplace in the interfaces of native applications, app stores, and things like carousels, but historically required JavaScript to implement.

> There have been different implementations and names for CSS Scroll Snap in browsers since 2014. However, it's taken time for a stable specification to emerge, along with compatible implementations. You can read the official specification at `https://www.w3.org/TR/css-scroll-snap-1/`.

Let's use CSS Scroll Snap to add scroll snap functionality to our horizontal "top-grossing films of 2014" container.

The scroll-snap-type property

First of all, we define the `scroll-snap-type` for our scrolling container. This is where we can decide whether we want the container to scroll snap in the x, y, or both, axes.

This property also allows us to define the strictness of the scroll snapping that is applied. The `mandatory` value is the one I always opt for unless I'm resetting scroll snapping, at which point you can use `none`. `none` will revert scroll snap to behave like a standard scroll container.

What `mandatory` does is ensure that if an item is partially scrolled within the container (for example, the left-hand side is off the viewport by a certain amount), then it will be "snapped" into or out of view.

There is also a `proximity` value. What this does is leave the snapping to the discretion of the browser.

It is important to understand why you may occasionally want and need to use `proximity`. Suppose you had items in a carousel that were always bigger than the viewport. Because, with `mandatory`, it would always snap, you may have trouble advancing the scroll panel. Setting it to `proximity` means that content will remain accessible as the browser will determine how much room should be left to accommodate scrolling.

Despite that, in our instance, since we know the width of our cells won't exceed the width of the viewport, we will apply `mandatory` for a consistent experience.

So, our container will be amended with this extra block. Note that we are wrapping it in a feature query:

```
@supports (scroll-snap-type: x mandatory) {
  .Scroll_Wrapper {
    scroll-snap-type: x mandatory;
  }
}
```

Now, if you refresh the browser and try the scroll panel, you will likely be disappointed. That, by itself, doesn't do anything. We now need to apply the `scroll-snap-align` property to the child items.

The scroll-snap-align property

The `scroll-snap-align` property controls where an item inside a scroll-snap container will snap to. The options are:

- `none` to reset an item
- `start` to snap the item to the beginning of a scroll snap area
- `end` to snap the item to the end of a scroll snap area
- `center` to snap the item to the center of the scroll snap area

So, inside our feature query, let's add `.Item` and set it to snap to the `start`:

```
@supports (scroll-snap-type: x mandatory) {
  .Scroll_Wrapper {
    scroll-snap-type: x mandatory;
  }
  .Item {
    scroll-snap-align: start;
  }
}
```

Now, if you scroll, you'll see that the items snap within their container. However, there's one little problem. As the items are snapping to the beginning, and we have the number positioned absolutely in the top left of each film, it's getting cut off. See for yourself:

Figure 11.5: We need to fix that number from being cut off on the left side

The scroll-padding property

Thankfully, the specification authors have considered such an eventuality. On the container, we can add some padding to our scroll snap area. This means that this distance is taken into account when the browser decides where to snap the items to. It's added here to the `.Scroll_Wrapper`:

```
@supports (scroll-snap-type: x mandatory) {
  .Scroll_Wrapper {
    scroll-snap-type: x mandatory;
    scroll-padding: 0 20px;
  }
  .Item {
    scroll-snap-align: start;
  }
}
```

Now, when we scroll, it takes that padding into account as it snaps our scrolling to a stop:

Figure 11.6: Applying scroll-padding solves our problem

The scroll-snap-stop property

By default, an excessive scroll action can send several items past the scroll snap point. With `scroll-snap-stop`, it should be possible to make the browser stop at each snap point. There are just two values to choose from: `normal`, which is what the browser does by default; or `always`, which ensures that no scroll snap points are skipped.

The bad news is that as I write this, `scroll-snap-stop` is only supported in Chrome and Edge. So, check the browser support before adding it to a project and wondering why it isn't working as expected!

CSS Scroll Snap is a hugely satisfying piece of functionality to use! In just a few lines, we are able to achieve in CSS what used to take whole libraries of JavaScript to achieve. And the best part is that we can apply this as an enhancement. If the user's browser supports it, great. If not, no big deal.

Smooth scrolling with CSS scroll-behavior

One of the oldest capabilities of HTML is the ability to anchor to different points in a document. You set a link on the page, and rather than it sending the user to another webpage, the user is instead instantly taken to a different point on the same page.

Typically, such functionality is in the y axis, or down a page. However, it works just as well horizontally in the x axis.

Historically, jumping to an anchor link has always been a little jarring. As the user is instantly transported to the new point on the page, there is no affordance to communicate to the user what just occurred. People have solved this common issue over the years with the help of JavaScript, by effectively animating the scroll action.

Now CSS has provided us with a simpler alternative: the `scroll-behavior` property.

I'm going to add "start" and "end" anchor points to each end of the scroll panel we just made and add two links below the scrolling panel. As you might imagine, by default, clicking on "end" instantly scrolls the panel to the end. However, if we add `scroll-behavior: smooth` to our scroll panel, we get a silky-smooth scroll behavior instead. Nice!

Sadly, this is something that images just don't convey. However, if you open `example_11-02`, then you can have a play with it for yourself.

Linking CSS breakpoints to JavaScript

Typically, with something web-based involving any sort of interaction, JavaScript will be involved. When you're developing a responsive project, it's feasible that you will want to do different things at different viewport sizes. Not just in CSS but also in JavaScript.

Let's suppose we want to invoke a certain JavaScript function when we reach a certain breakpoint in the CSS (remember that "breakpoint" is the term used to define the point in which a responsive design should change significantly). Let's suppose the breakpoint is 47.5rem (with a 16px root font size that would equate to 760px), and we only want to run the function at that size. There is a JavaScript API called `matchMedia`, which allows you to test in JavaScript, exactly the same as you would in CSS. The obvious solution would be to use that and create a comparable test as you have in your media query.

However, it would still mean two places to update and change those values when we are changing viewport sizes.

Thankfully, there is a better way. I first came across this technique on Jeremy Keith's website: `http://adactio.com/journal/5429/`.

You can find the full code for this at `example_10-01`. However, the basic idea is that in CSS, we insert something that can be easily read and understood by JavaScript.

Consider this in the CSS:

```
@media (min-width: 20rem) {
  body::after {
    content: 'Splus';
    font-size: 0;
  }
}
@media (min-width: 47.5rem) {
  body::after {
    content: 'Mplus';
    font-size: 0;
  }
}
@media (min-width: 62.5rem) {
```

```
body::after {
  content: 'Lplus';
  font-size: 0;
  }
}
```

For each breakpoint we want to communicate to JavaScript, we use the `after` pseudo-element (you could use `before` too, as either is just as good), and set the content of that pseudo-element to be the name of our breakpoint. In our example, I am using `'Splus'` for small screens and bigger, `'Mplus'` for medium screens and bigger, and `'Lplus'` for large screens and bigger. You can use whatever name makes sense to you and change the value whenever it makes sense to you (for instance, different orientations, different heights, different widths, and so on).

 Remember, the `::before` and `::after` pseudo-elements are inserted into the DOM as shadow DOM elements. The `::before` pseudo-element is inserted as the first child of its parent, and `::after` is inserted as the last child.

With that CSS set, we can browse the DOM tree and see our `::after` pseudo-element:

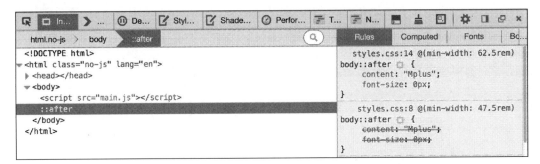

Figure 11.7: We can use pseudo-elements to communicate to JavaScript

Then, in our JavaScript, we can read this value. Firstly, we assign the value to a variable:

```
var size = window
  .getComputedStyle(document.body, ':after')
  .getPropertyValue('content');
```

And then once we have it, we can do something with it. To prove this concept, I have made a simple self-invoking function (self-invoking simply means it is executed as soon as the browser parses it) that writes our media query label into the body on page load; this can be a different value depending on the viewport size:

```
var size = window
  .getComputedStyle(document.body, ':after')
  .getPropertyValue('content');

(function alertSize() {
  if (size.indexOf('Splus') != -1) {
    document.body.textContent =
      size + ' I will run functions for small screens';
  }
  if (size.indexOf('Mplus') != -1) {
    document.body.textContent =
      size + ' Run a different function at medium sizes';
  }
  if (size.indexOf('Lplus') != -1) {
    document.body.textContent =
      size + ' I will run functions for LARGE screens';
  }
})();
```

So, depending on your screen size when you open this example, you'll see something like this:

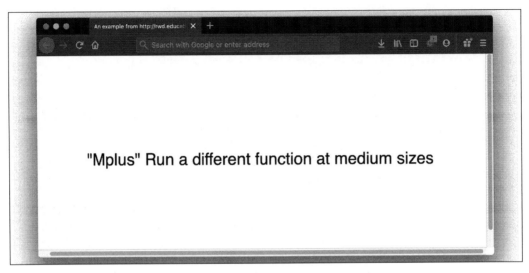

Figure 11.8: JavaScript can read in the value from CSS

Hopefully, you will find more interesting use cases for this technique. I think you will find great benefit in approaching the problem in this way. You'll never be in danger of your CSS media queries and your width dependent JavaScript functions going out of sync again.

You could also solve this problem using CSS Custom Properties, which we looked at in *Chapter 6, CSS Selectors, Typography, Color Modes, and More*, but I tend to stick with this older approach as it means it still works well in browsers like Internet Explorer 11, which lacks support for CSS Custom Properties.

 Note that I've tried to employ as many of the techniques that we covered in this book for the single-page `https://rwd.education` website. Hopefully, it's not too indulgent to suggest that if you want to see some of the techniques together, go and take a poke around there.

We've reached the end of the bonus techniques section. Hopefully, you have a few more handy tricks in your arsenal for the next project you embark on.

All that is left, in our final section of the chapter, and indeed the book (please, don't cry—you'll start me off), is for me to offer what I feel are the most important considerations for any responsive web project. Here goes.

Get designs in the browser as soon as possible

The more responsive web work I have done, the more important I have found it to get designs up and running in a browser environment as soon as possible. If you are a designer as well as a developer, then that simplifies matters. As soon as you have enough of a feel, visually, for what you need, you can get it prototyped and develop the idea further in a browser environment.

If you are primarily a developer, then this can aid the design process hugely in order to get the design living and breathing in the browser. Without fail, every project that I work on gets revised in some way as a result of the designs being built in the browser. That isn't a failure of the original flat designs, it's a consequence of realizing that the design is just a step towards realizing an idea. And seeing it working in a browser is one step closer.

There is a slew of problems that can only be solved by seeing the design in a browser. What about all those device and browser window sizes? What about the interactivity that occurs when the user opens a menu? How long should that introductory animation run for? And is it too much anyway? These are the kind of design decisions that can only be made when the design is realized in a browser.

Test on real devices

If you can, start to build up a "device lab" of older devices (phones/tablets) to view your work on. Having a number of varied devices is hugely beneficial. Not only does it let you feel how a design actually works across different devices, but it also exposes layout/rendering peculiarities earlier in the process. After all, no one enjoys believing that they have finished on a project only to be told it doesn't work properly in a certain environment. Test early, and test often! Buying extra devices need not cost the earth. For example, you can pick up older phone and tablet models on eBay, or buy them from friends/relatives as they upgrade.

Use tools like BrowserSync to synchronize your work

One of the biggest time-saving tools to incorporate into your workflow is BrowserSync. Once configured, as you save your work, any changes to things like CSS are injected into the browser without you needing to refresh your screen constantly. If that wasn't good enough, any other browsers on the same Wi-Fi and viewing the same URL refresh too. This saves picking each of your testing devices up and clicking refresh with each change. It even synchronizes scrolling and clicks too. It is highly recommended: `http://browsersync.io`.

Embrace progressive enhancement

In previous chapters, we have considered the notion of progressive enhancement. It's an approach to development that I have found so useful in practice that I think it bears repeating. The fundamental idea with progressive enhancement is that you begin all your frontend code (HTML, CSS, or JavaScript) with the lowest common denominator in mind. Then, you progressively enhance the code for more capable devices and browsers. That may seem simplistic, and it is, but if you are used to working the other way around, then by designing the optimum experience and then figuring out a way of making that thing work on lesser devices/browsers, you'll find progressive enhancement an easier approach.

Imagine a low-powered, poorly featured device. It has no JavaScript, no Flexbox support, and no CSS3/CSS4 support. In that case, what can you do to provide a usable experience? Most importantly, you should write meaningful HTML5 markup that accurately describes the content. This is an easier task if you're building text- and content-based websites. In that instance, concentrate on using elements like `main`, `header`, `footer`, `article`, `section`, and `aside` correctly. Not only will it help you discern different sections of your code, but it will also provide greater accessibility for your users at no extra cost.

If you're building something like a web-based application or visual UI components (carousels, tabs, accordions, and the like), you'll need to think about how to distill the visual pattern down into an accessible markup.

The reason good markup is so crucial is that it provides a base-level experience for all users. The more you can achieve with HTML, the less you have to do in CSS and JavaScript to support older browsers. And nobody, and I really mean nobody, likes writing the code to support older browsers.

For further reading and great practical examples on the subject, I would recommend the following two articles. They provide great insight into how fairly complex interactions can be handled with the constructs of HTML and CSS: `http://www.cssmojo.com/how-to-style-a-carousel/` and `http://www.cssmojo.com/use-radio-buttons-for-single-option/`.

It's by no means a simple feat to think in this manner. However, it is an approach that is likely to serve you well in your quest to do as little as possible to support ailing browsers. Now, about those browsers…

Define a browser support matrix

Knowing the browsers and devices a web project needs to support upfront can be crucial to developing a successful responsive web design. We've already considered why progressive enhancement is so useful in this respect. If done correctly, it means that the vast majority of your site will be functional on even the oldest browsers.

However, there may also be times when you need to start your experience with a higher set of prerequisites. Perhaps you are working on a project where JavaScript is essential, which is not an uncommon scenario. In that instance, you can still progressively enhance, but you are merely enhancing from a different start point.

Whatever your starting point, the key thing is to establish what your starting point is. Then, and only then, can you define and agree on what visual and functional experiences the different browsers and devices that you intend to support will get.

Functional parity, not visual parity

It's both unrealistic and undesirable to get any website looking and working the same in every browser. Besides quirks that are specific to certain browsers, there are essential functional considerations. For example, we have to consider things like touch targets for buttons and links on touch screens that aren't relevant to mouse-based devices.

Therefore, some part of your role as a responsive web developer is to educate whoever you are answerable to (your boss, client, or shareholders) that "supporting older browsers" does not mean it "looks the same in older browsers." The line I tend to run with is that all browsers in the support matrix will get functional parity, not visual parity. This means that if you have a checkout to build, all users will be able to go through the checkout and purchase goods. There may be visual and interaction flourishes afforded to the users of more modern browsers, but the core task will be achievable by all.

Choosing the browsers to support

Typically, when we talk about which browsers to support, we're talking about how far back we need to look. Here are a couple of possibilities to consider, depending on the situation.

If it's an existing website, take a look at the visitor statistics (for example, Google Analytics or similar). Armed with some figures, you can do some rough calculations. For example, if the cost of supporting browser X is less than the value produced by supporting browser X, then support browser X!

Also, consider that if there are browsers in the statistics that represent less than 10% of users, look further back and consider any trends. How has usage changed over the last 3, 6, and 12 months? If it's currently 6% and that value has halved over the last 12 months, then you have a more compelling argument to consider ruling that browser out for specific enhancements.

If it's a new project and statistics are unavailable, I usually opt for a "previous 2" policy. This would be the current version, plus the previous two versions of each browser. For example, if Safari 13 was the current version, look to offer your enhancements for that version plus Safari 12 and Safari 11 (the previous two). This choice is easier with the "evergreen" browsers, which is the term given to browsers that continually update on a rapid release cycle (Firefox, Chrome, and Microsoft Edge, for example).

Tiering the user experience

Let's assume your shareholders are educated and on board. Let's also assume you have a clear set of browsers that you would like to add enhanced experiences for. We can now set about tiering the experience. I like to keep things simple, so, where possible, I opt to define a simple "base" tier and a more "enhanced" tier.

Here, the base experience is the minimum viable version of the site, and the enhanced version is the most fully featured and aesthetically pleasing version. You might need to accommodate more granularity in your tiers, for example, forking the experience in relation to browser features; support for Grid or support for Scroll Snap, for example. Regardless of how the tiers are defined, ensure you define them and what you expect to deliver with each. Then you can go about coding those tiers. That's where techniques like feature queries, which we covered in *Chapter 6, CSS Selectors, Typography, Color Modes, and More*, will come in handy.

Avoid CSS frameworks in production

There are a plethora of free CSS frameworks available that aim to aid in the rapid prototyping and building of responsive websites. The two most common examples are Bootstrap (`http://getbootstrap.com`) and Foundation (`http://foundation.zurb.com/`). While they are great projects, particularly for learning how to build responsive visual patterns, I think they should be avoided in production.

I've spoken to plenty of developers who start all of their projects with one of these frameworks and then amend them to fit their needs. This approach can be incredibly advantageous for rapid prototyping (for example, to illustrate some interaction with clients), but I think it's the wrong thing to do for projects you intend to take through to production.

Firstly, from a technical perspective, it's likely that starting with a framework will result in your project having more code than it actually needs. Secondly, from an aesthetic perspective, due to the popularity of these frameworks, it's likely your project will end up looking very similar to countless others.

Finally, if you only copy and paste code into your project and tweak it to your needs, you're unlikely to fully appreciate what's going on "under the hood." It's only by defining and solving the problems you have that you can master the code you place into your projects.

Hiding, showing, and loading content across viewports

One of the commonly touted maxims regarding responsive web design is that if you don't have something on the screen in smaller viewports, you shouldn't have it there in larger ones either.

This means users should be able to accomplish all the same goals (such as buy a product, read an article, or accomplish an interface task) at every viewport size. This is common sense. After all, as users ourselves, we've all felt the frustration of going to a website to accomplish a goal and being unable to, because we're using a smaller screen.

This also means that as screen real estate is more plentiful, we shouldn't feel compelled to add extra things just to fill the space (widgets, adverts, or links, for example). If the user could live without those extras on smaller screen sizes, they'll manage just fine on bigger ones.

In broad terms, I think the preceding maxim is sound advice. If nothing else, it makes designers and developers question more thoroughly the content they display on screen. However, as ever in web design, there will be exceptions.

As far as possible, I resist loading in new markup for different viewports, but, occasionally, it's a necessity. Some complex user interfaces require different markup and designs at wider viewports. In that instance, JavaScript is typically used to replace one area of markup with another. It isn't the ideal scenario, but it is sometimes the most pragmatic.

By the same token, I think it's perfectly reasonable to have sections of markup hidden in CSS until they are appropriate. I'm thinking about things like headers. On more than one occasion, before Grid was well supported, I have wasted an inordinate amount of time trying to figure out how to convert one header layout for mobile into a different layout for larger screens, all while using the same markup. It was folly! The pragmatic solution is to have both pieces of markup and just hide each as appropriate with a media query. When the difference is a handful of elements and the associated styles, there are almost always more sensible savings to make elsewhere.

These are the choices you will probably face as you code more and more complex responsive web designs, and you'll need to use your own judgment as to what the best choice is in any given scenario. However, it's not a cardinal sin if you toggle the visibility of the odd bit of markup with `display: none` to achieve your goal.

Validators and linting tools

Generally speaking, writing HTML and CSS is pretty forgiving. You can nest the odd thing incorrectly, miss the occasional quotation mark or self-closing tag, and not always notice a problem. Despite this, on an almost weekly basis, I manage to befuddle myself with incorrect markup. Sometimes, it's a slip up, like accidentally typing an errant character. Other times, it's schoolboy errors like nesting a `div` inside a `span` (invalid markup as a `span` is an inline element and a `div` is a block-level element, which leads to unpredictable results). Thankfully, there are great tools to help out. At worst, if you're encountering a weird issue, head over to `http://validator.w3.org/` and paste your markup in there. It will point out any errors along with line numbers, helping you to easily fix things up:

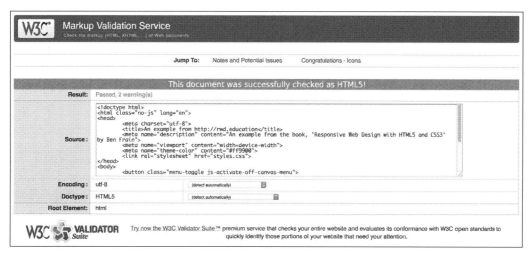

Figure 11.9: Skip the validation of HTML at your peril!

Better still, install and configure "linting" tools for your HTML, CSS, and JavaScript. Or, choose a text editor with some sanity checking built-in. Then problem areas are flagged up in your code as you go. Here's an example of a simple spelling error in CSS flagged up by Microsoft's Visual Studio Code editor:

```
_days-since.css preCSS
1  .post-DaysSince {
2      display: flex;
3      width|th: 100%;
4      alig   Rename to 'width'
5      marg   Rename to 'max-width'
              Rename to 'min-width'
6      font-size: 1.1rem;
7      line-height: 1;
8      border: 1px solid    #dedede;
9      background-color: $color-blockquote;
10     padding: 5px 0;
11 }
12
```

Figure 11.10: Embrace tooling that saves you from basic problems

Like a clown, I've clumsily typed "widtth" instead of "width." The editor has spotted this fact and pointed out the error of my ways and offered some sensible alternatives. Embrace these tools where possible. There are better uses of your time than tracking down simple syntax errors in your code.

Performance

Considering the performance of your responsive web designs is as important as the aesthetics. However, performance presents something of a moving target. For example, browsers update and improve the way they handle assets, new techniques are discovered that supersede existing "best practices," and technologies eventually get enough browser support that they become viable for widespread adoption. The list goes on.

There are, however, some basic implementation details that are pretty solid advice. These are:

- Minimize the page weight. If you can compress images to a fraction of their original size, you should. This should always be your first task with optimizing. It's possible to double the file size savings by compressing one image compared to compressing and minifying all of your CSS and JavaScript.

- Defer non-essential assets. If you can load any additional CSS and JavaScript until the page has rendered, it can greatly reduce the perceived load time.

- Ensure the page is usable as soon as possible, which is often a by-product of doing all the preceding points.

Performance tools

There are great tools available to measure and optimize performance. My personal favorite is `http://webpagetest.org`. At its simplest, you can pick a URL and click on **START TEST**. It will show you a complete analysis of the page, but even more usefully, if you choose the visual comparison option, it shows a "filmstrip" view of the loaded page, allowing you to concentrate on getting the rendered page completed sooner. Here's an example of the "filmstrip" view of the BBC home page:

Figure 11.11: Seeing the page load as a filmstrip can really tell the story of performance

There are also increasingly powerful performance tools built into browser developer tools. Lighthouse is part of the Google Chrome developer tools, which you can run from the **Audits** tab. Point it at a site and it will give you a breakdown of where improvements can be made:

Figure 11.12: The Lighthouse tools not only tell you what you can improve, but they tell you how to do it

This is useful as every piece of advice has links to additional documentation, so you read more about the problem and potential ways of addressing it.

Whenever you try to optimize performance, ensure you take measurements before you begin (otherwise, you will not understand how effective your performance work has been). Then make amendments, test, and repeat.

The next big things

One of the interesting things about frontend web development is that things change rapidly. There is always something new to learn and the web community is always figuring out better, faster, and more effective ways of solving problems.

For example, when writing the first edition of this book, responsive images (`srcset` and the `picture` element, which are detailed in *Chapter 4, Fluid Layout, Flexbox, and Responsive Images*) simply didn't exist. Back then, we had to use clever third-party workarounds to serve up more appropriate images to different viewport sizes. Now common need has been rationalized into a W3C standard, which has been implemented across browsers.

Similarly, only a few years ago, Flexbox was just a twinkle in a specification writer's eyes. Even when the specification evolved, it was still difficult to implement until a super-smart developer called Andrey Sitnik, along with his colleagues at Evil Martians (`https://evilmartians.com/`) created Autoprefixer. This was a tool that allowed us to write a single syntax and have our CSS be processed into code that could work across multiple implementations as if by magic.

Progress on the web shows little sign of abating. Even now, things like WebAssembly, or WASM, as it is often referred to, are gaining more and more traction. WebAssembly is a means of having web code that runs far more akin to the speed of a compiled language. In short, it will make things on the web feel a whole lot faster. Lin Clark, a developer at the browser-maker Mozilla, has a very accessible series on WebAssembly here: `https://hacks.mozilla.org/2017/02/a-cartoon-intro-to-webassembly/`.

CSS Grid, which we covered in-depth in *Chapter 5, Layout with CSS Grid*, has a Level 2 version in the works that will allow subgrids. Variable fonts, which we looked at in *Chapter 6, CSS Selectors, Typography, Color Modes, and More*, are going to become more and more commonplace, so expect interesting things in that space too.

In short, expect change, and embrace it!

Summary

As we reach the end of our time together, your humble author hopes to have related all the techniques and tools you'll need to start building your next website or web application responsively.

It's my conviction that, by approaching web projects with a little forethought and by potentially making a few modifications to existing workflows and practices, it's possible to embrace modern techniques that provide fast, flexible, accessible, and maintainable websites that can look incredible, regardless of the device used to visit them.

We've covered a wealth of information in our time together: techniques, technologies, performance optimizations, specifications, workflow, tooling, and more. I wouldn't expect anybody to absorb it all in one read. Therefore, the next time you need to remember this or that syntax, or to refresh your mind about one of the responsive-related subjects we've covered, I hope you'll dip back into these pages. I'll be right here waiting for you.

Until then, I wish you good fortune in your responsive web design quests.

See you again sometime.

Other Books You May Enjoy

If you enjoyed this book, you may be interested in these other books by Packt:

Django 3 By Example - Third Edition

Antonio Melé

ISBN: 9781838981952

- Build real-world web applications
- Learn Django essentials, including models, views, ORM, templates, URLs, forms, and authentication
- Implement advanced features such as custom model fields, custom template tags, cache, middleware, localization, and more

- Create complex functionalities, such as AJAX interactions, social authentication, a full-text search engine, a payment system, a CMS, a RESTful API, and more

- Integrate other technologies, including Redis, Celery, RabbitMQ, PostgreSQL, and Channels, into your projects

- Deploy Django projects in production using NGINX, uWSGI, and Daphne

Mastering Xamarin.Forms - Third Edition

Ed Snider

ISBN: 9781839213380

- Find out how, when, and why to use architecture patterns and best practices with Xamarin.Forms

- Implement the Model-View-ViewModel (MVVM) pattern and data binding in Xamarin.Forms mobile apps

- Incorporate client-side validation in Xamarin.Forms mobile apps

- Extend the Xamarin.Forms navigation API with a custom ViewModel-centric navigation service

- Leverage the inversion of control and dependency injection patterns in Xamarin.Forms mobile apps

- Work with online and offline data in Xamarin.Forms mobile apps

- Use platform-specific APIs to build rich custom user interfaces in Xamarin.Forms mobile apps

- Explore how to monitor mobile app quality using Visual Studio App Center

Leave a review - let other readers know what you think

Please share your thoughts on this book with others by leaving a review on the site that you bought it from. If you purchased the book from Amazon, please leave us an honest review on this book's Amazon page. This is vital so that other potential readers can see and use your unbiased opinion to make purchasing decisions, we can understand what our customers think about our products, and our authors can see your feedback on the title that they have worked with Packt to create. It will only take a few minutes of your time, but is valuable to other potential customers, our authors, and Packt. Thank you!

Index

Symbols

:empty selector 174, 175
:not selector 173, 174
-webkit-line-clamp
  reference link 346
"beginning with" substring matching attribute
     selector 160, 161
"contains an instance of" substring matching
     attribute selector 161
"ends with" substring matching attribute
     selector 161, 162
<a> element
  reference link 30
<a> tag
  reference link 30, 31
<address> element
  about 40
  reference link 41
<article> element
  about 33
  reference link 34
<aside> element
  about 34
  reference link 34
<audio> tag
  working 50
<b> element
  about 41, 42
  reference link 41
<details> element 39, 40
<em> element 42
<figcaption> element
  about 38
  reference link 38
<figure> element

about 38
reference link 38
<footer> element
  about 34
  reference link 35
<header> element
  about 34
  reference link 34
<i> element 43
<main> element
  about 32
  reference link 32
<nav> element
  about 33
  reference link 33
<p> element 37
<section> element
  about 32, 33
  reference link 33
<span> element 41
<strong> element
  about 42
  reference link 42
<summary> element 39, 40
<video> tag
  working 50
@font-face CSS rule
  about 184, 185
  used, for implementing web fonts 185, 186
@supports
  used, for code forking in CSS 181

A

Accessible Rich Internet Applications (ARIA)
  about 47
  reference link 46

Made in United States
Orlando, FL
17 July 2022